Cervantes and the Renaissance

Juan de la Cuesta
Hispanic Monographs

Thomas A. Lathrop, Editor

Series: *Documentación cervantina*, Nº 1

Cervantes and the Renaissance

Papers of the Pomona College Cervantes Symposium, November 16-18, 1978

Edited by Michael D. McGaha

Juan de la Cuesta

The publisher wishes to thank Professor R. M. Flores of the
University of British Columbia for providing the original
Juan de la Cuesta decorated capital letters which begin each article.

Contents

Preface

THE FOURTEEN PAPERS contained in this volume were first presented orally at the Pomona College Symposium on Cervantes and the Renaissance in November 1978. The symposium was intended to provide an opportunity for some of the world's leading Cervantes scholars to reassess Cervantes' work within the context of Renaissance thought and art.

In his keynote address Professor Juan Bautista Avalle-Arce attested that the description of Cervantes as a Renaissance writer is far more questionable than it might at first seem. Américo Castro definitively refuted the once widely held notion of Cervantes as *ingenio lego*, demonstrating beyond a doubt that he had thoroughly assimilated the intellectual attainments of the Renaissance. The canard that Spain was a country without a Renaissance has likewise been almost universally rejected. The classification remains problematical, however, because of questions of chronology and, more importantly, because of the uniqueness of the intellectual history of sixteenth- and seventeenth-century Spain. There is an enormous cultural gap between the Spain of Charles V and that of the Philips. Cervantes' work forms a complex and difficult bridge between the two periods. *Don Quixote*, Avalle-Arce concludes, can properly be considered a Renaissance work, but the posthumous *Persiles y Sigismunda* is an expression of the new cultural climate of Spain's Catholic Reformation. The secular treatment of the theme of self-knowledge and the disillusionment we find in *Don Quixote* reflect Cervantes' nostalgia for the earlier period of intellectual freedom

and speculation and his discomfort with the new emphasis on conformity and submission to authority. The *Persiles*, in which the protagonists seek the absolute truth of faith and dogma rather than the
relative one of self-knowledge, reveals how Cervantes finally succeeded in coming to terms with the new order.

Professor Juan Corominas sheds further light on this process in
his interesting comparison of Cervantes and Alonso de Ercilla.
Ercilla, fourteen years older then Cervantes and a decidedly Renaissance writer, was unable to make the transition to the new ideological and artistic climate. Instead of attempting to adjust to the new
values, he chose to withdraw from literary pursuits altogether. In
his *La Araucana* he had attempted to revive the classical epic. Corominas demonstrates that this work exercised a decisive influence on
Cervantes' tragedy *La Numancia*. Later, however. Cervantes was to
move beyond Ercilla's classicism.

According to Professor Elias Rivers, Cervantes' movement toward the new style is already evident in *Don Quixote*. Though in its
content the novel still reflects the humanistic preoccupations of the
Renaissance, its anti-classical medley of styles and levels of language
places it firmly within the confines of what we now know as the
Baroque. After reviewing the linguistic revolution brought about
by the Renaissance—the efforts of Renaissance writers to create a
neoclassical style in the vernacular languages—Rivers demonstrates
how Cervantes enthusiastically adopted this style in his *Numancia*
and *Galatea*, but later had more and more serious doubts about its
efficacy and finally rejected it in favor of a more complex and personal style which better expressed his ultimately ironic and problematical view of literature.

In my own essay I have examined the relationship of *Don Quixote*
to the single classic most admired and imitated in the Renaissance,
Virgil's *Aeneid*, arguing that the *Aeneid* offered Cervantes the fundamental model for his novel. Emphasizing the ideological affinity
between the two works, I have attempted to show that Cervantes
derived some of the most characteristic devices of his art—such as
foreshadowing, multiple allusion, perspectivism and implicit comment—from Virgil. However, just as Virgil had sought to surpass
Homer, Cervantes boldly attempted to improve upon Virgil by eliminating the flaws in Virgil's work which diminished its credibility.

Professor Luis Murillo ponders Cervantes' adaptation of material not only from the classical epic but from the epic poetry of the Renaissance. Though scholars have long recognized the presence of themes and motifs taken from epic poetry in *Don Quixote,* they have not succeeded in reconciling these elements with the comic and negative aspect of Don Quixote's adventures. Murillo argues that in his novel Cervantes both invests representational art with figurative meaning and demythifies and secularizes sacred and heroic themes. He states that Cervantes combines the sense of breadth or totalization which is indispensable to epic narrative with the absense of any overt movement toward transcendental meaning, thus creating a secularized version of life. One important way in which Cervantes accomplished this was by reducing chivalric themes to their counterpart in popular festival and ritual, especially the carnival.

Cervantes' use of symbolic motifs which originated in the carnival is examined in further detail by Professor Manuel Durán. Using the Russian Formalist critic Mikhail Bakhtine's studies of the symbol-system of the carnival in the work or Rabelais as a point of departure, Durán finds that *Don Quixote* abounds in carnival motifs—such as disguises, elaborate practical jokes, the coronation of a fool or madman as King of the Carnival and, most importantly, the use of laughter as a corrective agent against a religious and political hierarchy which tended to take themselves too seriously. Seen in the light of the carnival as an essentially subversive celebration which brought about a temporary but cyclically repeated restoration of primitive freedom and brotherhood among men, the Renaissance *topos* of the Golden Age, so important in *Don Quixote,* takes on a new meaning. Durán argues that a proper understanding of the carnival's significance is an indispensable first step towards comprehending the book's humor and its extraordinary attractiveness to the Spanish reading public of 1605 or 1615.

Professor Francisco Márquez Villanueva detects an important relationship between carnival motifs and the symbols of madness contained in the literature of folly which was so significant in the Renaissance. This literature had two aspects—a negative one (folly as sin), represented by Brant's *Narrenschiff* and a positive one (folly as wisdom), best exemplified by Erasmus' *Praise of Folly.* Both aspects were extremely influential in sixteenth-century Spanish literature and made important contributions to the iconography symbolic of folly, but it was the latter one which contributed most to *Don Quixote*. Using extensive examples from contemporary literature, Márquez demonstrates that Cervantes' use of symbols of madness—particularly symbolic colors, clothing and food—is a very important device for characterization in *Don Quixote*. This type of symbolism, though universally understood by Cervantes' contemporaries, requires explanation for us. Such explanation, like that of the equally forgotten carnival symbolism, offers a very valuable tool for the interpretation of *Don Quixote*. *Don Quixote,* Márquez concludes, was at once the culmination and the death certificate of the Renaissance literature of folly.

One of the most important sources of *Don Quixote* was the *Amadís de Gaula*. Concentrating on the treatment of the figure of the squire in the two novels, Professor Eduardo Urbina shows how Cervantes makes of Sancho Panza a much more interesting and autonomous character than his predecessor Gandalín in the *Amadís*. The dramatic tension in the *Amadís* results from the conflict between the knight's duty to his king and his love for his lady. Gandalín opposes Amadís' love for Oriana when it endangers his fame as a knight. However, his attempts to influence his master are futile and result finally in Amadís' abandonment of him. By 'enchanting' Dulcinea, Sancho removes the possibility of such conflict and at the same time precipitates the melancholy which will ultimately result in Don Quixote's abandoning his knightly role.

We have seen how in *Don Quixote* Cervantes created a multi-leveled synthesis of materials from Virgil, the epic poetry of the Renaissance, the romances of chivalry, the literature of folly and popular folklore, to mention only a few of his sources. Professor John J. Allen sees this "movement from an established genre to generic compendium and confrontation" as one of Cervantes' principal contributions to the creation of the novel. Most significant among Cervantes' other innovations were "the movement from the miraculous to the providential, which provided the solution to the problem of achieving *admiratio* without sacrificing verisimilitude" and "the movement from classical preoccupation with establishing the authority of a narrative to an exploration of the fertile possibilities in the management and manipulation of point of view." Allen's thoughtful comparison of the episode of the wedding of Silveria and Daranio in Book III of the *Galatea* and Camacho's wedding in Part II of *Don Quixote* reveals how Cervantes' art had developed in the thirty years between the publication of two books. *La Galatea* is a romance; its interest lies chiefly in what is told. *Don Quixote* is truly a novel. The focus is no longer on what happens but rather on how the characters assimilate their experience and shape themselves out of it.

Professor Ruth El Saffar finds that Cervantes' early works reveal a split between the author's individual consciousness and his society. In these works he depicts society and the material world as presenting insurmountable obstacles to his characters' desire for freedom and self-realization. The characters are seen as isolated and separated from their community. The conflict between the needs of the individual and the demands of society seems insoluble. Cervantes employs such devices as perspectivism, irony and the story-within-a-story to convey this tension. This situation persists as late as the 1605 *Don Quixote,* which ends in a stalemate. A corrupt but solid world seems temporarily to have vanquished Don Quixote, but we know that he will emerge from this defeat to continue his career undaunted. However, in the 1615 *Don Quixote* Cervantes at last sees the possibility of resolving the conflict. Don Quixote's expanding self-awareness leads him to a vision of truth which enables him to accept his whole self, not only that part of it with which he had previously identified. No longer resisting, he at last accepts the role assigned to him by divine providence. The acceptance is still melancholy, however, for there is nothing for the newly enlightened gentleman to do but die. In his last novel, the *Persiles*, Cervantes goes a step further, presenting a character "whose fortunes in this life are governed by the presence of the Divine and who lives to enjoy *here* the rewards of a harmonious interaction between himself and others, symbolized by his marriage to Sigismunda." The split between the individual and external reality has been healed. Persiles is "free to manipulate the material world, secure in an all-pervading consciousness of achievable harmony and perfection."

Professor Edward Friedman's study of Cervantes' complex attitude toward the roles played by individuals in society offers additional support for Professor El Saffar's thesis, and at the same time provides another case of Cervantes' "movement from an established genre to generic compendium," as described by Professor Allen. Friedman studies how Cervantes complicates the model of the *comedia de capa y espada* in *El laberinto de amor* and deflates or parodies that model in *La entretenida*. In the *comedia de capa y espada* literary characters usually adopt and invent roles in order to overcome obstacles to love. Finally, however, they resume their true identity, and these plays normally end with multiple marriages or promises of marriage. This is in fact what happens in *El laberinto de amor*, in which the characters thwart society's opposition to their love by an ingenious manipulation of reality. However, the characters who try to do the same thing in *La entretenida* find their clever schemes quashed by a reality which is impermeable to their manipulation. Friedman argues that the characters in *El laberinto de amor* are successful because their role-playing is only a temporary means to attain their providentially assigned place in society. The failure of the characters in *La entretenida* results from their fundamental dishonesty, their defiance not only of a repressive society but of the divine order in attempting to exchange their authentic roles for "better" ones of their own invention; Like the Don Quixote of 1605, they try to second-guess God and to substitute illusion for reality.

Just as he had overturned the conventions of the *comedia de capa y espada* in *La entretenida*, in his "exemplary novel" *La ilustre fregona* Cervantes created an unlikely amalgam of the pastoral and the picaresque, producing a work which transcends the limitations of both those genres. In examining how Cervantes accomplished this, Professor Robert Johnston gives us a perceptive and thought-provoking analysis of the similarities and differences between picaresque and pastoral.

Professor Bruce Wardropper surveys the characterization of figures representative of the academic world in Cervantes' fiction and then reviews what little is known about Cervantes' own educational experience in the attempt to discover what Cervantes really thought about educational institutions and the academic profession. Though always bearing in mind the caveat that it is dangerous to attribute the opinions of fictional characters to their author, Wardropper marshals an impressive body of evidence which strongly suggests that Cervantes had a negative or at least a suspicious view of the educational establishment and placed a higher value on education through experience than on mere book-learning. This judgment probably resulted at least in part from his own resentment at having been denied the advantages of a university education. However, it seems also to have been based on the philosophical notion that too much erudition, especially if acquired in an authoritarian situation, tends to stifle creativity. Much more important than these rather tenuous conclusions, however, is Wardropper's incisive demonstration of the fact that almost nothing is known with certainty about Cervantes' educational theory and experience. We need to be reminded of this, because many theories—particularly that of Cervantes' supposed Erasmian indoctrination by López de Hoyos— have been so often repeated and by such eminent scholars that they have come to be accepted as established facts, when in reality they are based on the shakiest circumstantial evidence.

Wardropper noted that Cervantes was apparently disturbed by an important change of emphasis in educational methods and goals which occurred during his lifetime. In his youth Renaissance humanists, for the most part laymen, had sought to endow their students with a critical spirit and with the ability to think independently. The educational establishment of Counter-Reformation Spain, largely controlled by the Jesuits, sought rather to impart an "elegance of expression which went hand in hand with conformity." Professor Helena Percas de Ponseti argues that the advice given by Don Quixote to Sancho in chapters 42, 43 and 51 of the 1615 *Don Quixote* implies a criticism of this new attitude. She sees Don Quixote's counsels as embodying two superimposed structures—a formal one, which is Baroque in style, i.e., highly structured and suggesting a conservative content; and an implicit ideological one, which is characteristic of the Renaissance, i.e., elastic, critical and original. She deduces Cervantes' ideas principally from a study of the internal contradictions in Don Quixote's words. Don Quixote's advice, she says, is expedient and utilitarian; he advises Sancho how to govern in order to be successful. Cervantes' implicit advice is ethical. Don Quixote's words are an implacable parody of the accepted moral code of contemporary society. They also serve to characterize him in this stage of his career (the stay in the ducal palace) as a disoriented intellectual. Analysis of the symbolism of the clothing worn by Don Quixote during this period and that of worn by Sancho Panza during his governorship offers further confirmation of Professor Percas' thesis and also usefully supplements the comments given by Professor Márquez on this subject.

This symposium was made possible by generous contributions

from the Del Amo Foundation and the Andrew W. Mellon Foundation.The Del Amo Foundation has also funded the publication of this volume. I am grateful to President David Alexander, Dean Robert Voelkel and Professors Virginia Crosby and Howard Young of Pomona College for their assistance in organizing the symposium. I also wish to express my heartfelt gratitude to Professors Carroll Johnson and Joseph Silverman for serving as moderators at the symposium.

MICHAEL D. MCGAHA

POMONA COLLEGE

Cervantes and the Renaissance

JUAN BAUTISTA AVALLE-ARCE

 HE GENERAL TOPIC of this symposium—*Cervantes and the Renaissance*—should be awe-inspiring, since it sets before us two of the most problematic issues of Spanish Literature. We know who Cervantes the man was, but poorly. All of the works that man wrote are readily available, but there is absolutely no consensus as to the means he used to give them ideological density, and as to the narrative techniques he used in order to bring these ideas to the reader's attention, they are still in polemical litigation. Needless to say, I am conscious of coming close to a critical hyperbole in my preceding statements, but I think we are in no danger of collision. Cervantes definitely is not The Great Unknown of Spanish literature, at least not anymore, and I trust that this symposium will more clearly trace some aspects of his profile.

The word Renaissance should make us shudder even more violently than the name Cervantes. Ever since the French historian Jules Michelet introduced it into the critical vocabulary back in 1859 critics have not been quite at ease with it. Probably a major cause in that professional uneasiness was the book that came out the year after, in 1860, by the celebrated Swiss historian Jakob Burckhardt: *The Civilization of the Renaissance in Italy.* It is well known that the analysis of the historical reality of Italy, in the 15th century and the centuries immediately preceding it, led the Swiss historian to sort out a number of characteristics of that reality, which, when systematically articulated, became the fundamental principles of the Renaissance as a concept. The conception of the state as a work of art, and the resulting development of the individual, were the two cornerstones of Burckhardt's concept of the Renaissance. The personal desire for fame and glory, the moral autonomy, spiritual freedom, were some of the elements with which Burckhardt finished off the structure of his concept.

Its success was nothing short of phenomenal, and quite deservedly so, because there are few instances in intellectual history of a whole age so neatly packaged and labeled. Everything was so clear and neat that it became almost a favorite scholarly pastime to superimpose Burckhardt's concept over historical realities other than the Italian. If the end-result of this extrapolation was not too divergent from the original set, then we had the Renaissance in France, or in England, or wherever else the curiosity of the historian led him, and history allowed such application.

But in Spain things turned out to be rather different. To start out with, Spain had led an anomalous life, by Occidental standards, for at least seven hundred years, from the invasion of the Moors in 711, to the conquest of Granada and the expulsion of the Jews in 1492. What made these seven long centuries anomolous was precisely the fact that they implied a coexistence, within a continuous war, between Christians, Jews and Moors. And this, in turn, could not but affect the very roots of the Spanish historical reality.

To cut a long story short, the year 1927 saw the publication in Germany of an article and a book, both denying the existence of a Spanish Renaissance. The article was authored by the historian and literary critic Viktor Klemperer, it came out in the journal *Logos,* and its title was a completely academic question, as far as the author was concerned: "Gibt es eine spanische Renaissance?" Needless to say, the answer was a rotund *no.* The book that came out at the same time in Munich was penned by Hans Wantoch, and was entitled *Spanien, das Lande ohne Renaissance.*

It is amusing to think that these German fireworks (in which was latent the question of the primacy of Protestantism over Catholicism), had been preceded by seven years by the book by Giuseppe Toffanin, *La fine dell'Umanesimo* (Torino, 1920), a work which, in retrospect, we must acclaim as epoch-making in our disciplines. In it Toffanin was at pains to insert Cervantes' name in that circle of first-rank international *literati* deeply affected by Italian 16th-century Neo-Aristotelianism;

The reading of Toffanin's masterful book set to work the intellectual gears of the extraordinary mind of Don Américo Castro. With this, and other critical helpmeets, Don Américo brought into the sharpest focus a completely new Cervantes, not the traditional *ingenio lego,* but rather the very distinct image of image of a Cervantes *a la altura de las circunstancias,* that is to say, the Cervantes that is still very much with us nowadays. The battering ram with which Don Américo pulverised the old *ingenio lego* image was, most particularly, his classic book on *El pensamiento de Cervantes* (Madrid, 1925), which was republished in Barcelona, 1972, with notes of Don Américo himself and Julio Rodríguez-Puértolas.

In *El pensamiento de Cervantes* Don Américo tried, and succeeded, in setting Cervantes in his historical and intellectual circumstance: Italy and Spain in the late 1500's. Miraculously, in view of Cervantine criticism until then, the novelist emerges from the pages of this classical work as a complete, integral man of the Renaissance. But if Cervantes was a man of the Renaissance and he lived and wrote in Spain, this implicitly means that Spain did have a Renaissance. So the book of Don Américo reactivated two not altogether unrelated fields: that of Cervantine studies, and, also, that of studies about the Renaissance in Spain. A half century after the Germanic intellectual fireworks I mentioned earlier, we can smugly smile and shrug our shoulders, because for us it is perfectly clear that there is no reason in the world why Spain should have an Italian Renaissance. A major contributor to our present smugness was Don Américo's great book.

By now we have established two things: one is the existence of a Cervantes who, far from being an *ingenio lego* was an active, dedicated and extremely complicated intellectual. And the second point established is that Spain did have a Renaissance. So far, then, the title of this symposium appears to be justified. But a doubt might linger in some minds. The title of the symposium can be completely justified only if Cervantes came after the Renaissance or was immersed in it. To put it another, clearer way: the chronology of the Renaissance cannot but affect out interpretation of its influence on Cervantes. We know he lived from 1547 to 1616, but do we know with equal certainty *when* the Renaissance took place? Of course not, especially now that we have any number of Renaissances, including one in the 12th century.

I do not want to give you the impression that I am creating imaginary giants to cut in half with the sharp edge of my erudition. A very serious and disturbing text of James Joyce has come out recently entitled "The Universal Literary Influence of the Renaissance". In this writing that most extraordinary of Irish story-tellers stands back to make place for James Joyce the literary critic. And this it what happens: Joyce the critic tells us that the Renaissance is the hurricane that cleans Europe of the likes of Saint Robert Bellarmino and Juan de Mariana. And since Bellarmino died in 1621 and Mariana in 1624, perforce the Renaissance did not happen before the third decade of the 17th century, and we know that Cervantes died in 1616. Horrors! So Cervantes antedates the Renaissance!

But James Joyce's unexpected intellectual torpedo has not quite sunk the ship of historical chronology, or so I would like you to think. For my purposes of today, and especially given the topic of our symposium, *when* the Spanish Renaissance began is irrelevant. I am far more interested at this moment in an approximate date, not for its demise (intellectual movements, like old soldiers, never die), but rather for its gradual metamorphosis into something else, a new movement which will gain little by little (or in an awful hurry) its own image and stature.

I want to make myself clear, and at the same time maintain a modicum of brevity, so I will say that for me, and at the present moment, when that famous verse of Hernando de Acuña that sings of "Un monarca, un imperio y una espada", when that verse has no longer historical validity in Spain, then the Spanish Renaissance is over. And if Acuña died in 1580, during the reign of Felipe II, the sonnet to which the quoted verse belongs gives a perfect epitome of the imperial movement, of the reign of Charles V, the first and last emperor of the Old World and the New.

The Spain that came after Charles V is known by many names, most of them centered around the idea of religious dogma, such as Tridentine Spain, the Spain of the Catholic Reformation, and many others. This new Spain, the Spain of Philip II, defines itself clearly in two government decrees signed by the King. The first one is a *pragmática* of the 22 of November of 1559, and I quote its heading: "Para que ningún natural destos reynos vaya a estudiar fuera dellos". The other one is a *real cédula* of the 12 of July of 1564, whereby the edicts of the Council of Trent (which had held its last session in that very same year), were made into laws of the land in Spain. It should be obvious now that if the Spain of Charles V saw the last moments of its own Renaissance, the Spain of Philip II was going to be magnetized by a massive re-dogmatization, which brought it very close to being a "born again Catholic".

Now I feel that I can come back to our main topic and say that when we talk about Cervantes and the Renaissance we are sailing with our eyes wide open through the strait of Scylla and Charybdis. Because the truth of the matter is that we must qualify that simple-sounding statement at almost every point. If the end of the Spanish Renaissance came in the reign of Charles V, yes, Cervantes did live to see it. But his very first published works (the mediocre poems to the death of Queen Isabel de Valois, which happened in 1568), already came out well into the reign of Philip II, and the rest of his production would be published in a minor part in the same reign (I am thinking of *La Galatea*), but most of it in the reign of his successor Philip III, who died in 1621.

I will not pursue this matter any further, because it is considerably more complex than I make it to be. It should be clear, however, that when we say "Cervantes and the Renaissance" we are acting like Pandora in front of her famous box, except that we have full knowledge, or intuition, of what is awaiting us. Cervantes felt as intellectually alienated in the Spain of the Philips as his hero Don Quijote de la Mancha, and for basically similar reasons: they are both out of step with their historical moment. To be sure, Don Quijote wants to go back to the Middle Ages for any number of reasons, many of which will be discussed in the course of this symposium. To be sure, also, Cervantes does *not* want to go back to the Middle Ages: he is very proud, and with complete justice, of having served in the army of Philip II, and he describes the battle of Lepanto as "the greatest occasion that the ages have seen." But he does not pine for the intellectual Spain of Philip II, but rather for the world of ideas that circulated quite freely in the Spain of Charles V, which had come to an almost stop during the reign of his son. I have

in mind a very concrete example. Erasmus and his works had mag-
netically attracted the Spain of Charles V, to the point that some of
the greatest intellectuals of the times were proud to call themselves
his disciples, and this went so far in the case of Alfonso de Valdés
that he has been called "más erasmista que Erasmo". Granted that
towards the end of the reign of Charles V a lukewarm persecution
against the *erasmistas* started to get underway, but nothing too
serious came out of it. The thunderbolt was going to fall in the very
first years of the reign of Philip II. In the *Index Librorum Prohibitorum* of
1559 of the Inquisitor General Don Fernando de Valdés, *all* of the
works "en romance" of Erasmus were prohibited. Nevertheless,
many years after such a categorical prohibition, the works of Cervantes appear to be permeated by Erasmian ideas and attitudes,
many of them known to us since the time of Américo Castro and
Marcel Bataillon, but some others of more recent identification, and
which, in part, will be presented to you by Professor Francisco
Márquez Villanueva.

　　If at this point I say that Cervantes evidently had a very complex
personality, I am making very pointed use of an understatement.
Because, as it happens, it will be Don Quijote himself who will say
at one point: "cada uno es hijo de sus obras" (I, iv). Without entering
into Logic (the Logic of Pero Grullo, to be sure), it is only fitting and
proper that the complexity of the works mirror the complexity of
the personality, or vice versa, *as you like it.* We cannot, at the risk of
our professional reputations, print a flat statement about Cervantes
and his works without having to qualify it from one point of view,
at least. Let us look at the two great novels of Cervantes in search
of illustrations

　　The *Quijote*, as we all know, came out in 1605 and 1615; the
Persiles came out posthumously in 1617, but I hope to have demonstrated in my edition of it that its composition was pretty much
simultaneous with that of the *Quijote*. What we have in the *Quijote,*
among a myriad of other things, is an *hidalgo manchego* who loses his
mind, disguises himself and chooses a false personality, that of Don
Quijote de la Mancha, the defender of the order of knight errantry.
It is obvious that his personality has reached the heights, or depths,
of delusion, but nevertheless, he will always fight for the supremacy
of self-knowledge. It should be no surprise then that when in the

Second Part Sancho Panza is ready to start for his coveted Ínsula Barataria, his master will give him a long list of advice, which begins like so: "Primeramente, ¡oh hijo!, has de temer a Dios; porque en el temerle está la sabiduría, y siendo sabio no podrás errar en nada. Lo segundo, has de poner los ojos en quien eres, procurando conocerte a ti mismo" (II, xlii). The privileged place that self-knowledge takes in the scale of values of Don Quijote is underlined by the fact that it comes immediately after a Biblical text of the book of Job: "Timor Dei est initium sapientiae". At this point let me just add that Persiles solemnly agrees with Don Quijote when he says: "Las verdades que uno conoce de sí mismo no nos pueden engañar" (II, xii).

Self-knowledge had already played a decisive role in the very complex episode of the *venta* of Juan Palomeque el Zurdo, where all kinds of mismatched lovers appear at various times: Don Fernando, Dorotea, Cardenio, Luscinda, the Captive Captain, Zoraida, Doña Clara and Don Luis. But all bloodshed is avoided, all recriminations quelled, all violence averted, and all lovers leave the inn with complete sentimental gratification. The model of all this was, as I pointed out years ago, the episode in the *Diana* of Montemayor which tells of the palace of Felicia and her administration of *el agua encantada,* all of it *esperpentizado,* to be sure, in the *Quijote*. At the inn of Juan Palomeque it is the use of self-knowledge on the part of the most violently reluctant of the lovers, Don Fernando, which eases in the pacific and permanent solution: "Don Fernando se ablandó y se dejó vencer de la verdad, que él no pudiera negar aunque quisiera" (I, xxxvi).

But in spite of the highest esteem in which Don Quijote holds self-knowledge, and in spite of the capital role to which it is put by the author in the first part of the novel, in spite of all this, poor Don Quijote is totally incapable of practising what he preaches. He seems to know himself ("Yo sé quién soy", he will proudly exclaim in I, v), but when he says this he is referring to his carvival masque of Don Quijote, for the *hidalgo manchego* remains subsumed by the false identity. It is true that close to the climax of his *desengaño* Don Quijote will publicly admit: "Yo hasta agora no sé lo que conquisto a fuerza de mis trabajos" (II, lviii). Self-knowledge is slowly inching its way forward in the consciousness of Don Quijote, but it will only make its solemn appearance when the battered *hidalgo manchego* doffs his masque and in his deathbed admits in front of all of his family and intimate friends: "Dadme albricias, buenos señores, de que ya yo no soy don Quijote de la Mancha, sino Alonso Quijano, a quien mis costumbres me dieron renombre de *Bueno*" (II, lvxxiv). The only time that self-knowledge appears in the masquerade lived by Don Quijote is enough to shatter everything in his world, to leave only a poor, dying, old man, ready now, yes, but *only* now, to meet his Maker.

The role of self-knowledge in the *Persiles y Sigismunda* is just as evident, central and important as in *Don Quijote*, and I hope you will remember the words of Persiles I just quoted to that effect. We need not single out any of the episodes of the *Persiles* to show this. It will be enough to remind you that from the very beginning of the novel the protagonists are not identified by their right names (Persiles and Sigismunda), but rather by the ones they have assumed (Periandro and Auristela). They want to be known as Periandro and Auristela and that is how they introduce themselves throughout the corpus of this long novel. It is only towards its very end that the chapter-heading clues us: "Donde se dice quién eran Periandro y Auristela" (IV, xii). Don Quijote lives his masquerade to the bitter end, and only doffs his masque in order to let his true self meet his Maker at the moment of death. Periandro and Auristela also live a masquerade, and just as stubbornly as Don Quijote, but instead of beatings and broken teeth the new protagonists will suffer from storms at sea and almost mortal separations. The story of Don Quijote falls into the category of what the great German folklorist Johann Georg von Hahn called the *Arische Aussetzungs- und Rückkehr-Formel* (Aryan Expulsion and Return Formula), in the sense that he is forced to leave his village (A case of self-exile, of course), and returns to die in it. The story of the protagonists of the Persiles begins in the *ultima Thule* of Vergil, that is to say, at the very edge of the known world, but from then on the course of the novel will make a slow but steady progress towards Rome. Early in the novel we are told that "Roma es el cielo de la tierra" (II, vii), and it is when they arrive at this *cielo terrenal* that the protagonists are ready to doff their masques and regain their true identities. But not to die, to be sure, but rather, since they have been sufficiently catechized in the tenets of the Catholic faith, to enter with all due solemnity, and in the ideal place, the Church of God, which they cannot do with aliases.

So, to this extent, and only to this extent, the *Quijote* is a masquerade with total oblivion of the original self which brings about defeat, abdication and death. The self was lost until the minute before entering Eternity. The *Persiles* is also a masquerade, but this is not a flight of the imagination, but rather it is imposed by the centripetal force of the Catholic faith. There are, in consequence, no defeats, just the triumphant acceptance of the protagonists into the bosom of the Catholic Church, and in the appropriate ante-chamber, Rome. There are no abdications, because giving up assumed aliases can hardly be called that; there are, instead, re-integrations of the protagonists to the identities they want to keep through Eternity. And, of course, there cannot be the death of the protagonists, because the recuperation of their true identities is a symbolic baptism, and Saint Paul had written as follows about the sacrament of Baptism: "For we were buried with him by means of Baptism into death, in order that, just as Christ has risen from the dead through the glory of the Father, so we also may walk in newness of life." (VI, 4)

The fundamental difference between the two novels in their plots is in that in the *Quijote* the protagonist is defeated, whereas in the *Persiles* the protagonist is triumphant. But then, for Don Quijote "truth is but a point of view", as Ortega y Gasset liked to say. Don Quijote himself will admit as much, and at the dramatic moment of the enchantment of Dulcinea, thanks to the wiles of Sancho: "Pues yo te digo, Sancho amigo, dijo don Quijote, que es tan verdad que son borricos o borricas como yo soy don Quijote y tú Sancho; *a lo menos, a mí me parecen tales"* (II, x). I do not see any point in dwelling on the truism that Don Quijote is not concerned at all, at any time in his life, with transcendental, religious, absolute truth. Let us not forget that the one that dies in the novel is Alonso Quijano, who has previously abdicated to his assumed *persona* of Don Quijote. The life of Don Quijote is a paean to the relativeity of truth. because the concept of truth with which he deals is in the *hic et nunc,* "la verdad de tejas abajo."

The case of the *Persiles* is extremely different, because just as the plot of the novel undeviatingly takes the protagonists to Rome, so the whole of the novel is attracted by the absolute truth of religion. This faith-centered living which Persiles and Sigismunda demonstrate in every moment of their lives had been reaffirmed and buttressed some fifty years before by the Catholic Reformation and the edicts of the Council of Trent, which we have seen converted into laws of the land by the zeal of Philip II. The *Persiles*, therefore, is dedicated to this aspect of truth, as the fruit of faith and dogma, and the differences of targets between the two novels (relative truth in the *Quijote*, absolute truth in the *Persiles*) should begin to explain the seemingly absurd position that Cervantes gives it among the works of fiction, and this is in no other place than the dedication of the Second Part of the *Quijote:* "Con esto me despido ofreciendo a V. E. los *Trabajos de Persiles y Sigismunda*, libro a quien daré fin dentro de cuatro meses, *Deo volente:* el cual ha de ser o el más malo o el mejor que en nuestra lengua se haya compuesto, quiero decir de los de entretenimiento; y digo que me arrepiento de haber dicho *el más malo*, porque, según la opinión de mis amigos, ha de llegar al estremo de bondad posible."

Cervantes, the child of the Renaissance, has finally some to terms with the new laws of the land. In his mind *Persiles* is the best novel of the Catholic Reformation in Spain because it was not the predictable picaresque novel, such as the *Guzmán de Alfarache* of Mateo Alemán. *Persiles* is, most definitely, the novel adumbrated by the Council of Trent; *Don Quijote de la Mancha*, regardless of whatever else we might think of it, definitely is not. In this respect, and only in this respect, *Don Quijote* could be called the novel of the Renaissance, whilst *Persiles* would be the novel of the Catholic Reformation.

UNIVERSITY OF NORTH CAROLINA

Cervantes y Ercilla

Juan M. Corominas

 PESAR DE la enorme cantidad de estudios literarios que se han hecho sobre Cervantes y su obra, no creo que se haya estudiado bastante la relación que media entre él y Ercilla, autor de *La Araucana*. El objeto del presente estudio, por su misma naturaleza sintético, es indicar y revelar esta relación: ver cómo Cervantes menciona encomiásticamente a Ercilla en algunos lugares de su obra literaria; cómo en otros, incluso lo personifica y dramatiza; y finalmente, cómo se inspira en obra ercillana para componer, para crear dos de sus dramas: *El gallardo español* y *El cerco de Numancia*. Interés especial de este estudio es hacer ver que la relación Ercilla-Cervantes es una relación renacentista.

Referente a esto último, creo que no hay dificultad en admitir que Alonso de Ercilla es un autor decididamente renacentista. Toda su formación humana y literaria es del tiempo del Emperador. En su misma persona, a través de su obra y de otros documentos, se nos ofrece siempre como un perfecto cortesano renacentista cortado sobre el patrón de Castiglione. Cuando Ercilla en la corte de Felipe II se ve en la precisión de ser un escritor barroco, se calla y se dedica a la censura de libros o a otros quehaceres muy ajenos a la literatura. Bastante más complejo es el caso de Cervantes a pesar de ser sólo

catorce años más joven que Ercilla. Debido a ciertas circunstancias
de su vida, le tocó cabalgar sobre el lomo de centurias culturalmente
diferentes.[1] Para algunos autores Cervantes fue siempre un autor
renacentista.[2] Yo diría que dichos críticos confunden e identifican el
renacimiento con el humanismo. Para otros críticos Cervantes en
cuanto escritor, fue siempre un autor decadente, que es lo mismo
que decir barroco.[3] Si admitimos que la vocación de escritor en Cervantes es desvelada por un acorralamiento de la vida y una obligada
retirada a la interioridad, no se puede negar que se dan en él dos
épocas. Una de ellas, la renacentista; es breve y es debida al impulso
renacentista remanente aun en su espíritu, a pesar de los graves
desengaños personales y del descalabro nacional de la Armada
Invencible. La segunda época es más prolongada y definitiva, es la
que corresponde al período barroco. Pero tanto en una como en
otra, Cervantes conserva siempre el humanismo de la Contrarre-
forma. Ortega y Gasset y Américo Castro no consideran la Contra-
rreforma como la causante del aislamiento y retraso de España.[4]
Con la terminología de Pfandl[5] se podría decir que el siglo XVI es el
siglo de la universalidad, y el siglo XVII el de la nacionalidad. En
consecuencia Cervantes sería un nacionalista a la manera de los de la
generación del 98. Pero ateniéndonos a la nomenclatura tradicional
se puede afirmar que Cervantes es renacentista en *La Galatea* y *El
cerco de Numancia*, las dos obras que más se relacionan con Ercilla.

Relación Personal

Según Toribio Medina, Ercilla y Cervantes de debieron encontrar y conocer por primera vez en Lisboa, cuando la campaña de
Portugal. Por documentos consta que por aquellas fechas Ercilla
estuvo en dicha capital. Allí se encontraba de seguro, el 16 de julio de
1582. Aprovechó esta oportunidad para solventar el asunto de una
publicación subrepticia de *La Araucana* que allí se había hecho. Casi
seguro que durante su estancia en Portugal posaba en casa de don
Álvaro de Bazán, Marqués de Santa Cruz, con el cual le unían víncu-
los de amistad y de parentesco por parte de su esposa doña María de
Bazán. Incluso es muy probable que participara al lado del Marqués
en la conquista de Las Azores y en la batalla naval del 22 de julio del
mismo año. Esto se puede conjeturar por el espíritu aventurero de
Ercilla, por su deseo reiteradamente manifestado de participar en
una batalla naval, y sobre todo por un romance que de él se conoce

compuesto con motivo de la dicha batalla.[6] Por aquellos mismos días, Cervantes, vuelto del cautiverio de Argel, se trasladó a Lisboa por hallarse allí la corte. El objetivo de su ida era recabar alguna ayuda económica con que saldar la deuda de su rescate, y a la vez hallar manera de reorganizar y encauzar su vida.[7] En Lisboa, necesariamente tuvo que visitar al Marqués de Santa Cruz, uno de los grandes generales en la batalla de Lepanto y a quien él en *El Quijote* celebra en los siguientes términos: «rayo de la guerra», «padre de los soldados» y «venturoso y jamás vencido capitán.»[8] Para afianzar más esta suposición téngase en cuenta, que después, Felipe II va a nombrar al Marqués encargado general del abastecimiento de la Armada Invencible y que Cervantes, con este mismo fin, fue comisario de abastos de Sevilla. Para cuando Cervantes fue a Lisboa, hacía por lo menos cuatro años que se había publicado la segunda parte de *La Araucana* en donde aparece un canto dedicado a la batalla de Lepanto, y lo más natural es que Cervantes lo hubiese leído y tuviera sumo interés en conocer a su autor. «Cervantes—escribe Medina—era un desconocido aun en las letras, pero las alusiones que a Ercilla hizo en su *Galatea* bajo nombre arcádico, y que había de publicar en 1584, prueban que intimó con él, para recordarle, por último, en elogiosos términos en su obra maestra.»[9]

Relación literaria

En *La Galatea*

Medina nos acaba de hablar de unas alusiones a Ercilla en *La Galatea* y de unos elogios en *El Quijote*. Veamos cuales fueron estas alusiones y estos elogios, empezando por los últimos.

En el celebrado escrutinio de los libros, en el capítulo VI de la primera parte, el barbero presenta al cura *La Araucana, La Austriada* y *El Monserrate*. «Todos tres libros—dijo el Cura—son los mejores que en verso heroico, en lengua castellana, están escritos, y pueden competir con los más famosos de Italia; guárdense como las más ricas prendas de poesía que tiene España.»[10] Y en la segunda parte del *Quijote,* en el capítulo XIV, cuando el desafío con el Caballero del Bosque, se citan unos versos de *La Araucana:*

> y tanto el vencedor es más honrado
> cuanto más el vencido es reputado;[11]

En *La Araucana* el refrán reza así:

> pues no es el vencedor más estimado
> de aquello que el vencido es reputado.[12]

En *La Araucana,* en el Canto xxvii el poeta, a través del globo prodigioso del mago Fitón ve el Cairo, que incluye tres ciudades, «y el palacio de Dultibea.» No sería nada extraño que esta Dultibea fuese la madrina de Dulcinea del Toboso.

En *La Galatea,* en el Canto de Calíope se dice de Ercilla:

> Y el que con justo título merece
> gozar de alta y honrada preeminencia,
>
> un don Alonso es, quien florece
> del sacro Apolo la divina ciencia;
> y en quien con alta lumbre resplandece
> de Marte el brío y sin igual potencia.[13]

Con las palabras «de Marte el brío. . .» seguramente que Cervantes hace alusión a *La Araucana.* Y no sería nada extraño que con «del sacro Apolo la divina ciencia» hiciera alusión a una glosa lírica de Ercilla, que según Medina fue su primera producción poética. Cervantes al igual que Lope de Vega conocieron dicha glosa antes que dos siglos después apareciera en el *Parnaso español.*[14]

En cuanto a la personificación de Ercilla en la persona del pastor Lauso, el autor de *La Galatea* lo introduce con las siguientes palabras: «Lauso amante de Silena y antiguo amigo de Damón. Fue cortesano y guerrero, habiendo visitado Asia y Europa.»[15] En una obra líricopastoril, difícilmente Cervantes podía referirse a Ercilla como autor épico; más bien debía considerarlo como un autor lírico. En la glosa de Ercilla el poeta se nos ofrece como un amante con el alma aprisionada por el eros-pasión y a la vez quebrantada por el desdén de la amada a la manera de los lances amorosos cortesano-renacentistas:

> Amor me ha reducido a tanto estrecho
> y puesto en tal extremo un desengaño
> que ya no puede el bien hacerme provecho
> ni el mal, aunque se esfuerce, mayor daño;
> todo lo que es posible está ya hecho;
> y pues no puede ya el dolor extraño
> crecer ni declinar sólo un momento
> *seguro estoy de nuevo descontento*[16].

Y así, con esta actitud llega a desearse la muerte. En *La Galatea,* Lauso se nos presenta en un proceso de superación. Si en los primeros libros se halla como el poeta de la glosa ercilliana, después, consigue triunfar del amor-pasión y se adueña de nuevo de su libertad.[17] Y eso, ni más ni menos es lo que ocurre históricamente a Ercilla. Según Medina, y en contra de la opinión general, la glosa vendría a ser la expresión real de un desengaño amoroso que le llevó a tomar la heroica resolución de abandonar la corte e irse a Chile.[18] Pero en *La Araucana* Ercilla triunfa del amor-pasión y recupera su libertad.[19] Sin embargo no por eso se deja de estimar el eros-voluntad, el eros platónico, como se puede inferir por lo que dice sobre el amor: «¿Qué cosa puede haber sin amor buena?» Y en lugar de hundirse en un resentimiento misógino, continúa, como buen humanista y renacentista venerando el eterno femenino. Como conclusión de todo lo dicho se podría decir que en *La Galatea* Cervantes presenta y dramatiza a Ercilla en la persona del Pastor Lauso, presentántole en su doble dimensión de épico y lírico.

Antes de seguir adelante con *El cerco de Numancia,* creo oportuno para ver la influencia de Ercilla en la obra de Cervantes parangonar algunos de los nombres propios usados en ambas obras y advertir su parecido poético y fonético:

En *La Araucana*	En *La Galatea*
Glaura	Claurara
Leocato y Leocotón	Eleuco
Lautaro	Lauso
Orompelo	Orompo
Crepino, Galbarino, Crino	Carino y Crisino

Los de *La Araucana* se suponen reales y originales, los de *La Galatea* son ficticios y creados.

En *El cerco de Numancia*

Con lo que hasta aquí llevamos dicho queda fuera de duda que Cervantes no sólo conocía personalmente a Ercilla, sino que también le eran familiares sus obras. Ahora vamos a dar un paso más y demostrar la última parte de la tesis que hemos asentado y probar que la obra de Ercilla inspiró a Cervantes en la creación de dos de sus obras dramáticas: *El cerco de Numancia* y *El gallardo español.* La que aquí nos interesa es *El cerco de Numancia,* por ser una obra cervantina renacentista.[20]

Por lo que a *El gallardo español* se refiere, la primera obra dramática de la segunda época cervantina, Cotarelo y Mori dice que debe relacionarse con el viaje que por encargo de Felipe II hizo a Orán. Ahora bien, sabemos que este encargo le fue hecho en Lisboa y en la misma ocasión en que tuvo que conocer a Ercilla. El drama podría considerarse renacentista por el fondo de tema morisco. Con ello entraría en la órbita de las novelas y crónicas moriscas como *Las guerras civiles de Granada* de Ginés Pérez de Hita, de las crónicas de Hurtado de Mendoza y de los romances moriscos, todo ello de la época del Emperador. Pero, es ya barroco por la forma de enredo, por los lances de capa y espada y por la figura del gracioso. Dicho drama indudablemente se inspira en lo esencial en *La Araucana.*

En el segundo canto de la obra el poeta nos narra el primer ataque de los araucanos después de elegido Caupolicán. En su avance inesperado hallaron desprevenidos a los españoles en tres fuertes de vanguardia. El primero que acometieron fue el fuerte de Tucapel, cercándolo y estrechándolo de mala manera. Los españoles sitiados, ante la multitud del enemigo y vista la imposibilidad de todo socorro, comenzaron a desmoralizarse. Entonces un mozo de la guarnición, para infundir ánimo a los compañeros, caló sobre el puente y retó a los enemigos con las siguientes palabras:

> «Salga adelante, salga el más valiente
> y a mil no negaré este cuerpo mío».

Y el poeta prosigue:

> No porque tantos vengan temor tiene
> el gallardo español, ni esto le espanta, . . .[21]

No cabe duda de que este gallardo español cuyo nombre desconocemos va a ser el modelo y el prototipo del otro gallardo español cervantino cuyo nombre conocemos y que en contra de las órdenes de don Alonso de Córdoba, saltó el foso y se apresuró a contestar al reto de Alimuzel:

> a pesar de todo el mundo
> que lo quiera defender[22].

Huelga decir que este cerco de Orán, este foso que se tiene que vadear y el capitán Fernando de Saavedra nos traen a la memoria otro cerco cervantino, otro foso y el desafío de Carabino en *El cerco de Numancia*. Y tanto uno como otro, el de Numancia y el de Orán, dependen literariamente del Tucapel en *La Araucana*.

Pero dejando de lado *El gallardo español* vengamos ya a *El cerco de Numancia*.

Es tanta la afinidad material y formal que existe entre las dos obras que se puede advertir a simple vista la dependencia de una de la otra. Voy a indicar solamente algunos de los puntos de semejanza, no todos, y sin bajar a pormenores y análisis. Con el sólo parangón se advertirá inmediatamente la influencia.

En primer lugar se trata de dos obras literarias renacentistas que intentan restaurar dos géneros clásicos—la epopeya y la tragedia—y ambas carecen de protagonista individual. Por esta razón los preceptistas y los críticos neoclásicos negaron el carácter de epopeya a *La Araucana* y el de tragedia a *El cerco de Numancia*. A propósito de esta última, Menéndez Pelayo replicó diciendo que en *La Numancia* la tragedia de todo un pueblo es tan humana y sentida que produce tanta o más impresión de terror y de compasión que las tragedias personales.[23] Y varios críticos han hecho notar que Esquilo también tiene algunas tragedias de personaje colectivo como *Los siete contra Tebas* y *Los Persas*.[24]

Lo primero que vamos a ver en la relación comparativa de las dos obras es que los motivos que producen el conflicto bélico son los mismos. Ni en Numancia ni en el Arauco, contra lo que se podrá creer, la guerra es el resultado de la resistencia a la invasión o la conquista, sino una sublevación posterior, después de haberse dejado conquistar por los que ellos tomaron por superhombres. Pero una vez cayeron en cuenta del error, al ver que eran mortales como ellos; y sobre todo ante la extorsión, crueldad, opresión e injusticia de que eran objeto, se determinaron a sublevarse y rebelarse.[25] Y lo mismo que ocurre en el Arauco, ocurre en Numancia. Jamás se hubieran los numantinos apartado de la sujeción al senado romano a no ser por los desafueros y desmanes de los cónsules.[26] En ambas obras se hace hincapié sobre la avaricia y la explotación por parte de los conquistadores: «la hambrienta y mísera codicia» *(La Araucana)*, «y con su extraña condición avara» *(Numancia)*.

Lo mismo en Numancia que en el Arauco la guerra se prolonga indefinidamente con alternativas de una y otra parte por falta de un hombre estratega y enérgico en el bando de los conquistadores. Únicamente empieza a llevar buen camino en el momento que llegan dos enérgicos generales que lo mismo literaria que históricamente tienen mucho de parecido. Tales personajes son Escipión el Africano, en Numancia, y García Hurtado de Mendoza, Marqués de Cañete, en el Arauco. Los Numantinos y los Araucos advierten inmediatamente que las cosas van a cambiar y tomar otro sesgo en su perjuicio, y se aprestan a negociar un armisticio. Pero visto que tanto uno como otro imponen una rendición incondicional y sin garantías, se deciden a continuar desesperadamente la guerra hasta la extinción. En ambos casos se hace notar que más por las armas o la táctica militar, son vencidos por la enfermedad, la peste y hambre. En último término los únicos que triunfan son la muerte y la fama. Tanto en una como en otra obra los vencidos antes de darse la muerte practican lo que hoy se llama política de la tierra quemada. Los Araucanos y los Numantinos queman sus enseres y su riqueza. «Nada encontrará el invasor. Nada útil encontrará cuando entre. El fuego, más misericordioso, recogerá los ajuares y prendas.» En ello el sacrificio se trueca en un perfecto holocausto.

El idilio trágico de Marandro y Lira en *La Numancia* aúna y sintetiza, como no podía ser menos en una obra teatral, todos los caracteres de los idilios trágicos de *La Araucana*: el de Gualcolda y Lautaro cuando en los momentos de intimidad conyugal presienten y presagian la muerte que se acerca para destruirles para siempre el amor; el de Tegualda que viene a recoger el cuerpo de su esposo Crepino para llevárselo a enterrar a su tierra;[30] el de Lauca que malherida junto al cadáver de su esposo considera como la peor de las crueldades de los españoles su compasión para con ella y el intento que muestran de curarla.[31] Adviértase de paso como lo hemos hecho con *La Galatea,* el parecido poético y fonetico de algunos nombres, incluso tienen parecido en su papel dramático: Galvarino en *La Araucana* y Caravino en *Numancia,* el de Mareguano en *La Araucana* y el de Marandro en *Numancia,* Leocato y Leocotón en *La Araucana* y Leonicio en *Numancia.* En *Numancia* también Lira y Marandro presagian el próximo fin de su amor debido a la muerte que se les viene en cima.[32] Lira, lo mismo que Tegualda, tiene en su regazo a su esposo muerto, y ambas desaparecen de la escena llevándose a su esposo a enterrar.[33] Lira al igual que Lauca a los españoles, suplica a un soldado numantino que por favor no use de piedad para con ella, antes bien la trate con rigor y acabe de matarla.[34]

En las dos obras los hechiceros con sus augurios, escudriñando el vuelo de las aves vaticinan la próxima destrucción y ruina de la nación. En *La Araucana* Tucapel mata a uno de los hechiceros, en *La Numancia* el hechicero Marquino se precipita dentro de la tumba abierta del muchacho que por arte de magia negra había hecho aparecer. En ambas obras se invoca al diablo: en *La Araucana* se le llama Epanomón y en *La Numancia,* Plutón. E incluso en ambas se hace visible. También es común en ambas obras la antropofagia en los momentos extremos del hambre. En *Numancia* se comen la carne de los enemigos, en *La Araucana* la de los propios familiares.[35]

Con todo lo visto hasta el presente, se nos hace evidente la semejanza que media entre las dos obras. Sin embargo el hecho contundente de esta semejanza y por tanto de una influencia directa entre ambas obras, es el suicidio del último superviviente. En *Numancia* realiza la hecatombe trágica un muchacho que primeramente, horrorizado ante la visión de la muerte huye a esconderse en lo más alto de una torre. Inadvertido por la espada exterminadora, es el único superviviente de toda la ciudad. Yugurta lo descubre y Escipión intenta apresarlo con el halago de joyas y de riquezas. Pero Bariato, que así se llama el muchacho, impresionado por el lúgubre silencio de muerte que reina en la ciudad, y visto el sacrificio heroico de todo su pueblo, increpa al vencedor y entonando una oración fúnebre a los muertos, a «cuantos ya son muertos en este pueblo,» se suicida a la manera de Melibea, precipitándose desde lo alto de la torre y cayendo muerto a los pies de Escipión. En *La Araucana,* en el último canto de la primera parte, como una resolución dramática, también se realiza una hecatombe trágica del único superviviente. Villagrán había sorprendido a los araucanos dentro de una fortaleza. Igual que los numantinos, los araucanos fueron atacados y apremiados hasta el extremo. Villagrán les intimidó la rendición y ellos exclamaron:

> Los ojos contra el cielo vueltos, braman,
> «¡Morir, morir! no dicen otra cosa.
> Morir quieren, y así la muerte llaman
> gritando: ¡Afuera vida vergonzosa!»
>
> Ningún bárbaro en pie quedó en el fuerte,
> ni brazo que mover pudiese espada:
> sólo Mallén que al punto de la muerte
> le dio de vivir gana acelerada. . .[37]

Pero al igual que Bariato, viendo a todo el pueblo muerto se suicida:

> Aquí cerró la voz, y no dudando,
> entrega el cuello a la homicida espada;
> corriendo con presteza el crudo filo,
> sin razón de la vida cortó el hilo.

En ambas obras se hace resaltar la presencia impresionante del silencio: «todo está en calma y silencio puesta» (Cervantes); «Que como dije, ya la muerte había—puesto silencio con airada mano» (Ercilla). Como un triunfo de la muerte sobre los dos montones de cadáveres, ambos autores, mayormente Ercilla debido a la índole de la obra, describen con un realismo naturalista el espectáculo de los muertos. Este espectáculo impresiona a Mallén como había impresionado a Bariato.

Finalmente, lo mismo en *La Araucana* que en *La Numancia,* por más que Ercilla diga en alguna ocasión que se movió a escribir para dejar constancia del valor de los castellanos, al igual que Cervantes, la fuerza que les impulsa a escribir es el ardiente deseo de dar vida inmortal a través de la fama a los que supieron morir libres antes que vivir con vituperio esclavos de un pueblo que a su vez era esclavo. Según Ercilla el castellano era esclavo de la avaricia y rapacidad; y según Cervantes el romano lo era de la libidinosidad y crápula. En *La Numancia* la última que tiene la palabra es la fama.[38] En *La Araucana* es el autor que tiene la primera al decirnos en el prólogo que quiere pagar tributo de admiración a un pueblo que «con duro valor y porfiada determinación hayan redimido y sustentado su libertad, derramando en sacrificio della tanta sangre así suya como de los españoles, que con verdad se puede decir haber pocos lugares que no estén della teñidos y poblados de huesos. . .[39]

Creo que muy poco se ha estudiado la relación Ercilla-Cervantes. Y sin embargo, es evidente que medió entre ellos una relación, sobre todo por parte de Cervantes; relación de admiración por la obra de aquel, trato personal e influencia literaria en su época renacentista. Los dos autores mirando el pasado clásico quisieron hacerlo renacer —renacimiento—en sus tiempos, e infundiéndole una fuerte carga de humanismo. Este humanismo; fruto de la reviviscencia platónica y el Evangelio, es la característica del renacimiento español. Humanismo que va a permanecer durante la época barroca en los tiempos de decepción y de decadencia. Este humanismo es el que se halla en toda la obra de Cervantes y que ha hecho pensar a algunos críticos que Cervantes fue siempre renacentista. Ciertamente fue renacentista, lo fue en sus primeras obras, pero no lo fue siempre. Cuando Ercilla optó por callarse antes que dejar de ser renacentista dentro de la línea de Garcilaso, entonces le tocaba el turno a Cervantes que comenzaba a escribir.

CALIFORNIA STATE UNIVERSITY, DOMINGUEZ HILLS

NOTAS

[1]Juan Luis Alborg, *Historia de la literatura española*, 2a. ed., tomo II (Madrid: Gredos, 1974), p. 25.

[2]A. Bell, *El renacimiento español*, (Zaragoza: Ebro, 1944).

[3]Ramiro de Maeztu, *Don Quijote, Don Juan y La Celestina*, 10a. ed. (Madrid: Espasa-Calpe, 1968).

[4]Américo Castro, *La realidad histórica de España*, 4a. ed. (México: Editorial Porrúa, 1971), p. 3.

[5]Ludwig Pfandl, *Historia de la literatura nacional española en el siglo de oro*, trad. por J. Rubió (Barcelona, 1932).

[6]José Toribio Medina, *Vida de Ercilla* (México: Fondo de Cultura Económica, 1948), págs. 131-2.

[7]Martín de Riquer, *Aproximación al Quijote* (Estella, Salvat, 1970), p. 24.

[8]Miguel de Cervantes Saavedra, *Obras completas*, 10a. ed. (Madrid: Aguilar, 1956), p. 1209. Todas las referencias a obras de Cervantes van a ser tomadas de esta edición.

[9]Medina, p. 134.

[10]Cervantes, p. 1316.

[11]Cervantes, p. 1316

[12]Alonso de Ercilla, *La Araucana*, 4a. ed. (México: Editorial Porrúa, 1977), p. 15. De aquí en adelante todas las citas de *La Araucana* serán tomadas de esta edición, citando el canto y la página.

[13]Cervantes, págs. 745-6.

[14]Medina, p. 13.

[15]Cervantes, p. 607.

[16]Medina, p. 31.

[17]Cervantes, p. 690.

[18]Medina, p. 31.

[19]Ercilla, Canto I, p. 15.

[20]Edilberto Marbán, *El teatro español del renacimiento* (New York: Las Américas, 1971), p. 247.

[21]Ercilla, Canto II, p. 42;

[22]Cervantes, p. 187.

[23]Marcelino Menéndez Pelayo, *Estudios de crítica histórica y literaria*, tomo I de *Obras Completas* (Madrid: C.S.I.C., 1941), p. 260.

[24]Alborg, p. 57.

[25]Ercilla, Canto I, p. 26:

> Crecían los intereses y malicia
> a costa del sudor ajeno,
> y la hambrienta y mísera codicia,
> con libertad paciendo iba sin freno:

[26]Cervantes, p. 150:

> Dice que nunca de la ley y los fueros
> del Senado romano se apartara
> si el insufrible mando y desafueros
> de un consul y otro no le fatigara.

[27]Ercilla, Canto XII, p. 173:

> Que se llame victoria yo lo dudo
> cuando el contrario a tal extremo viene,
> que en aquello que nunca el valor pudo
> la hambre miserable poder tiene:
> y así por bajo modo y estrecheza
> viene a parecer fuerte la flaqueza.

[28]Rafael Alberti, *Numancia* (Madrid: Turner, 1975), p 78.

[29]Ercilla, Canto XII, p. 196.

[30]Ercilla, Canto XXI, p. 296.

[31]Ercilla. Canto XXXII, p. 443.

[32]Cervantes, p. 165:

> Pienso cómo mi contento
> y el tuyo se va acabando;
> y no será su homicida
> el cerco de nuestra tierra:
> que primero que la guerra
> se me acabará la vida.

[33]Cervantes, p. 179; Ercilla, Canto XXI, p. 297.

[34]Cervantes, p. 170:

> Lira
>
> Esa piedad que quies usar conmigo
> valeroso soldado, yo te juro,
> y alto Cielo pongo por testigo,
> que yo la estimo por rigor muy duro.

[35]Ercilla, Canto IX, p. 126; Cervantes, p. 164.

[36]Cervantes, p. 175.

[37]Ercilla, Canto XV, p. 215.

[38]Cervantes, p. 176.

[39]Ercilla, Prólogo, p. 11.

Cervantes and the Question
of Language

ELIAS L. RIVERS

HE RENAISSANCE may be defined, in one of its most fundamental aspects, as a linguistic revolution. We all know that humanism, in the strict sense of the word, began as a radical attempt to restore Classical (written) Latin: that is, the humanists recognized that what passed for Latin in medieval schools, churches and universities was very different from the *Latinitas,* the elegantly written Latinity, which they so admired in Virgil and Cicero, in Horace and Tacitus. They realized that something long ago had happened culturally which they could see only as a barbarous corruption and decline; for them, to restore true Latinity was to return to the wholesome primitive roots of European civilization, to encourage its rebirth. Such was the polemical, anti-scholastic stance of those militant humanistic scholars, such as Petrarch and Boccaccio, who began to write Neolatin eclogues and epistles for a new and growing European public. By the end of the 15th century Nebrija had written a new Latin textbook for schools in Spain; and Queen Isabel la Católica was encouraging even her elderly courtiers to learn to read and write this restored Classical Latin.

You and I, of course, have a somewhat more complex historical perspective. But we have to admit that the humanists basically knew what they were talking about. As we now know, Virgil and Cicero had in fact invented Classical (written) Latin by imposing upon the vernacular dialects spoken around Rome the written models of the Greek culture: they used the Greek dactylic hexameter, Greek philosophical concepts, and Greek cadences and figures as templates, so to speak, filtering the vulgarity out of the spoken language and giving an elegant texture to their Classical Latin writings. But Vulgar Latin continued to be spoken among the lower classes, of course, and later on, with the Christian revolution, the language of slaves and criminals imposed itself, counterculturally, in written form: St. Jerome's translation of the Bible and St. Augustine's sermons shocked the pagan aristocrats (who still wrote like Cicero and Virgil); it shocked them because this new church Latin smelled strongly of the gutter, of lower class religious fanatics and anti-intellectuals who had the bad taste to insist upon crucifixion and other vulgar forms of martyrdom intended for common criminals, a bad taste which was naturally reflected in their uncouth style of writing. Later on Charlemagne tried to restore Classical Latin for his own imperial purposes; but the Carolingian reform only complicated the situation by introducing a new sophistication. Such were the roots of medieval European diglossia: there was a growing split between the way people spoke their mother tongues (Celtic and Germanic and Romance dialects) and the way the educated minority wrote the Latin academic language of Church, Empire and university (whether is was the Latin of the Church fathers or neoclassical Carolingian Latin).

By the time our Renaissance humanists appeared on the scene, literature was already being written in the modern European languages: oral French epics had been transcribed and imitated in the *romans courtois;* folk poetry of love was being absorbed by written courtly love lyrics in Provençal, French, Italian, Catalan, Portuguese and even German; and in Italian the *Divina Commedia* was a great medieval monument, in which, according to Auerbach, we can first hear again echoes of Virgil's sublime style. And it was Dante himself who, in *De vulgari eloquentia,* first defended the use of the vernacular, in opposition to Latin, as a vehicle of serious literature. So we can see that once again a great Christian writer was defending the language of the people against the language of an élite, whether clerical or humanistic.

I have said that we may define the Renaissance as a cultural, and therefore a linguistic, revolution. The real linguistic revolution turned out to be, not the pan-European humanists' restoration of Classical Latin, but the national vernacular writers' invention of neoclassical styles in the modern European languages. This starts, as we have seen, in the Tuscan dialect of Italy, with Dante, Petrarch and Boccaccio; their neoclassical written language imposed itself culturally upon the other spoken dialects of Italy, giving rise to great continuing debates concerning the establishment of a standard written vernacular as the vehicle of high literary culture. By the 16th century the Italian *questione della lingua* was spreading to Spain, France and England. Bembo advocated Dante, Boccaccio and Petrarch as the only models of Italian style; Castiglione attacked this rigidly conservative program and advocated a more fluid modern basis for a national prose style. Nebrija was Spain's Bembo, holding up Juan de Mena as a model of Spanish style; Boscán translated Castiglione's ideas about language into a new Spanish prose, and Juan de Valdés, in his *Diálogo de la lengua,* strongly attacked Nebrija's *Gramática de la lengua castellana* and proposed a *rapprochement* of courtly Spanish speech and a written prose which was perfectly exemplified in his dialogue itself. Just as Virgil and Cicero long ago had invented a Classical (written) Latin by imposing Greek literary patterns and ideas upon Roman vernaculars, so in the 16th century Garcilaso and Boscán invented a classical written Spanish verse and prose which reflected Classical Latin patterns and ideas, as mediated, of course, by the Italian of Boccaccio and Petrarch, Castiglione, Sannazaro and Bernardo Tasso.

Cervantes was born thirteen years after the publication of Boscán's *Cortesano* (1534) and only four years after that of Garcilaso's poetry (1543). He read them both early in his life, and his first literary maturity, in the 1580's, was firmly based on these established classical idioms of Spanish verse and prose. Cervantes probably did not read Juan de Valdés' *Diálogo de la lengua,* which was not published until late in the 18th century; but we can learn from this radical Christian reformer what it was that Boscán and Garcilaso thought they had accomplished. Valdés' dialogue was written in

Naples in the 1530's while Garcilaso was also there, at the height of his poetic career. Valdés was a Christian humanist who, unlike Erasmus, wrote in his own vernacular, his mother-tongue; like St. Augustine and Dante, like the Protestants, like Fray Luis de León later on, Valdés chose the vernacular because he believed "vox populi vox Dei", that God speaks in the language of the people. But Valdés was also a courtly aristocrat, who strongly believed in his own good taste. Avalle-Arce has shown better than anyone else just how sophisticated in structure Valdés' *Diálogo* really is: whether such a dialogue ever actually took place or not, Valdés transcribed or imagined it in an elegantly written prose, with no signs of the "hemming and hawing" of actual redundant oral conversation. In his dialogue Valdés advocated the establishment of a clearly written expository style of Spanish prose which should be as close as possible to the Spanish vernacular spoken by cultured people in the city of Toledo. Garcilaso in his poetry did something very similar; he wrote a Spanish with very few words which were not common in the spoken language of his native city; but, as Lapesa has shown, in a subtle way Garcilaso imposed upon these common words certain syntactical and semantic patterns that derive from Latin poetry. This fusion of the vernacular with a pre-existing literary tradtion was in fact the creation of the classical idiom of Spanish poetry. And Boscán's translation of Castiglione's *Cortegiano* was a similar linguistic and stylistic feat. Cervantes undoubtedly read Garcilaso's prologue to this translation, in which he says: "It being in my opinion as difficult to translate a book well as to write it from scratch, Boscán was so able in this matter that each time I begin to read this book of his, I have the feeling that it doesn't exist in any other language. . . He has managed to accomplish in the Spanish language what very few have achieved, which is to avoid affectation without falling into flatness, and with great purity of style he has used terms which are quite courtly and acceptable to refined ears, neither too new nor yet fallen into disuse among the people."

Cervantes was still a young man when the classical achievement of Garcilaso was canonized academically, in the 1570's, by the critical editions and commentaries of the great Latin grammarian of Salamanca Francisco Sánchez de las Brozas, or El Brocense, known in Europe as Sanctius, and by the monumental edition and commentaries of Fernando de Herrera, the scholar-poet of Seville. Cervantes, in the 1580's, had this edition available while writing the *Cerco de Numancia* and the *Galatea*. They helped him complete his own education as a Renaissance man who had traveled in Italy and had read the Italian classics.

More than one scholar has pointed out some of the many echos of Garcilaso's poetry which are found everywhere in Cervantes' works, from beginning to end, in verse and in prose. He also knew the poetry of Ariosto and Ercilla. For his prose he had other models, both Italian (Boccaccio, Castiglione) and Spanish (Boscán, Montemayor). We find an original synthesis of such classical models in his heroic play on the destruction of the Iberian town Numantia by the Roman army under Scipio; although the language and versification is classical, the theme is radically Christian, for the death of this town is presented as a paradoxical *felix culpa,* a grim physical martyrdom that will lead to the resurrection of Catholic Spain under Charles V, who will sack the Pope's Rome, and under Philip II, whose brother will defeat the Turks in the battle of Lepanto. Despite its classical pretensions, this play reminds us less of Garcilaso's Italian humanism than of the Spanish and Christian humanism of Fray Luis de León.

If we focus upon a central episode in Cervantes' *Galatea* (1585), we find a similar synthesis of Classical and Christian elements. The funeral of a great shepherd-poet, representing Don Diego Hurtado de Mendoza, takes place in a classical landscape like that of Garcilaso's eclogues; but the tall trees of the grove inevitably remind us of the columns of a Gothic Cathedral. Garcilaso's Tagus Valley near Toledo is revisited in a pantheistic mood: the river and the land embrace each other, and God's nature reaches its plenitude in its synthesis with agricultural man's technology, whose waterwheels, for example, are able to irrigate the fields which are far from the river. This is Cervantes' syncretistic vision of a pastoral utopia, of a Platonic return to nature; and the beautiful flow of Cervantes' classical prose here reflects what seems to be the fundamental nature of a harmonious universe *(Galatea,* VI):

> La tierra que abraza [al río], vestida de mil verdes ornamentos, parece que hace fiesta y se alegra de poseer en sí un don tan raro y agradable; y el dorado río, como en cambio, en los brazos de ella dulcemente entretejiéndose, forma como de industria mil entradas y salidas, que a cualquiera que las mira

> llenan el alma de placer maravilloso, de donde nace que,
> aunque los ojos tornen de nuevo muchas veces a mirarle, no
> por eso dejan de hallar en él cosas que les causen nuevo placer
> y nueva maravilla.

Here we have, fully achieved, the "zero degree" of the classical, periodic Renaissance style of writing in Spanish.

But Cervantes' career as a writer did not, of course, end in 1585. If it had, if Cervantes had been no more than the minor Renaissance author of the *Numancia* and the *Galatea,* we wouldn't be here now at this Cervantes symposium. His career was interrupted, for almost ten years; and when he began writing again, he was no longer the same Renaissance man. We don't know exactly what happened to him, spiritually, during these ten years of silence; we do know that, socially, he suffered financial difficulties, that he was excommunicated and sent to prison. There was also the defeat of the Invincible Armada, which had presumably been destined to liberate Catholic England from Protestant tyranny. Should we speak of a *desengaño,* a spiritual crisis in the life of Cervantes? Whatever it was, exactly, it seems to correspond to something akin to what Hyram Haydn has called the "Counter-Renaissance," the skeptical disintegration of that early optimistic synthesis reflected in a classical style of language.

To see what this meant in Spanish terms, we need only recall Acuña's famous sonnet in which he sings of the reunification of Catholic Europe under the rule of the Spanish Empire:

> . . .una grey y un pastor solo en el suelo. . .
> un monarca, un imperio y una espada. . .

In sharp contrast to this sonnet, we have two sonnets by Cervantes dating from the 1590's: one on the English invasion and prolonged sack of the Spanish port of Cádiz, and the other on the catafalque erected in the cathedral of Seville for King Philip II's requiem mass. The tone of these two sonnets is far from that of solemn unity of church and empire: their tone is a surprisingly light one of detached amusement. A certain Captain Becerra had drilled Spanish troops to reenter Cádiz, and Cervantes writes with colloquial irony in the first tercet:

> Bramó el becerro, y púsoles en sarta;
> tronó la tierra, oscurecióse el cielo
> amenazando una total rüina. . .

And then, in the second tercet, after the Count or Earl of Essex had
left Cádiz completely of his own accord, the Duke of Medinaceli
calmly entered in triumph:

> y al cabo, en Cádiz, con mesura harta,
> ido ya el conde sin ningún recelo,
> triunfando entró el gran duque de Medina.

This is a vision of the Spanish Empire and its myths that anticipates the modern satirical vision of a Juan Goytisolo, for example;
but instead of bitter satire, we have Cervantes indulging in light
laughter. Even lighter in tone is his more famous sonnet on Philip
II's funeral; it's much more subtly indirect. In this sonnet Cervantes
doesn't even mention the king himself, except in the title "Al
túmulo de Felipe II," and he refers only indirectly to the impressive
pseudo-coffin erected in the central aisle of the cathedral; a profane
soldier exclaims about its grandeur in the first eleven lines:

> Voto a Dios que me espanta esta grandeza. . .
> Por Jesucristo vivo, cada pieza
> vale más de un millón. . . *etcetera*

Then, in the second tercet, a tough guy backs him up, swagger-
ing out meaninglessly in an *estrambote:*

> Esto oyó un valentón, y dijo: «es cierto
> cuanto dice vuacé, señor soldado,
> y quien dijere lo contrario, miente.»
> Y luego incontinente
> caló el chapeo, requirió la espada,
> miró al soslayo, fuése, y no hubo nada.

It all ends in nothingness, anticipating later sonnets by Góngora
and Sor Juana Inés de la Cruz. In both of these "Counter-
Renaissance" sonnets by Cervantes the classical language of Garcilaso and Acuña has disintegrated; it has been infiltrated by colloquial
vulgarities. And it is burlesque sonnets such as these that introduce
the first part of *Don Quijote;* one, for example, is a dialogue between
the Cid's horse, Babieca, and Don Quijote's Rocinante, with the
brilliant line about the relationship between being philosophical and
not eating:

«Metafísico estáis.» «Es que no como.»

The novel *Don Quijote* itself is, as we might expect, Cervantes' major commentary upon Renaissance and post-Renaissance language. The mad knight fights to maintain classical humanistic standards of diction. His famous speeches on the Golden Age, for example, or on arms and letters, or his courtly advice to Sancho on how to behave as governor, are all direct reflections of Renaissance handbooks, and—out of context—they may be read "straight", that is, as serious rhetorical elaborations upon traditional classical commonplaces:

> Don Quijote. . . tomó un puño de bellotas en la mano y, mirándolas atentamente, soltó la voz a semejantes razones:
> —Dichosa edad y siglos dichosos aquellos a quien los antiguos pusieron el nombre de dorados. . . Eran en aquella santa edad todas las cosas comunes: a nadie le era necesario para alcanzar su ordinario sustento tomar otro trabajo que alzar la mano y alcanzarle de las robustas encinas, que libremente les estaban convidando con su dulce sazonado fruto. . . Todo era paz entonces, todo amistad, todo concordia: aún no se había atrevido la pesada reja del corvo arado a abrir ni visitar las entrañas piadosas de nuestra primera madre; que ella, sin ser forzada, ofrecía, por todas las partes de su fértil y espacioso seno, lo que pudiese hartar, sustentar y deleitar a los hijos que entonces la poseían. . .

This, taken in itself, sounds like a return to the zero-degree of Renaissance writing which we saw in the *Galatea*. But then we recall that it is being declaimed in the presence of the goatherds and Sancho Panza, people who don't understand how anyone could actually *prefer* to eat acorns and other such natural foods. Sancho's language provides constant cointerpoint to Don Quijote's Renaissance style, not by representing a later period, but an earlier one: the essentially medieval Spanish peasant, the "cristiano viejo" who hates Jews and can neither read nor write, much less Latin, and whose encyclopedia is the *refranero*, that inexhaustible store of traditional wisdom passed on orally from generation to generation. Don Quijote corrects Sancho's grammar, trying in vain to impose upon peasant speech the bookishness of Latinizing humanism: "Don't say *regoldar*, Sancho: the proper word is *eructar*." So then, if Sancho represents a medieval style of speech and Don Quijote the Renaissance style, who represents the Baroque? There is obviously no single character to be a gongoristic mouthpiece: it is rather a matter of the total linguistic context, the range, mixture and interplay of styles, presided over by an elusive narrator, reworking an imaginary series of narrators and making ironic fun of the whole complicated linguistic structure.

The prologue to the first part of the *Quijote* is where we can see Cervantes' playful burlesque in its purest form, for in it he masterfully "deconstructs" the prologue itself as a Renaissance genre. A prologue is textually ambiguous and transitional, standing between the external author, as an historical human being of flesh and blood, and the internal narrator, as a fictitious *persona* of paper and ink. A literary text is the disembodiment of real human speech, which is always centered upon an *ego hic et nunc,* a first person singular who gestures with body language in the middle of his world, trying to convince a second person, or persons, nearby, with a torrent of illocutionary speech acts. But when the first person singular, instead of standing there and asserting his physical presence in a unique here-and-now, is discovered to be inscribed upon a piece of paper, with no real person present in that present tense of the verbs which he seems to be speaking from within that piece of paper, what is the reader to think? For no one ever really said those words as an authentic performative act of speech *in praesentia;* they first came into existence as writing, addressed to an imagined or anticipated reader: "Desocupado lector. . ."

Even an orthodox prologue cannot avoid ambiguities of this sort. If the author is a serious humanist, he takes academic scholarship seriously and is obliged to present himself on paper as a learned authority. But he has another rhetorical task, which is to capture the good will of his reader, by making himself seem modest, *simpático.* Cervantes decided to resolve this dilemma by making fun of academic scholarship, disclaiming it altogether. His literary style becomes colloquial in the very first sentence of the prologue: "Desocupado lector: sin juramento me podrás creer que quisiera que este libro, como hijo del entendimiento, fuera el más hermoso, el más gallardo, y más directo que pudiera imaginarse." Thus he begins taking the reader into his confidence by declaring, with winning modesty, that his book is not beautiful and doesn't deserve a prologue, which he is *at this moment* (*hic ego et nunc*) finding very difficult to write, even as the reader is reading it, a simultaneity which is, of course, impossible: "aunque me costó algún trabajo componerla [his-toria], ninguno tuve por mayor que hacer esta prefación que vas leyendo." It is shortly after this point that a friend of the author's just happens to come into his study; the rest of the prologue is, as you may recall, a dialogue with this friend, who advises him to use second-hand humanistic erudition in his prologue to heighten by contrast the authentic values of the story itself.

What is the meaning of this strange anti-prologue about the difficulties of writing a prologue? I think its meaning is closely related to the meaning of the novel as a whole, which questions whether texts, no matter how fictitious, can ever be radically separated from the truth of human existence; but they can't be identified with human existence, either, as Don Quijote in his madness tries to claim. In the prologue we see a writer as an old man trying to write, to invent a new *écriture*, and his struggle becomes the substance of the text; in the novel we see a reader as an old man trying to live what he reads, and his struggles to convert texts into the substance of his life becomes in fact the substance of another super-text. All texts, for writer and reader alike, are rooted deeply in human existence; but human existence is something more physical, as well. This problematical view of literature, of disembodied language as part of our human substance, marks a decisive step beyond the simple faith of Renaissance humanism and non-problematical, or classical, language.

For further commentaries upon questions of language, style and poetry, we may turn to his *Viaje del Parnaso,* published in 1613. In form this poem is a mock epic, a classical parody, with traces of the Spanish picaresque; it is a poem about the status of poetry and poets in the Spain of Cervantes' own time. The first-person narrator and protagonist, named Miguel de Cervantes, seems to be nostalgic for an earlier Renaissance humanism; but he is actually aware that, in Spain at least, humanism has broken down and that there are no firm classical standards in literature anymore: "bad" poetry is praised and rewarded financially, while "good" poets starve to death. Cervantes has deep dark doubts in his mind: could poetry as literary texts be kept at a classically controlled distance in order solemnly to teach us morality and truth? Or was poetry, the literary text, really a picaresque illusionistic game which only a quixotic madman could take seriously? These are some of the radical questions which Cervantes implicitly poses in his rather bitterly satirical *Viaje del Parnaso:*

> Y cuando encuentro algún poeta honrado
> (digo poeta firme y valedero,
> hombre vestido bien y bien calzado),
>   luego se me figura ver un cuero,
> o alguna calabaza, y de esta suerte
> entre contrarios pensamientos muero.

The financially rewarded poet, socially accepted, well dressed and well shod, is seen to be really a hollow windbag or floating pumpkin, after Cervantes' imaginary voyage, dream vision, and battle of the books; his last line ("entre contrarios pensamientos muero") is borrowed from the classical poetry of Garcilaso's *Elegía II* to express, in a burlesque way, his own doubts about the literary and social status of good classical poetry, at least in Madrid.

In the *Viaje del Parnaso* Cervantes praises Góngora's poetry in the highest terms, calling it "inimitable". For us, of course, Góngora's poetry must represent the Baroque transformation, or disintegration, of Garcilaso's classically unified idiom: instead of Garcilaso's perfect balance of Spanish and Latin vocabulary and syntax, Góngora's poetry represents an explosion in which, on the one hand, we have the preliterate colloquial diction of a schoolboy talking to his sister in "Hermana Marica" ("mañana es fiesta, no irás a la amiga, ni iré a la escuela"), and on the other, we have an inscription on El Greco's tomb which is so heavily condensed that we must decipher it like Latin:

> *YACE EL GRIEGO. HEREDÓ NATURALEZA*
> *ARTE, Y EL ARTE ESTUDIO; IRIS COLORES*
> *FEBO LUCES, SI NO SOMBRAS MORFEO*

There is also the slangy burlesque of Pyramus and Thisbe, a classical tale told as though it had taken place in Carabanchel. If Góngora, then, is the "superación" of Garcilaso in Spanish poetry, similarly, Cervantes transcends classical Spanish prose, transforming the pastoral utopia and the picaresque dystopia into a baroque interplay of different styles and characters, of written and oral acts of speech, an interplay which amounts, as we can now see, to the invention of that anti-classical genre which is the modern novel.

STATE UNIVERSITY OF NEW YORK AT STONY BROOK

Cervantes and Virgil

Michael D. McGaha

 ON QUIXOTE purports to be a parody of the novels of chivalry, and many of its best-known episodes are indeed modeled after passages in those novels.* However, modern critics have amply demonstrated that Cervantes' imitation and parody of literature in *Don Quixote* is not restricted to the novels of chivalry but reflects the influence of scores of other works which Cervantes had come to know during a lifetime of voracious and intelligent reading. In the present article I would like to propose the hypothesis that the parody of the novels of chivalry was in reality only a smokescreen intended to mask Cervantes' primary intention in *Don Quixote,* which was to imitate and improve upon Virgil's *Aeneid.*

It is hardly surprising that Cervantes would have chosen the *Aeneid* as the fundamental model for his work, since Renaissance literary theorists constantly recommended the imitation of Virgil.

[1]This paper was first published in the June 1979 issue of *Comparative Literature Studies* and is reprinted here by permission of the University of Illinois Press.

Even the classical doctrine of the imitation of nature was subordi-
nated to the imitation of Virgil. Julius Caesar Scaliger taught that
since Virgil alone had imitated reality perfectly, the modern poet
should imitate Virgil.[1] By the time of Cervantes the *Aeneid* had
acquired a reputation for authority and perfection which made it
comparable only to the sacred scriptures. Don Cameron Allen has
pointed out that "the early editions of Virgil's *Opera* are the most
profusely annotated classical texts the world has ever seen. Each ten
lines of the *Aeneid* is surrounded by hundreds of lines of exposition."[2] Medieval commentators had embellished—or disfigured—
Virgil's text with allegorical interpretations to such an extent that
the poem came to be viewed as expressing a wisdom beyond the
capacities of ordinary mortals. This gave rise to the belief that Virgil
was a sorceror, magician or divinely inspired prophet who had
obtained his knowledge by supernatural means.[3]

Early commentators on *Don Quixote* were aware in a general way
of Cervantes' imitation of the *Aeneid*. In the *Vida de Cervantes y análisis
del Quijote* prefixed to his 1780 edition of the novel, Vicente de los
Ríos pointed out several parallels of content and theme between the
Aeneid and *Don Quixote,* relating such episodes as Camacho's wedding
(Don Quixote II, 20) and the description of the games in *Aeneid* 5; Don
Quixote's stay in the ducal palace (II, 30-57; 70) and Aeneas' sojourn
in Carthage (*Aeneid* 4); the Clavileño episode in *Don Quixote* (II, 41) and
the story of the Trojan horse (*Aeneid* 2). John Bowle in his edition of
1781 and Martín Fernández de Navarrete in his *Vida de Miguel de
Cervantes Saavedra* (1819) spoke of Cervantes' imitation of Virgil as an
established fact, though mentioning few specific examples.[4] In his
important commentary on Cervantes' novel (1833-1839) Diego Clemencín identified a number of passages in which Cervantes quotes
the *Aeneid*.

Arturo Marasso demonstrated in his *Cervantes y Virgilio*—later
expanded into *Cervantes, la invención del Quijote*—that Cervantes' imitation of the *Aeneid* was far more extensive than had previously been
recognized. Marasso's careful research indicated that Cervantes
was familiar not only with the Latin text of the *Aeneid* but with both
sixteenth-century Spanish translations of the work: that of Grego-
rio Hernández de Velasco (1555) and that of Diego López (1600).
The genuine importance of Marasso's discoveries went largely
unrecognized, probably because of the fact that he limited himself

to pointing out verbal and episodic parallels between Virgil and Cervantes, failing to realize that these similarities were but the superficial symptoms of a much more profound indebtedness of Cervantes to Virgil. In order to reveal this indebtedness it is necessary to look beyond similarities of plot and wording and to examine the overall objectives of both works and the characteristic techniques the two authors employed to achieve those objectives.

Albert G. Richards has taken a valuable first step in this direction in his unpublished dissertation *The Aeneid and the Quijote: Artistic Parody and Ideological Affinity.*[6] Richards, while largely working with parallels pointed out by Marasso and earlier scholars, has studied how Cervantes transformed the material he borrowed from Virgil, reducing what in the *Aeneid* was sublime tragedy to bittersweet comedy. He emphasizes the parallels between Aeneas' stay in Carthage and Don Quixote's stay in the ducal palace and between Aeneas' descent into Hades *(Aeneid* 6) and *Don Quixote*'s descent into the cave of Montesinos (II, 23), pointing out some hitherto unnoticed symbolic and thematic similarities between those episodes.

Richards notes that both Cervantes and Virgil had passed the age of fifty when they began composing their masterpieces, and that the elaboration of both works was a long and difficult process, consuming more than a decade in each case. Both men had seen their countries drained and brutalized by decades of wars, all supposedly fought with the best of intentions. Both set out in their works to redefine the heroic ideal, recognizing that the soldier's training, "though it provides a ready answer to the situations of battle, is a poor guide when the situation is not clear-cut, but demands moral or humane insight, an ability to reckon with the more far-reaching consequences of our first response to an emergency."[7] Both depict men whose mechanically "heroic" behavior results in disastrous consequences for themselves and others. And both writers ultimately point to to the moral lesson that heroism lies not so much in "heroic" behavior as in the conquest of self.

Aeneas and Don Quixote are guided by their authors through a series of learning experiences which purge them of egotism and impulsiveness and lead them to self-mastery. Aeneas thus becomes *pius* and Don Quixote is transformed back into Alonso Quijano *el Bueno*. The essential difference between the two characters is that Aeneas has been entrusted with a divine mission to lead his people to their destined home—a mission which he attempts over and over to evade before finally submitting to it—while Don Quixote attempts to usurp a messianic mission for which he was not "destined" and is only gradually brought to the acceptance of his proper role as a humble Christian hidalgo. The antithesis is only apparent. Richards goes beyond the earlier critics who had commented on the influence of Virgil on Cervantes when he insists that in spite of differences of form, genre and tone, the basic ideology underlying the *Aeneid* and *Don Quixote* is identical.

I would now like to explore some of the other areas in which Cervantes learned from Virgil.

Don Quixote abounds in allusions—some obvious and some oblique—to literary works of all periods and genres. The simplest reason for this constant use of allusions was to secure the reader's pleasure in recognition and to acknowledge the author's indebtedness to writers he had admired or to poke fun at those whom he was parodying. Beyond this, however, the use of multiple allusions in a single episode creates the impression of receding levels of meaning. Like the use of metaphor in poetry, the superimposition of several allusions "packs tightly all objects into one word: and makes you see them one inside the other in an almost miraculous way. Hence your delight is greater, because it is a more curious and pleasant thing to watch many objects from a perspective angle than if the originals themselves were to pass successively before one's eyes."[8] The sustained use of literary allusion is an important and characteristic device of the *Aeneid*. Virgil constantly evokes Homer, not only in superficial borrowings but in ways which challenge some of the fundamental principles and techniques of Homer's art. In fact, the *Aeneid* not only imitates Homeric epic but boldly attempts to surpass it. In addition to the constant references to Homer, the *Aeneid* contains hundreds of allusions to post-Homeric epic, Greek tragedy, the works of the Hellenistic poets and Virgil's predecessors in Latin poetry.

One of the most famous scenes in the *Aeneid* is that in which Aeneas comes upon a series of paintings in the temple of Juno at Carthage which represent episodes in the Trojan war in which he he himself had been a major participant. Imitating the moving scene in which Homer had made Odysseus weep when he heard the blind bard Demodocus sing of the fall of Troy in Book VIII of the *Odyssey*, Virgil gives a new depth and illusion of reality to his protagonist by making making him see himself already portrayed in art. Sadly pondering the paintings, the "real" Aeneas asks Achates:

> . . .is there anywhere,
> Any place left unhaunted by our sorrows?[9]

We know that this scene made a profound impresion on Cervantes. Not only did it inspire the ingenious idea of making the 1605 *Don Quixote* an important literary element in the 1615 novel—as in the cases of Odysseus and Aeneas, Don Quixote's fame will precede him, causing the other characters to compare the "real" Don Quixote with his literary representation—but Cervantes created a parodic imitation of Virgil's scene in *Don Quixote* II, 71. There Don Quixote and Sancho arrive at an inn and are given lodgings in a room,

> the walls of which were covered with some old bits of painted serge of the kind found in villages in place of leather hangings. On one of these was depicted, by a very crude hand, the abduction of Helen, when the bold guest bore her off from Menelaus, and on the other was represented the story of Dido and Aeneas, with the queen standing on a high tower and signaling with half a sheet to the fugitive, who was now at sea on a frigate or brigantine. Helen did not appear very reluctant about going, for she was laughing slyly and roguishly, but the beauteous Dido was shedding tears the size of walnuts.
>
> "These two ladies," observed Don Quixote as he surveyed the paintings, "were most fortunate not to have been born in this age, and I above all men, am unlucky not to have been born in their time. Had I encountered those gentlemen, Troy would not have been burned nor Carthage destroyed, for all I should have had to do would have been to slay Paris, and all the ensuing misfortunes would have been avoided."
>
> "I will wager you," said Sancho, "that before long there will not be an alehouse, inn, tavern, or barbershop where the history of our exploits will not be painted on the walls, but I'd like it done by a better hand than the one that did these."[10]

It happens that the scene from the *Aeneid* which Cervantes was imitating here is also a good example of how Virgil used the technique of multiple allusion. Kenneth Quinn has written of this scene that "the pictures on the walls of Dido's temple are a direct challenge to Homer, but they incorporate non-Homeric material—for example, references. . . to Troilus, Memnon and Penthesilea. And not only do the pictures imply a reassassment of Homer's judgments. . .; the scenes chosen are a kind of foreshadowing of Virgil's own story: Achilles on his chariot foreshadows Turnus, whose symbol is also the chariot. . . ; the horses of Rhesus foreshadow the escapade of Nisus and Euryalus in *Aeneid* 9; the brutal murder of Troilus foreshadows the murder of Polites in *Aeneid* 2; the temple of Pallas is prominent in *Aeneid* 2; the confrontation of Priam and Achilles foreshadows Camilla in *Aeneid* 11."[11] Virgil based his reference to Troilus on a lost play by Sophocles, and the description of Memnon and Penthesilea is derived from Arctinus' *Aithiopus,* although Memnon is also a character in the *Odyssey.*

The technique of foreshadowing or thematic preparation is also characteristic of Cervantes. His Virgilian use of multiple allusion is well exemplified in the episode of Marcela and Grisóstomo. Just as Virgil's Turnus is in part a synthesis of Homer's Menelaus and Hector, Marcela is presented as simultaneously analogous to Diana, Ovid's Daphne, Seneca's Hippolytus, and Eurydice. The episode also contains a complex counterpoint of allusions to the *Aeneid,* Lucan's *Pharsalia,* St. Ambrose's *De Virginibus,* Boccaccio's *Genealogie Deorum* und Leone Ebreo's *Dialogues on Love,* among other works.

Cervantes follows the example of Virgil when he employs dialogue, and to a lesser extent action, as his primary device for characterization. Both writers refrain from explicit comments on the character of their protagonists and both are extraordinarily reticent about presenting even the most basic information about their characters' physical appearance. The importance of dialogue accounts for the essentially dramatic quality of both the *Aeneid* and *Don Quixote.*

One of the most attractive features of the *Aeneid* and of *Don Quixote* is the amazing comprehension of the complexity of human nature expressed in both works. Neither the *Aeneid* nor *Don Quixote* contains a single character who can be categorized as totally good or bad. All attract our sympathy to a greater or lesser extent and all of the characters who play a significant role are dynamic, involved in a constant process of change and development.

Both the *Aeneid* and *Don Quixote* contain numerous internal contradictions which have led some critics to charge that Virgil and

Cervantes were careless and forgetful. Some of these critics have even been so presumptuous as to attempt to rewrite sections of both works in order to make them consistent. Fortunately, both Virgilian and Cervantean scholars now tend towards a greater respect for the integrity of the text. In the case of both writers, it has been suggested that even the internal contradictions may have been intentional. We know that both Virgil and Cervantes were constantly preoccupied by the problem of the elusiveness and many sidedness of truth. The contradictions which appear in the two works may well have been meant to emphasize just how hard it is to arrive at the truth.

Nevertheless, there can be no doubt that both the *Aeneid* and *Don Quixote* were intended by their authors to be "exemplary" and didactic works. However, both Virgil and Cervantes had to overcome formidable obstacles in order to achieve this goal. It is much easier to be didactic when one holds an essentially simplistic view of life. The task then is merely to show how all the apparently complex and disordered phenomena of reality can be reduced to a simple, univocal explanation. Neither Virgil nor Cervantes could do this. Both were clearly religious and patriotic men, but both were equally well aware of the dangers of religious fanaticism and jingoism. Both surely shared the universal human desire to find simple answers for life's complicated problems, but this wish was sabotaged by the rebellious voice of reason, which sometimes led them to view even their most deeply held beliefs with a certain skeptical relativism. How could they dare to present themselves as authoritative exponents of a version of reality about which they themselves had doubts?

They could do so because, in spite of their doubts, both men had an essentially optimistic view of human nature and believed that their readers, if confronted with the data of reality, would, at least in matters of fundamental concern, be able to draw the correct conclusions. Virgil and Cervantes had too much respect for their reader to take him by the hand and offer him a simple solution to all the problems presented in their works. To do so would have been to impoverish those works,for one of the greatest pleasures of reading the *Aeneid* and *Don Quixote* is precisely the intellectual challenge that they pose for the reader. Our experience of the *Aeneid* and of *Don Quixote,* and the conclusions we draw about the

meaning of the books, like our experience and interpretation of
life itself, is conditioned by our native intelligence and education.
Both writers wisely employ the Socratic method in their teaching;
they answer every question with a new question, thus forcing the
reader to find his own answers. Kenneth Quinn has compared the
Aeneid to Graham Greene's novel *The Power and the Glory*, writing
that in both works "The reader is invited to enter into a kind of
compact not to take the story at face value, to regard it as a kind of
sustained, richly-textured, fundamentally ironic parable—not one
in which the writer's beliefs are rammed down our throats, but an
imaginative invitation to have another look at the world in the
light shed on it by acceptance of certain beliefs about it"[12] And
Helena Percas de Ponseti's description of Cervantes' use of indirect exposition applies equally well to the *Aeneid*: "In order to seem
true, fiction must be visually precise, concrete and indivisible but
unstructured and multivalent, like life, which it imitates. Thus,
each reader can understand it according to his own conventions,
presuppositions, premises and ideologies. The author, on the other
hand, should narrate the facts clearly and succinctly. . ., withhold-
ing his personal opinions—not hiding them, which is not fair
play—by means of eliminating ideological or preferential data. In
order to achieve this, he employs techniques of indirect exposition: the presentation of the characters' varying points of view
regarding the events described; recourse to the superimposition of
levels of reading which facilitate thematic, ideological and social
perspectives in the reader, and, finally, use of symbol, allegory and
metaphor, instruments of the 'mother of the sciences,' Poetry, as a
means of creating a superreality which, like the Platonic cosmos,
will irradiate images of the world and, like painting, will offer
visual esthetic qualities. The object of this technique is to induce
in the reader a spontaneous and immediate interpretation of life
as presented in fiction."[13]

Having examined some of the fundamental areas in which
Cervantes imitated Virgil, I shall now attempt to explain how *Don
Quixote* differs from the *Aeneid*, and in doing so I shall clarify the
implied criticism of the *Aeneid* in *Don Quixote*. Just as the *Aeneid*
constitutes both an imitation and a challenge of Homeric epic, so
Don Quixote attempts not only to imitate but to excel the *Aeneid*.

Modern Virgilian critics are unanimous in the opinion that

Virgil meant for his poem to express strong reservations about the character of Aeneas. These reservations are not conveyed by intrusive editorial judgments but by the technique of implicit comment which, as we have seen, is one of the hallmarks of Virgil's art. Aeneas is presented not as a superman or as a saint but as a human being. If indeed the epithet most often applied to him is *pius*, he comes to deserve that title only at the end of the poem, after undergoing a long series of ordeals which have molded his character. Renaissance readers were less likely to perceive the gradual development of Aeneas' character, because the medieval commentators— determined to make the *Aeneid* didactic in a sense that it was never intended to be—had gone through extraordinary mental gymnastics to explain away every sign of weakness in Aeneas. Thus Boccaccio saw in Aeneas a compendium of all the Christian virtues. He advises those who doubt Virgil's power to stimulate his readers to virtue to "re-read those lines in the *Aeneid* where Aeneas exhorts his friends to endure patiently their labors to the last. How fine was the ardor of his wish to die a fair death from his wounds, to save his country! How noble his devotion to his father when he bore him to safety on his shoulders through the midst of the enemy and a shower of flying weapons, while buildings were ablaze and temples crashing down at every turn! What gentleness he showed to his enemy Achaemenides! What strength of character in spurning and breaking the chains of an obstreporous passion! What justice and generosity, too, in distributing well-earned rewards among friends and aliens alike, at the conclusion of the anniversary games to Anchises at the court of Acestes! What circumspect wisdom he showed in his descent into Hades! What noble exhortations to glorious attainment were those of his father! There too was his tact in cultivating friendly relations, and his high and loyal courtesy in keeping them afterwards; and there were his devoted tears for the death of his friend Pallas, and his frequent admonitions to his friend's son."[14]

The modern reader would have to object that Aeneas' wish to die a fighting death was in fact an impulsive attempt to find an easy escape from the more onerous duty of leading his people to a new land. When he expressed this rebellious wish, he had already been warned that resistance was useless and informed of his divine mission by a dream in which Hector appeared to him and by a miraculous vision of his mother Venus. He may have been gentle to Achaemenides, but what about his brutal and unnecessary slaughter of Lausus and Turnus and his execution of eight defenseless prisoners in revenge for the death of Pallas? We may concede that he showed strength of character in breaking away from Dido, but only after an explicit warning from Mercury that he was defying the gods by needlessly tarrying with her. Moreover, even if we believe that Dido deserved her fate, we cannot altogether exempt Aeneas from responsibility for her death. But if all of this seems self-evident to us, we must remember that Cervantes saw the *Aeneid* through the prism of centuries of allegorical commentary. Strange though it may seem to us, his Aeneas was the same saintly figure we find described in the works of Dante and Petrarch, and was therefore on a plane with the idealized heroes of the novels of chivalry.

This explains why Cervantes has Don Quixote tell Sancho in I, 25 that "he who would achieve a reputation for prudence and long-suffering must and does follow in the footsteps of Ulysses; for in describing his character and the hardships that he endured Homer gives us a lively picture of the virtues mentioned. Similarly, Vergil, in the person of Aeneas, portrays for us a dutiful son and the sagacity of a brave and intelligent leader. And these personages, be it noted, are not depicted or revealed to us as they were but as they ought to have been, that they may remain as an example of those qualities for future generations." (p. 198) And in II, 3 he remarks that "You may be sure that Aeneas was not so pious as Vergil would have us believe. . ." (p. 528)

As we have seen, the essential message which Cervantes sought to convey in *Don Quixote* was identical to that expressed by Virgil in the *Aeneid*. If Cervantes chose to write about a poor, obscure, pathetically ridiculous fifty-year old hidalgo instead of a handsome young hero, it was surely because he felt that this was a better way to demonstrate the futility of mechanically "heroic" behavior. Aeneas was forced to learn the lesson of self-control and Stoic submission to his fate, but his fate, after all, was that of a genuine hero and savior of his people. Such a calling, Cervantes must have thought, was not really so difficult to accept. How much harder it is to resign oneself to behaving decently and virtuously in Don Quixote's depressingly monotonous situation, in which he could not even console himself for his hardships with the promise of fame and glory!

Aeneas and his companions spent a dark and fearful night on a Sicilian beach, terrified by the thunderous sounds of Mt. Etna's eruptions:

> That night we hid in the woods, enduring those gigantic Phenomena, and unable to see what caused the din. . .(III, 583-4, p. 76)

Cervantes will carefully evoke this scene when in *Don Quixote* I, 20 he has Don Quixote and Sancho pass just such a night, lost in the woods and alarmed by a "sound of measured blows, together with the rattling of iron chains, accompanied by so furious a thunder of waters as to strike terror into any other heart than that of Don Quixote." (p. 145) When morning came, Aeneas found that his fears were amply justified, for he was in the dangerous land of the Cyclops. Don Quixote, on the other hand, was humiliated to discover that the source of the noise was six fulling hammers. The parallel implies a parodic putdown of the *Aeneid*—after all, Cervantes knew that there were no Cyclops—and Don Quixote is made to look somewhat ridiculous because of his vain display of bravado. However, Cervantes also meant for the reader to understand that the fact that Don Quixote's "adventure" turned out in a most unheroic way did not diminish the reality of the courage he had shown. Lest the point be missed, Cervantes had Don Quixote ask Sancho: "supposing that, in place of fulling hammers, this really had been another dangerous adventure, did I not display the requisite courage for undertaking and carrying it through?" (p. 154) Even heroic intention is not enough, however. It must be accompanied by the prudence which comes from self-mastery. The most heroic thing Don Quixote does in the entire book is to renounce his absurd mission.

Another aspect of the *Aeneid* which Cervantes found objectionable was Virgil's use of magic. The *Aeneid* contains numerous references to magical armor. The most important examples are the armor which Venus obtained from Vulcan for Aeneas and the sword, also made by Vulcan, whcih belonged to Turnus. For Cervantes the use of these magic weapons must have seemed not only distinctly unheroic but positively ridiculous. It detracted unnecessarily from Aeneas' stature as a hero and from the *Aeneid*'s verisimilitude. Cervantes parodies this preoccupation with magical armor in Don Quixote's desire to obtain a sword like that which belonged to the "Knight of the Flaming Sword." This sword not only protected its bearer from enchantment but was able to penetrate any suit of armor.[15] However, the most notable burlesque of the theme of magic in *Don Quixote* is the knight's theft of the magic helmet of Mambrino—in reality a brass barber's basin—which, far from rendering him invulnerable, brings him only woe. One of the galley slaves whom Don Quixote liberated in I, 22, "seizing the barber's basin from the knight's head,. . . struck him three or four blows with it across the shoulders and banged it against the ground an equal number of times until it was fairly shattered to bits." (p. 176) Don Quixote will again encounter the barber from whom he stole the "helmet" in I, 44, and in the following chapter, while all present at the inn engage in a mocking discussion of whether the object is a helmet or a basin, the argument will attract the attention of some rural policemen to Don Quixote, causing them to recognize him as the man whom they have been assigned to arrest on the charge of liberating the galley slaves. As if this were not enough punishment for his ill-gotten gains, in II, 7 Sancho uses the helmet to hold some curds which he buys from some shepherds and when Don Quixote impatiently demands his helmet, Sancho, not daring to tell Don Quixote of the ignoble use to which he has put it, returns it to him without a word. Don Quixote instantly puts on the helmet and, as the curds begin to ooze down his forehead, he has the terrifying sensation that his brains are melting. In all of this, Cervantes may have had in mind the helmet of Messapus, which was stolen by Euryalus and which brought about the latter's downfall. As Euryalus and his friend Nisus were attempting to sneak through the Italian ranks, a flash of moonlight gleaming on the stolen helmet gave them away, causing their death. He may also have thought of the beautifully decorated belt which Turnus stole from the body of his victim Pallas. It was the sight of this belt on the shoulder of the conquered Turnus, who was pleading for his life, that reminded Aeneas of Turnus' arrogant slaughter of Pallas and convinced him to slay Turnus in revenge.

In book XII of the *Aeneid* Aeneas suffers a wound from an arrow. The physician Iapyx is unable to extract the arrow and treat the wound until Venus intervenes, pouring a magical potion consisting

wound until Venus intervenes, pouring a magical potion consisting
of dittany, ambrosia and panacea into Iapyx's basin. The arrow then
slips from the wound, and Aeneas' limb is miraculously cured. Cervantes wryly mocks the use of such magic healing potions in the
episode of the balm of Fierabrás. Don Quixote informs Sancho that
with this balm "one need have no fear of death nor think of dying
from any wound. I shall make some of it and give it to you; and
thereafter, whenever in any battle you see my body cut in two—as
often happens—all that is necessary is for you to take the part that
lies on the ground, before the blood is congealed, and fit it very
neatly and with great nicety upon the other part that remains on
the saddle, taking great care to adjust it evenly and exactly. Then
you will give me but a couple of swallows of the balm of which I
have told you, and you will see me sounder than an apple in no time
at all." (I, 10, p. 76) When Don Quixote finally prepares the balm in
chapter seventeen, it turns out to be a powerful emetic. The seizure
of vomiting it produces leaves Don Quixote purged and much
relieved. The balm fails to produce the desired effect on Sancho,
however, causing instead an agony of cramps, nausea, perspiration
and convulsions which finally leaves him "so tired and weak that he
was not able to stand." (p. 152) In the following chapter, Don Quixote learns the futility of trusting in such remedies. While being
stoned by a group of angry shepherds, "believing himself dead or
badly wounded, and remembering his potion, he took out his vial,
placed it in his mouth, and began to swallow the balm; but before he
had had what he thought was enough, there came another almond
(i.e., pebble), which struck him in the hand, crushing the tin vial and
carrying with it a couple of grinders from his mouth, as well as
badly mashing two of his fingers." (p. 135) Later, the balm takes
effect, causing Don Quixote to vomit profusely in Sancho's face.
Sancho, nauseated by the smell of the balm, in turn vomits all over
his master. So much for magic remedies.

The aspect of the *Aeneid* which Cervantes seems to have found
most disturbing was the constant meddling of the gods in the affairs
of men. Virgil adopted this divine machinery from Homer and he,
too, seems to have felt some uneasiness about it. The intervention
of the gods in the *Aeneid* is considerably less frequent than in
Homeric epic, and Virgil took pains to provide an alternate, rational
explanation for his characters' behavior in every case in which that

behavior was apparently caused by divine intervention. "Not only. . .
do their individual actions make psychological sense in the immediate context in which they act: the whole complex of the actions of
a character suggests a coherent personality."[16] It is most unlikely
that Virgil really believed that the gods interfere in human life in
the ways he describes in the *Aeneid*; what he was apparently trying
to express in a metaphorical way was the conviction than man is not
a completely free agent, that his behavior is determined by forces
beyond his control. Cervantes was not alone in seeing the use of
divine machinery as a major flaw in the *Aeneid*. Kenneth Quinn has
observed that "here, perhaps more than in any other single aspect
of (Virgil's) structure, success has eluded him. His attempt to res-
trict the divine machinery so that it will not overshadow the heroic
action has resulted in a serious loss of dramatic plausibility."[17] We
can see Cervantes' implied criticism of the device in Don Quixote's
constant insistence that all of his misfortunes come about because
he is persecuted by hostile enchanters, when it is evident to the
reader that they are in fact caused by his own foolish mistakes.
Aeneas likewise blamed his troubles on the persecution of Juno and
her cohorts, but the reader finds this rationalization just as uncon-
vincing as Don Quixote's.

However, although Virgil did not believe in the traditional
anthropomorphic version of the pagan gods, he does seem to have
believed in the concept of fate, which he failed to distinguish clearly
from fortune.[18] The *Aeneid* demonstrates the inevitability of fate;
whatever resistance men offer to their destiny, fate will find a way
to make even their rebellious behavior subserve her ends. Even the
gods, with the sole exception of Jupiter, are powerless to resist fate.
The only acceptable way to deal with fate is to accept it stoically,
resigning oneself to the belief that whatever happens must be good,
since it is destined. The Stoic doctrine rests on the notion that the
universe is ordered and properly ruled. Fortune, on the other hand,
refers to the superficial ups and downs of human life which somehow escape the inexorable control of fate. Though it is difficult to
reconcile the two concepts, the Roman idea of fate seems not to
have excluded the existence of mutable and haphazard forces which
play a lesser, but still significant, role in influencing the life of men.
Unlike fate, however, fortune could be conquered. As H. R. Patch
has written, "as the Roman. . . came to regard himself as at the

mercy of Fortune, so he tried to save himself by limiting her powers. One way to be successful in this was to show courage. Another was to oppose reason against unreason, to live the life of wisdom; and another, less widely used, perhaps, was to devote one's self to those concerns in which Fortuna has no part—the activities of virtue. It is 'prudentia' which Juvenal advocates (*Satires,* X, 363); and Seneca. . . also writes as follows 'Vnum Bonum esse, quod Honestum est. . . nam, qui alia bona iudicat, in fortunam uenit potestatem,. alieni arbitrii fit' (*Epistles,* lxxiv, 1). These methods of dealing with Fortuna move actually in the direction of putting her out of existence. Her power is at least not universal, if one may successfully take a stand against her."[19]

The only sort of fate which Cervantes could accept was that of divine providence and predestination which, as the Catholic theologians of the Counter-Reformation emphatically insisted, does not exclude free will. Don Quixote is at first subject to the batterings of fortune because of his vanity and ambition. In expressing this idea Cervantes frequently plays with the ambiguity of the word *aventura,* which can mean both "adventure" and "fortune." Don Quixote often consoles Sancho for the disastrous outcome of their early adventures with the idea that "It's always darkest before the dawn," and that the only thing that can be said about fortune with any certainty is that she is constantly changing. Don Quixote's courage provided a partial escape from the psychological consequences of fortune's upheavals. Cervantes quotes Virgil's dictum (*Aeneid* 10, 284) that "fortune favors the bold" in the first of the poems which he prefixed to the 1605 *Don Quixote.*

However, Don Quixote really ceases to be a plaything of fortune only when he stops defying the will of God as it is manifested in the events of his life. Sancho had warned him as early as I, 20 that it is wrong to tempt providence and had quoted to him Christ's words to St. Paul: "Saul, Saul, why persecutest thou me? it is hard for thee to kick against the pricks." (Acts 26:14) But it is not until after his defeat by the Knight of the White Moon—the moon is of course the most common symbol for the ceasingly changing aspect of fortune —that Don Quixote frees himself by resignation to the will of God and by recognizing that he is responsible for his actions. At first he is tempted to explain his defeat as resulting from the adversity of fortune. His reference to Troy shows that Cervantes was conscious of Virgil's presentation of Aeneas as persecuted by fate when he wrote these lines: "Here was Troy; here my ill luck and not my cowardice robbed me of the glory I had won; here it was that fortune practiced upon me her whims and caprices; here my exploits were dimmed; and here, finally, my star (*ventura*) set never to rise again." (II, 66, p. 943) Sancho attempts to console him, saying that "I have heard it said that what they call luck (*Fortuna*) is a drunken wench who does not know her own mind; above all, she is blind and cannot see what she is doing, nor does she know who it is she is overthrowing or exalting." It is only when he hears his sentiments echoed by his squire that Don Quixote realizes how lame this explanation really is. Then, finally, he expresses Cervantes' ultimate judgment on the matter: "I can tell you one thing: that there is no such thing as luck in this world, and whatever happens, whether it be good or bad, does not occur by chance but through a special providence of Heaven; hence the saying that each man is the architect of his own fortune. I was the architect of mine, but I did not observe the necessary prudence, and as a result my presumptuousness has brought me to a sorry end."

Cervantes was moved to imitate the *Aeneid* not just because Renaissance theorists considered it the ideal literary model but because he sensed a deep affinity with Virgil's world-view. The influence of the *Aeneid* on *Don Quixote* is immediately apparent to any reader familiar with both works in Cervantes's borrowing of felicitous turns of phrase and admirable plot situations. A more thoughtful and probing comparison of the two works reveals that Virgil offered Cervantes a model for such devices as foreshadowing, multiple allusion, perspectivism, implicit comment and the creation of dynamic characters through the use of dialogue as a primary device for characterization. The importance of the influence of Virgil can be seen in the fact that these are the very devices which modern critics have singled out as most characteristic of Cervantes' art. There is absolutely no question of plagiarism in Cervantes' imitation of Virgil. The Spanish writer assimilated Virgil's work so thoroughly that he made it his own, and in *Don Quixote* he transformed it into something quite new and different. Not content to imitate Virgil, Cervantes sought to surpass him. He achieved this objective by eliminating the flaws in Virgil's work which had diminished its credibility: the reliance on magic and divine machinery. He Christianized Virgil's doctrine of fate and created a modern hero who, in his thoroughgoing humanity, was more "exemplary" to the suffering masses of mankind than the plaster saint which medieval and Renaissance commentators had made of Aeneas.

POMONA COLLEGE

NOTES

[1] See E. C. Riley, *Cervantes's Theory of the Novel*, (London: Oxford University Press, 1968), p. 46.

[2] *Mysteriously Meant* (Baltimore: The Johns Hopkins University Press, 1970), pp. 140-41.

[3] See Domenico Comparetti, *Vergil in the Middle Ages*, trans. E. F. M. Benecke (London: Swan Sonnenschein & Co., 1895).

[4] See Rudolph Schevill, "Studies in Cervantes. *Persiles y Sigismunda:* III. Virgil's *Aeneid*," *Transactions of the Connecticut Academy of Arts and Sciences*, 13 (1908), 499n.

[5] Buenos Aires: Libr. Hachette, 1954.

[6] Ohio State University, 1973.

[7] Kenneth Quinn, *Virgil's Aeneid* (Ann Arbor: The University of Michigan Press, 1969), p. 20.

[8] Emanuele Tesauro, *Il Cannocchiale Aristotelico*, (Venice, 1655), cited in Mario Praz, *Studies in Seventeenth-Century Imagery* (Rome, Edizioni di Storia e Letteratura, 1964), p. 18.

[9] *Aeneid* I, 459-60, trans. C. Day Lewis, Doubleday Anchor Books (Garden City, New York: Doubleday, 1953), p. 26. All subsequent quotes are from this translation and will be cited in my text by page number.

[10] *The Ingenious Gentleman Don Quixote de la Mancha*, trans, Samuel Putnam (New York: The Modern Library, 1949), p. 972. All subsequent quotes from *Don Quixote* are from this translation and will be cited in my text by page number.

[11] *Virgil's Aeneid*, pp. 283,84.

[12] Ibid, p. 292.

[13] *Cervantes y su concepto del arte* (Madrid: Gredos, 1975), I, 22-23; my translation.

[14] *Boccaccio on Poetry*, trans. Charles S. Osgood (Princeton: Princeton University Press, 1930),. pp. 74-75.

[15] See *Don Quixote* I, 18.

[16] Quinn, *Virgil's Aeneid*, p. 303.

[17] Ibid., p. 306.

[18] See Quinn, *Virgil's Aeneid*, p. 321.

[19] *The Goddess Fortuna in Mediaeval Literature* (New York: Octagon Books, 1974), p. 13.

Don Quixote as Renaissance Epic

L. A. MURILLO

F THE TERM "RENAISSANCE EPIC" has any valid-
ity beyond describing a group of poems, it
conveys some idea of the prestige and preemi-
nence given in the age of rebirth to the imitation of the rarest and most difficult of classical
forms. My subject in this paper is not the relation of Cervantes' book in literary history to
these poems, nor an analysis of it according to
theories and polemics about the epic form in the sixteenth century,
nor in what way *Don Quixote* constitutes a "prose epic" along the
lines of Homeric, Vergilian, or Heliodorian models. These matters
have been treated satisfactorily or to some extent in contemporary
criticism.[1] Nor do I propose to discuss, after Lukács, the "genesis" of
the modern novel from a parody of chivalry and the epic. My subject is *Don Quixote* seen as an epical structure according to some of
the historical and esthetic considerations that constitute our concept of the Renaissance. Although most of what I have to say is
intended to shed some new light on Cervantes' story and characters, I think that it may suggest also some new ways of looking at
the epic poems of his forerunners and contemporaries.

What meaning, or meanings, can the term "Renaissance epic"
convey? *Epic* itself is difficult enough to define; in what way does

Renaissance simplify or complicate mattrs? Given the differences between the various poems usually included within this group— from *Orlando furioso* to *Os Lusíadas* and *La Araucana,* to *Gerusalemme liberata* and the *Faerie Queene* to *Paradise Lost*—what can we say (other than that they are 'literary epics') that would specify their qualities as those of Renaissance epic poems?[2]

In their book *The Nature of Narrative* Scholes and Kellogg describe epic narrative in this way: if from a fixed point which we consider to be Homer we draw a line to another point which we think of as Vergil, we describe not only the direction taken by Vergil in his imitation of Homer, but also the only direction that was possible thereafter for the written epic form.[3] Now, if we assume that our "Renaissance epics" can be thought of as a third point of reference to which we can extend our line, we describe the direction and fix the point of reference for any enterprise of this nature, be it Ariosto's, Ercillas', Tasso's, or Milton's. But of course here we are not dealing with one poet and his achievement, but with a group of poets who have in common an historical or cultural period, however different the artistic qualities of their poems. What, then, constitutes this third point of reference for the epic narrative? In at least one way the answer is simple, and this is why I press it. We can agree that Renaissance implies a resurgence of classical influence if not classical culture after centuries of medieval, that is, Christian culture and belief. The distance between Vergil and the Renaissance epics, or between Homer and Vergil and the Renaissance epics, is calculable by all that we identify as the culture of the Middle Ages, with its own heroic age, its own 'primitive' epics, legends, artistic traditions and history. In this sense our Renaissance epics are those poems which are related to Homer's and Vergil's or to any other classical epic such as Lucan's, by their contiguity with medieval culture and history, as well as by their concomitance with contemporary culture and history in the sixteenth century. In this view "Renaissance" does not mean a "pure" resurgence and re-birth of classical art and ideology, uncontaminated by medieval, Christian elements, but rather the opposite: the gathering up of various medieval materials, popular or learned, Christian or "barbarian"— and their assimilation into classical form.

Or, to put it another way: it was from the vigor of medieval culture, infused with the powerful mythological and popular elements of the northern barbarian peoples, that the 'literary' epic poetry of the Renaissance would take its decisive character. Medieval history and legend, Christian belief and sentiment provided it with a heroic conception of life, of Christian knighthood. It was, after all, the force of the several "barbaric" mythologies and popular legends—whether we think of them together as Celtic and Teutonic, or break them down to particular peoples or races, Irish, Welsh, Scandinavian, Norse, Norman, Germanic, Anglo-Saxon, etc., that provided the heroic impulse that sustained both the epic narratives such as the *Chanson de Roland* or *Beowulf* and the later verse romances that propagated the legendary materials of Britain and France (the Arthurian and Carolingian legends) and that shaped so much of the 'matter of Rome'.[4] And it was, after all, the history of medieval Europe that had provided the conditions by which Spain France, England, and even Italy and Germany, shaped their new national identities within European Christianity after 1500. It seems to me basic to say that the Renaissance epic came forth from the legendary materials diffused throughout the fabric of medieval life and letters.

The polemics in Italy about the relative merits of *Orlando Furioso* as an epic, and later the comparisons with Tasso's poem, turned on questions of form, the unity of action, and the observance of rules for the epic based on Aristotle's *Poetics*.[5] The medieval or Christian content of these poems was hardly a matter of argument. Even the use of the vernacular rather than Latin was more debatable. It is possible that in this audience there are some who would maintain that the *Furioso* is not, strictly speaking, an epic, but a romance, or *romanzo*, a point on which so much of that polemic turned. Most of us, however, will agree that it is the first undoubted triumph of Renaissance heroic if not epic poetry—and what does it represent in literary history, if not the absorption and refinement on the part of Ariosto of medieval materials both popular and learned into a poetic style and artistic control that is modern or Renaissance for its avoidance of doctrinaire subjects, its secularization of Christian legend, and its political point of view? Perhaps the most serious charges leveled at Ariosto by the purists were that he had not maintained a sufficiently high level of 'epic dignity'; and that his multiplicity of plots and digressive interlacings, and his free-roaming fantasy, were inspired by the desire to please an unlearned and popular taste. In other words, he was not sufficiently 'aristo-cratic'. From the other direction, it is evident that the *Furioso* repres-ents a decisive and perhaps culminating moment in the populariza-tion of aristocratic or feudal and courtly epico-chivalric themes. The process by which the epico-chivalric narratives developed in Italy, fusing Carolingian and Arthurian themes, from *L'Entrée d'Espagne* and its continuations to Pulci, Boiardo and Ariosto is so well known that I mention it only to emphasize my point: that the *Furioso* is the major achievement in the long evolution of narrative that began with the oral tradition of feudal epics and moved by stages toward written and eventually printed form. The Castilian *Romancero* is another body of poetry in which epic and chivalric themes and legends undergo a parallel development and survive into the age of printing in both popular and learned form. The poems of Boiardo and Ari-osto and the Old Castilian *romances caballerescos* have in common a disposition to treat the solemn themes of love and honor with humor,° though the intellectual quality of the Italian poems is such that we describe this disposition as ironical. They are equally impor-tant as precedents for Cervantes' story for their comical, popular, or modernized versions of chivalric legends. The relation of the *Furioso* to *Don Quixote* is unique, because it is the precedent that is both a *romanzo* (chivalric romance in verse) and an epic poem.

I propose that the quality most nearly indispensable to epic nar-rative is a certain spirit of expansiveness or totalization and that for his strength in this respect Ariosto belongs alongside Camoens, Ercilla, Tasso and Milton. Ariosto's irony, in our post-romantic age, would seem to be a confirmation of this view of him, rather than any hindrance to it. I cannot, however, go into this matter. It is sufficient to bear in mind that Orlando's madness is a medieval theme broadened and deepened by Ariosto's artistry and sensitivity, or his irony, to the proportions of epic in the classical sense.

The origins of Orlando's madness, as Pio Rajna[7] showed many years ago, are to be found in the Arthurian legends of Tristan and Lancelot. They are the same sources of Amadís' love sickness. The 'love madness' of a chivalric hero, with the accompanying motifs of 'wild man' and 'penitent lover', is a theme deeply rooted in medical and folk beliefs of the Middle Ages and is traceable in the main to Celtic mythology.[8] Its persistence in chivalric and courtly romance may be said to constitute a myth (or story pattern) in the literary

sense. It is the theme—or literary myth—that connects Cervantes'
book most directly with Ariosto's poem as an epical conception, and
Don Quixote with Orlando, in the sense that their elect status of
hero within the work is the condition by virtue of which their
respective narratives attain epical qualities.

To see Don Quixote as an epic hero is to recognize that his
madness has inspired him to assume the heroic personality of an
over-reacher. The abnormity of his illusion is on the scale of one
who defies, in the name of a more solemn and direct relationship
with superior forces, the limits of his will and freedom imposed by
the existing social order. That an *hidalgo* should fancy himself to be
an heroic *caballero* is of course comical and satirical. But it will make
no difference to insist that his book is only a comic epic, or a comic
epic in prose, because his situation is in any case that of the epic
hero. The narrative depicts him as having assumed for himself the
elect status of hero, and it presses the point that the entire appara-
tus of himself related to supernatural enchantments, and magical
and mythological entities, is a pathological delusion. In this way the
character conceives and carries out an 'imitation' of the heroic role
(of literary models, that is) which is framed within the narrative
that is an 'imitation' of nature.

The consensus of critical opinion has placed Cervantes' originality in this conception beyond any doubt with respect to poetic theories of imitation current in his time, and both learned and popular
sources and literary precedents. Following the studies of Iriarte and
Otis H. Green,[9] on the other hand, we can admit a profound
indebtedness on the part of Cervantes to Renaissance versions and
interpretations of the humoral theory of temperaments, characte-
rology and pathology, for the possible medico-physiological 'cause'
of Quixote's madness, for the correspondence between his physical-
physiological characteristics and his behavior and moral ideas, and
even for some subtle correspondences between the human temperaments, the elements, and the planets and seasons of the year,which
border on the esoteric. The influence of Huarte de San Juan's *Examen
de Ingenios* (1575) appears to have been decisive. Had Menéndez Pidal
been able to take it into account when he wrote on the 'genesis' of
Don Quixote in 1920, he could not have placed, in my opinion mis-
placed, the importance that he did on the 'popular' influence of an
anonymous *Entremés de los romances;* nor did Américo Castro allow any

importance to Huarte or to the humoral medical theories in *El pensa-miento de Cervantes* (1925-1972).

In the narrative, the psycho-moral characteristics of the *hidalgo ingenioso* are developed as an interaction of choleric and melancholic humor. To date several critics, myself included, have traced the hidalgo's career through the book from the initial stages of his cho-leric outbursts to the later stages of melancholic depression, manif-ested fully in the episode in Sierra Morena, where he imitates the madness of Orlando and the penance of Amadís, and eventually to his death in Part II. Don Quixote as a psycho-moral case can be related to the Renaissance psychosomatic theories of character, and very meaningfully, I think. But behind the humoral theories that illuminate his choleric-melancholic development there are other ideas and themes about which we know much less at the present time. It seems evident, as his madness is a literary one, and issues from and expresses his choleric-melancholic temperament, that it is related to the 'heroic' excesses of the epic tradition: the wrath of Achilles, the fury of Hercules and Orlando, that is, his choleric side aligns with Achilles , Hercules and Orlando, while his melancholic side aligns with the 'heroic melancholy' of Hercules, Ajax, and pos-sibly Aeneas. In their book *Saturn and Melancholy* (1964), Klibansky, Panofsky and Saxl pointed out that, as early as the fourth century B. C. *humor melancholicus* was designated by a rationalist approach to poetic subjects as "a disease of heroes," (like Hercules. . . punished with madness by an insulted godhead) of the man of action, that is. Eventually, and due to Ficino, it became the disease of reflective heroes.[10]

The hero's conception of himself, then, occupies the center of the narrative, whose linear unfolding is a succession of episodes or mock adventures tracing a story pattern and disclosing a structure of mythopoetic themes and motifs, so that, though the explicit meaning of his actions is comical and negative—the hero is ineffec-tual in the material world—the effect is that of investing the historico-realistic narrative with poetic qualities of epical propor-tions. The themes and story patterns that comprise Quixote's adventures in Part I have been related to the traditions of epic poetry for at least a century. Yet an important element that would explain that relationship is missing. I suggest it is the unifying ele-ment that is missing, the element that would explain the connection between Quixote's illusion of himself as hero-knight of elect status and the breadth and power of the narrative that acquires for his adventures the encyclopedic and universalizing breadth of epic narrative. Laying aside for now the incidents of the first sally, in the second—from the fight with the windmills (mythological giants) to the battle with the sheep flocks, the episodes of the corpse and fulling hammers, barber's basin, galley slaves, and the retreat into the Sierra Morena, where Quixote and Sancho meet up with Cardenio—each episode contains and is constructed on one or more epic motifs, not exclusively, of course, but in combination with others that are chivalric and popular. Let us look briefly at two episodes, the attack on the sheep flocks and the freeing of the galley slaves.

The attack on the sheep has been described as epical mainly for the 'catalogue' of warriors that Quixote enumerates. It has been pointed out also that here Quixote, in his illusion, joins up with an army or collective body representing an entire people or nation (the Christian army of Pentapolín), assuming a role that resembles that of the hero-warrior in both classical and medieval epic. Before charging at the sheep Quixote describes in an exalted and ecstatic way the scene of the battle, the chieftains, and the *causa belli* that has brought their armies to fight on the plains of La Mancha. By virtue of the character's verbalized 'imitation' (not the author's) the scene takes on the significance of a universal event. We leave aside the fact that it is all comical. The epic majesty of the scene, an audio-visual fallacy, is reducible to Quixote's illusion. Sancho was deceived into believing his master only initially. Quixote's passionate fury is an expression of his *ingenio* and choleric humor. But here his *furor bellicus* built up to a climax to the moment of his charge through *furor poeticus*. Quixote is isolated in his hero's role. His madness insures his isolation, his elect status. He is isolated for his uniqueness or singularity, as is Achilles or Aeneas; but of course he is isolated from reality, as they are not. Unlike them he can maintain the heroic stance and the illusion of a war adventure on the condition that he be the maker or poet and the warrior-actor of his imagined battle world.

I selected an episode that illustrates the fusion of literary reminiscences of classical epics and of epico-chivalric themes from verse or prose romances, including Ariosto, and representative in every way of Renaissance art, in order to point out popular elements in it not usually associated with the epic. Quixote believes that evil enchanters turned the chieftains and warriors into sheep, and thus introduced the theme of enchantments and transformations, a version of the supernatural machinery of the learned epic. That machinery works in reserve here, since the effect of the story is to make us reflect on the pathetic turn of the hero's isolation rather than the grandeur of his efforts supported or thwarted by divine forces. While the sheep flocks were merely flocks—before his hallucination lifted them to the scale of poetic vision—they could not be attached to any literary species. But when Quixote claims that the contending armies have been changed into sheep, he twists the outcome of his adventure in the direction of folk tales, where the motif of men turned into animals abounds. It is one of numerous popular motifs that give the narrative its power, and surface at decisive moments. Their presence is felt most directly in the constant intervention of animals in the story—Rocinante and Dapple are main characters in this respect—and the immediacy with which Quixote's adventures revolve around the human body, its senses organs, its needs and urges and deficiencies. The vomiting scene with Sancho is the necessary climax imposed by this physiological counterforce in the narrative.

We have been instructed by the literary criticism of several centuries to explain this attention to physiological acts, and to bodily and even animal pain as Cervantes' comic realism. We are unaccustomed to think of it as a counterforce to the learned materials of the epic, that is, as popular epic material.

At this point I must say something about Sancho's role. He would seem to be the realistic, popular, even rustic, tradition incarnate, at least for Spanish literature. His role is that of squire to a knight. But Sancho's role exceeds by far the role of any squire in chivalric literature. He belongs as well, for his role as counselor, meddler and instigator, to the epical tradition of the companion to the hero, who remains at his side in the face of danger, and admonishes and reproaches out of a sense of loyalty. I have seen some references to this role as the 'sage companion' to the hero, as Olivier is to Roland, or Enkidu to Gilgamesh.

In the episode with the galley slaves there is no occasion for Quixote to disfigure or misperceive what he sees or hears. It is a stark encounter between heroic-chivalric idealism and a criminal, roguish or 'picaresque' mentality. Yet for all its realism it is an analogue of the descent of the epic hero to the underworld. Arturo Marasso pointed out that, as an emphasis on seeing and hearing, it is meant to recall those moments in the *Aeneid* (Bk. VI, vss. 548-633) when Aeneas gazes at the torments of the condemned in the underworld.[11] Quixote, however. is in the real world, and he goes one step further: he liberates the condemned, and his adventure is comparable to his descent into the cave of Montesinos in Part II. One is a scene of harsh even hellish realism, unrelieved by any allusions to enchantments and the like (the allusions to the picaresque are incomprehensible to Quixote); the other is a dream-journey to the underworld described with a plethora of epic ornaments. The epical significance of this episode grows out of the confessions of the condemned men (strung out like a chain of autobiographical picaresque narratives), for their testimony confirms for Quixote that he should free them. Here the gratuity of his action corresponds to material effectualness. He does free them, and through force, like the effective epic hero. To what end? What purpose does Cervantes have in depicting the megalomaniac hidalgo as an arbiter of social justice? I suggest that by depicting an explicit liberation of oppressed men in realistic terms Cervantes is disclosing the formula (though he would not complete it until much later) by which a representational or mimetic art is invested with its corresponding levels of figurative meaning. The outcome and meaning of Quixote's deed is not only the fragmentation or de-mythification of the sacred theme of heroic liberation, which would be satirical, but the translation of its sacred and ritualistic meaning into secular terms.

The theme is justice as conceived by the participants and carried out by the hero, but his deed is rendered problematical from every side. Notwithstanding, it is conceived as "ethical" in the absolute sense, and no doubt Cervantes exemplified here the requirements of those Renaissance theorists like Salviati[12] who argued that the 'invention' of the epic poet must rise from and follow the logic of necessity, probability and of verisimilitude. Quixote's madness, as if in contact with the marvelous and celestial, tells him he is called on by some higher power (an ideal of justice) to bestow a Christian act of charity, to relieve *out of feeling,* the physical suffering of the oppressed, though these oppressed are self-confessed criminals. They prove to be unworthy of his act, which is foolish as an act of justice, but right as one of *Charitas*. The outcome only underscores the bleakness of his liberation. It is devoid of transcendental significance, as it is of immediate social justification. This was implicit in a social encounter in which neither the liberator nor the oppressed qualified unconditionally for their roles.

Quixote's action was right by the most profound law of Christian belief, yet it cannot serve to illustrate unreservedly the workings of that law in the social life of Cervantes' real world or in the artistic (fictional) world of his story. The episode has indeed a psychological, social and even philosophical content, but it does not illustrate any specific doctrine, humanistic or religious. Its referential meaning excludes the allegorical and I dare say the symbolical. In this respect it differs from the major trend in epic poetry in the later sixteenth century. So wide, undogmatic and problematic are its possibilities, or rationalistic and tolerant, that I think no term better describes them than 'secular.' There is no other episode just like it in the book (later on I offer an explanation for this). It exemplifies the means and ends of his narrative posed between the sense of breadth or totalization and (however) the absence of any overt movement toward transcendental meaning. What emanates from it is simply experience, exhilarating to the senses and problematical to reason, a secularized version of life.

At this point in the story of Part I Cervantes consummated one phase of Quixote's epical delineation and began another. After this episode, fearing the Holy Brotherhood, Quixote and Sancho seek hiding in Sierra Morena and meet Cardenio. In the Sierra Morena Quixote will imitate Orlando and Amadís; his actions constitute what I call the Orlando phase of his delineation and is significantly wedged between the first, the Achillean phase, in which his actions have the effect of testing his 'heroic' illusion, and a third phase, which I call the Odyssean phase. This third phase will begin on the appearance of the priest, barber and Dorotea. The story pattern in the first phase is that of a withdrawal (like Achilles) and a quest (in prose terms, he leaves his village and seeks adventures). The story pattern in the Odyssean phase is the return or homeward journey, and essential to it is that Quixote be elevated to the status of a recognized and celebrated hero. Part II of 1615 will consist of one phase. Obviously it is the Aenean phase.

But the question I want to pursue is about the means by which Cervantes invested his narrative with the breadth or all-inclusiveness of epic narrative, in particular from the moment the first hoax or *burla* is played on Quixote by the priest, barber and Dorotea, which begins the return phase of Part I. The diversity of narrative forms, styles, and characters—pastoral, picaresque, etc.; or the poetic forms, learned and popular; or the hierarchy of cultural levels from the high humanistic and scholarly (almost consistently introduced in a burlesque tone) to the middle level, represented by the books in Don Quixote's library, to the popular forms of tales and legends; or the importance conceded to proverbs, dialects and folk expressions; all of this is sufficiently known, so what I have to say is meant to move and establish the question beyond these subjects.

By applying the term 'secular' to the referential possibilities of his narrative, I mean to affirm how it is a divestment of solemn and sacred rituals and themes in spirit of a 'festive' mythology,' whose antecedents are to be found in what we call popular culture or tradition. Now *'festivo'* is a consecrated term in Cervantean criticism for the style of *Don Quixote*. 'Festivo' and 'burla' are intimately related. Our use of them recognizes that much of the book is "festivo" and "burlesco," rather than realistic or parodistic, but we have no way of making our apprehension explicit in a critical concept. The meaning of *festival* or *celebration* (Fr. *fête*) is closely associated with ceremony and ritual in popular culture, but more directly with the rituals of popular feasts and entertainments than with the solemn religious feasts of which these are in some respects a mock verison. Now the popular festival with the most persistent characteristics developed in the Middle Ages, and with an immemorial tradition behind it, is Carnival, the festival that precedes Lent in the Christian liturgical calendar.[13] One of the contributions of twentieth-century anthropology to literary criticism has been the elevation to the status of a literary or critical concept of *Carnival*, not only 'Carnival spirit' or 'Carnival world,' but even I suppose a 'structure of Carnival.' The semiologists and structuralists, among others, have been prominent in its application. I know of some studies of this nature on *Don Quixote*, the most notable a study of Sancho's government of Barataria by Agustín Redondo, and some general remarks by Mikhail Bakhtine in his book on Rabelais.[14] My own inclinations are not in the direction of semiotics, structuralism, or cultural anthropology, and I offer only a tentative outline of how the concept of Carnival is applicable to *Don Quixote*. My point of view is that it is applicable to its all-inclusiveness as a 'secular' epic.

The order of episodes in Part I and II actually discloses an entire evolution of motifs from popular culture of which Carnival is one. They constitute a popular mythology elevated to the dignity of the mythology of classical culture, and with which they are combined in many instances. Most of them are associated in some way with popular feasts and diversions, particularly with Carnival: mock rituals, coarse tricks and hoaxes, disguises, masks, songs and games. Their use in the story follows the course and trajectory of Don Quixote, of his adventures and characterization, and they become intensified as the story progresses, in an ascending arc toward the fulfillment of his illusion and of his role as *caballero* in Part II. The ritualistic motifs are apparent from the beginning, when Quixote takes on the attributes of knighthood by naming his horse, himself and Dulcinea. To think of these scenes and those at the inn when he is dubbed a knight by the innkeeper and the two women, as parody alone is to have a very incomplete view of them. They are comical in the positive spirit of a festive popular ritual. The scene where Sancho is thrown in a blanket *"como perro por carnestolendas"* (I, 17) is an explicit instance. This is the same spirit that delights in picturing animals and men in close association, the prominence of Rocinante and Dapple in the story having practically no chivalric antecedents.

In the principal action leading up to the episode of the galley slaves, Quixote undergoes the trials of isolation, and in this phase is subjected to the roughest and cruelest bodily punishment. He is beaten and abused repeatedly. We can believe that his choleric temperament and his constitution inure him to this abuse and ensure that he will survive it. On the other hand, those beatings and humiliations can be related to the traditions of folk humor, where it is usual to inflict the cruelest physical punishment in both real and mock form on the fool figure, or a scapegoat, in whose case the ritualistic meaning of those blows is all but explicit. The inescapable presence of body functions in the story, from character physiology to the play of the senses, bears of course a similarity to preferences for physical facts and materialism in folk humor. The so-called ritualistic actions of eating, drinking, sleeping, even talking, are invested with suggestions of the ritualistic sense that these actions have in the classical epic. Their literary verisimilitude as epic material is derived from both the popular and the learned or classical conceptions.

In this respect, Quixote's imitation of the 'mad' knight in Sierra Morena is a penitential ritual for reasons of love, and carried out in physical actions. When the priest, barber and Dorotea appear with disguises, in order to convince him to leave the Sierra and return to his village, the narrative acquires the explicit array of Carnival hoaxes and disguises, meant to revolve around the person of a madman and fool, a famed knight. Beyond this turning point in Part I Quixote's actions are ritualistic by the semblance of adventure sustained by the hoax: he ceases to be the object of physical blows but instead is both elevated and humiliated by deceptions played according to his chivalric illusion, the prophecy of his marriage to Dulcinea, his confinement in the cage. As a ritual figure of popular humor, he has passed from physical beatings to be a figure of festival ritual, as the scene of his homecoming in the village indicates. In the second half of Part I the elements of *burla* and *artificio,* complete with a mock plot, costumes and masks, have come to substitute for the hero's will and incentive for action. The *festival* illusion is one with the chivalric illusion of Quixote.

In my study on temporal configuration in *Don Quixote* I described the time of the action of Part I as the summer of Quixote's exemplary depiction, and of Part II as the summer of the mythical depiction.[15] While I concluded that the narrative time of his story had necessarily to be spring and summer, I could not there emphasize sufficiently the element of popular feasts and celebrations, assumed disguises (impersonations) and personalities, that constitute and, magnified, sustain the epic structure of Part II. In that study I pointed out that the course of Quixote's and Sancho's adventures in Part II follows the trajectory of spring festivals, from Carnival and Easter to Midsummer. This temporal pattern is derived from chivalric stories and chronicles of the Arthurian tradition, with its roots in Celtic rituals and folk tales. It follows one of the oldest narrative traditions, whose Christian version is that the "creation of the world" took place in spring. Spring and summer, in any case, constitute the season of romance and of the golden age of mythology. In the folk tradition of medieval Europe spring is associated with the

Carnival season, which is not confined to a brief period of days before Lent, but is a time of festival that can be invoked variously during spring and into early summer.[16]

The adventures of Part II begin with the staging of a popularized version of the abduction motif (the mythical folk motif behind Helen's abduction in the *Iliad*). Quixote is convinced by Sancho's deception that Dulcinea is enchanted. Her disenchantment or rescue is the motif that will be mounted on progressively more complicated levels of deception. Eventually the ducal pair and their servants will convince Quixote and Sancho that she can be disenchanted by a peculiar folkish solution: Sancho is to subject his body to a hyperbolic sum of lashes. This meshing of the hero's quest (to rescue his lady) to his squire's fat body discloses the very center of the process by which one after another chivalric theme is reduced to its counterweight in popular festival and ritual in the form of a hoax or staged deception.

The encounter with the traveling players brings Quixote and Sancho in direct contact with the theatrical otherworld disguises of the festival play of *Corpus Christi;* and in the person of the "Caballero de los Espejos" and his long-nosed squire with the Carnival world of burlesque transformations. These give way to the meeting with the "Caballero del Verde Gabán" (another festive outfit) and the mock triumph over the African lions (another epic motif). The unifying element running through the action up to the cave episode is the 'festival mythology,' with its hoax transformations bringing together classical themes (such as the comical figure of Hercules for Sansón Carrasco and the Pyramus and Thisbe story for Basilio and Quiteria) and popular and medieval ones. The ceremonial visit to don Diego de Miranda's home is followed by the feast at Camacho's wedding, a particularly explicit combination of popular and classical themes, a hoax, ritual, festival, and celebration, with an abundance of food and drink, music and dances. From this high point of rustic celebration, of *fête,* the hero's trajectory will be lifted to the lavish spectacles performed in the ducal palace and on Barataria, and brought to a climax at Barcelona, in a mock celebration and pageantry of Renaissance *fêtes* staged for the arrival of royalty at a great city.[17] This trajectory traces the Aenean phase of adventures that closes with the mock funeral for Altisidora, who, like Dido, dies from being spurned, but is restored to life by Sancho consenting to a form

of ritualistic torture from feminine fingers, vaguely suggestive of
inquisitorial punishments.

The sustained effect of ritualized hoaxes, ceremonial receptions,
festive mythology and celebration, is to invest the realistic action
with an inherent sense of adventure and the fictional semblance of a
higher transcendency we expect of epic narrative. It is secular in
that its entire movement upward emanates from a secularized version of transcendental possibilities: the redemption of social life
through the exertion of the hero who incarnates it.

The cave episode does not happen in the real world, so it cannot
have the form of a carnival occasion. Yet many of its grotesque
deformities are in the way of festival caricatures. If the 'Carnival
world' can take the form of its own travesty, then Quixote's dream
experience in the underground world of enchanted spirits can be
said to have approximated this inversion.

Over the years the cave of Montesinos episode has attracted an
enormous amount of critical and interpretative commentary. While
the similarities in it to the visit to the other world of classical heroes
have been studied several times over, its relation to the cave episodes of numerous Spanish epic poems of the sixteenth century has
gone unnoticed. Indeed, the cave—both theme and motifs—is so
prominent as to qualify for prototypal status in the Renaissance
epic, and particularly in Spanish. In this respect *Orlando Furioso*
offered an indispensable model, but Cervantes' most important
antecedent in Spain is Alonso de Ercilla's *La Araucana,* where in Can-
tos 23 and 26 the author-poet undergoes an initiatory experience in
"La cueva de Fitón." Equally important is the case of *El Monserrate,* the
poem about the monk Garín and the founding of the monastery
(you will recall that these two poems are mentioned with *La Austriada* by the priest in the scrutiny of Quixote's books), in which there
are four different major episodes that take place in a cave. There is a
'cave episode' in nearly all the important epic poems of the Golden
Age. I propose that the Cave is a major theme of Renaissance artistic expression in the epic, in chivalric romance, and probably in the
theatre and the pastoral as well, and merits a major critical study.

The cave episodes of the *Odyssey* and the *Aeneid* show the hero
descending to the underworld to visit the place of departed spirits.
Their experience in the cave is one more mythological theme
absorbed into the epic tradition from the religious beliefs of very

ancient peoples. Among stone-age tribes it was thought that the ghosts of the dead survived in the caves in which they were buried. The subject is one that overlaps into the study of ritual and myth among primitive peoples by anthropology and comparative religion. Since the 1930's when Jackson Knight[18] published his study on Vergil's episode as an initiation ritual for Aeneas, and similar in fascinating respects to the cave beliefs of stone-age cultures, the descent of the hero to the underworld has been interpreted as a ritual pattern of initiation in epic poetry. In July of this year, at the Congress on Cervantes in Madrid, Agustín Redondo presented a paper on the *cueva de Montesinos* episode as an initiation ritual leading to Quixote's renovation (based partly on Mircea Eliade's theories), but without relating it to the cave theme in the classical epic.[19] We should assume, in any case, that the cave experience in chivalric prose romances, like Rosicler's in "la cueva de Artidón" (*Espejo de príncipes y cavalleros*),[20] will disclose an initiatory pattern as a legacy of epic narrative.

My interest here is to stress the importance of the popular medieval legend that is the content of Quixote's experience in the cave of Montesinos. The primary sources for this material are three or four *romances* belonging to the pseudo-Carolingian cycle.[21] In Quixote's experience or dream, Montesinos, Durandarte and Belerma have been 'enchanted' by the sorceror Merlin in the form they had at the time of Durandarte's death. (There is no explicit mention in Quixote's account that these personages are 'the dead' of 'the other world.' Indeed, if they were, it would not be possible to disenchant them. But this is just one more incongruity in his fiction.) Their 'immortal' state is one and the same with their fame in the traditional ballads. Quixote's narrative centers on the most obvious detail, the heart of Durandarte, which was extracted by Montesinos according to the knight's dying wishes at Roncesvalles, and taken to Belerma as a token of undying fidelity. In the state of her enchantment Belerma is compelled to show her grief for his loss by leading a procession of damsels through the underground palace with the mummified heart. Quixote's entire narrative is a dream deformation of the popular legend. But it is evidently full of ritualistic details; they bear a religious significance, yet one so close to pagan or heathen customs and superstitions that we do not associate it with Christian beliefs. Durandarte's heart carried in procession is a profane emblem of eternal fidelity. We cannot overlook the fact that for modern spirituality the 'sacred heart,' revealed through a wound in the side of the living body, is an emblem of divine love, but a product of the increasing abstraction of religious pictorial representaton since the Renaissance, oriented to avoiding anthropomorphism and inspired by Reformist tendencies.[22] It is remarkable that Cervantes suggests a 'secularized' heart, because it was a mystical current in sixteenth-century religious life, in which the Jesuits played a prominent role, that was formative for modern Catholic dogma.[23] Folk mythology about the heart is universal, of course. The theme in the ballad of Durandarte is one classified according to the lover's plea, "Take out my heart."[24] Another version of the theme leads to "the legend of the eaten heart," which of course we find in Boccaccio[25] (*Decameron*, 4th day, 9th story).

In any case, as told in the ballads, Durandarte's dying request is that his heart be extracted from his breast and taken to Belerma. It is a theme and no doubt a reality of medieval life and culture. Among various peoples of western Europe (in particular the Celts, it appears) there existed the custom of extracting the heart of a deceased, in order to give it burial in a different place, or to preserve it as a relic. It was also a custom carried out by various kings of England, France and Spain down to the close of the Middle Ages.[26] What I want to stress is that in Cervantes' episode the extracted heart is a popular epic-chivalric motif that gathers to it all the poetic force of Quixote's fabrication. The mummified heart is the relic, or, better, the cipher that contains the sense of what Quixote sees in the cave, the marvelous object of his initiatory experience. Can a shrunken heart qualify as a fertility symbol? we ask. Can Quixote presume to 'disenchant' Durandarte, Belerma, Montesinos, and the rest, if he has not the power to restore Durandarte's heart to his body? It would be tantamount to restoring him to life. Would it be tantamount to restoring him to love as well? The cave episode is a triumph of narrative art, whether we believe Quixote is a failure or not. I can think of no other episode of epic narrative in the Renaissance that is a more intense interweaving of classical and medieval, learned and popular traditions. Its modernity is as subtle as it is transparent. Whether Quixote dreamt what he saw and heard, or fabricated it in a semi-conscious state, the fact remains that, as initiatory ceremonies end in sleep for the newly initiated,[27] Quixote was pulled out of the cave to the sunlight asleep.

Cervantes' approach to the materials of epic and romance was at no time exclusively that of the classicist, or the Latinist, the learned theoretician or humanistic scholar. He was influenced by them, decisively at times, but his own approach has to be seen as that of a story teller who subordinates all elements and influences from either learned or popular traditions into one fabric of narrative.

Whereas the higher humanist ideology would have prescribed the elevation of medieval chivalric legends to a doctrinal framework—in this case, perhaps, satirical—(cf. Quevedo's "Necedades de Orlando") that included allegorization and the learned ornaments of classical myth, Cervantes opted for combining in *Don Quijote* those legends and those myths with the traditions of folk humor and its festival mythology. He subverted the ends of epic narrative as understood in his time, not because he was a poet writing in prose, nor because his ends were those of the modern novelist, but because he worked with story and characters in the timeless manner of a mythologist.

University of California, Berkeley

Notes and References

¹See my Bibliography (Madrid: Castalia, 1978), items 098, 107, 108, 130, 370, 373, 473.

²Bibliography on Renaissance epic poetry is extensive. My listings here are limited to works to which I am in some way obligated. I must cite first of all the article by Robert M. Durling, the last word on the subject: "The Epic Ideal" in *Modern Literature and Western Civilization* [vol. 3], *The Old World: Discovery and Rebirth*, gen. eds. David Daiches and Anthony Thorlby (London. Aldus, 1974), pp. 105-146.

[Anthologies]

Candelaria, Frederick H., and William C. Strange, eds., *Perspectives on Epic* (Boston: Allyn and Bacon, 1965).

Yu, Anthony C., ed.,*Parnassus Revisited, Modern Critical Essays on the Epic Tradition* (Chicago: American Library Association, 1973). Includes an extensive selected bibliography.

Abercrombie, Lascelles, *The Epic: an Essay* (London: Martin Secker, 1922).

Cook, Albert, *The Classic Line, a Study in Epic Poetry* (Bloomington: Indiana University Press, 1966).

Bowra, C. M., *From Virgil to Milton* (London/New York: Macmillan/St. Martin's Press, [1945] 1962).

———, *Heroic Poetry* (London/New York: Macmillan/St. Martin's Press, 1966).

Gilbert, A. H., "Qualities of the Renaissance Epic," *South Atlantic Quarterly*, 53 (1954), pp. 372-378.

Lord, Albert B., *The Singer of Tales*, (Cambridge: Harvard University Press, 1974).

Pollman, Leo, *La épica en las literaturas románicas* (Barcelona: Planeta, 1973).

Durling, Robert M., *The Figure of the Poet in Renaissaince Epic* (Cambridge: Harvard University Press, 1967).

Giamatti, A. Bartlett, *The Earthly Paradise and the Renaissance Epic* (Princeton: Princeton University Press, 1966).

Greene, Thomas,*The Descent from Heaven, a Study in Epic Continuity* (New Haven: Yale University Press, 1963).

Belloni, Antonio, *Il poema epico e mitologico,* (Milano: F. Vallardi, 1912 [Storia dei generi letterari italiani]).

Ruggieri, Ruggero M., *L'umanesimo cavalleresco dan Dante al Pulci* (Roma: Edizioni dell' Ateneo 1962).

Brand, C. P., *Ludovico Ariosto, a Preface to the 'Orlando Furioso'* (Edinburgh: Edinburgh University Press, 1964).

———, *Torquato Tasso, a Study of the Poet and his Contribution to English Literature* (Cambridge: Cambridge University Press, 1965).

Arce, Joaquín, *Tasso y la poesía española* (Barcelona, Planeta, 1973).

Bertini, Giovanni Maria, "Torquato Tasso e il Rinascimento spagnolo," *Torquato Tasso*. Comitato per le celebrazioni di Torquato Tasso (Ferrara, 1974).

Pierce, Frank, *La poesía española del Siglo de Oro*, versión española por J. C. Bethencourt, 2nd ed. (Madrid, Gredos, 1978).

———, "Some aspects of the Spanish Religious Epic of the Golden Age," *Hispanic Review*, 12 (1944), 1-10.

———, "Some Themes and Sources in the Heroic Poems of the Golden Age," *Hispanic Review*, 14 (1946), 95-103.

³Robert Scholes and Robert Kellogg, *The Nature of Narrative*, (Oxford University Press, 1966), p. 70.

⁴W. P. Ker, *Epic and Romance* (1896; New York: Dover, 1957 [reprint]); *The Dark Ages* (New York: Charles Scribner's Sons, 1911).

⁵Bernard Weinberg, *A History of Literary Criticism in the Italian Renaissance* (Chicago: University of Chicago Press, 1961), II, chs. 19-20.

⁶See my article *"Lanzarote* and *Don Quijote" Folio* (State University of New York, Brockport), 10, 55-68.

⁷Pio Rajna, *Le fonti dell' "Orlando Furioso,"* 2nd ed. (Firenze, 1900), ch. 13, p. 393-408.

⁸In addition to my notes and bibliographical references in *The Golden Dial*, pp. 166-68, see Judith Silverman Neaman, "The Distracted Knight: a Study of Insanity in the Arthurian Romances," unpublished dissertation, Columbia University, 1968; Penelope B. R. Dobb, *Nebuchadnezzar's Children, Conventions of Madness in Middle English Literature* (New Haven: Yale University Press, 1974), ch. 4, "The Unholy and Holy Wild Man."

⁹See my Bibliography, items 400-408. The humoral doctrines were throughly absorbed into Spanish culture by 1500 and were transported to America, where they have persisted into modern times in medical folklore. See George M. Foster, "Humoral Pathology in Spain and Spanish America," *Homenaje a Julio Caro Baroja* (Madrid, 1978), pp. 357-370.

¹⁰Raymond Klibansky, Erwin Panofsky and Fritz Saxl, *Saturn and Melancholy, Studies in the History of Natural Philosophy, Religion and Art* (London. Thomas Nelson & Sons, 1964), pp. 16 ff.

¹¹Arturo Marasso, *Cervantes, la invención del Quijote* (Buenos Aires: Librairie Hachette, 1954), p. 80.

¹²Weinberg, p. 1017; Durling, pp. 120-21.

¹³See Julio Caro Baroja, *El Carnaval (análsis histórico-cultural)* (Madrid: Taurus, 1965).

¹⁴Agustín Redondo, "Traición carnavalesca y creación literaria, del personaje da Sancho Panza al episodio de la Ínsula Barataria . . ." (To be published in *BulHisp*, 80, 1978), paper read at VI Congreso, Asociación Internacional de Hispanistas, 26 August 1977, Toronto, Canada. Mikhail Bakhtine, *Rabelais and His World*, trans. by Hélène Iwolsky (MIT Press, 1968), p 23.

¹⁵*The Golden Dial, Temporal Configuration in 'Don Quixote'* (Oxford: Dolphin, 1975), pp. 126-28.

¹⁶See Claude Gaignebet and Marie-Claude Florentin, *Le Carnaval, essais de mythologie populaire* (Paris: Payot, 1974).

¹⁷See Jean Jacquit, ed., *Les Fêtes de la Renaissance* (Paris: Éditions du Centre National de la Recherche Scientifique, 1956). Contains: Miguel Querol-Gavaldá, "Le Carnaval à Barcelone au début du XVII siècle, pp. 371-75.

¹⁸W. F. Jackson Knight, *Vergil, Epic and Anthropology*, (London: George Allen & Unwin, 1967), Part II, *Cumaean Gates*, originally published in 1936 (Oxford: Basil Blackwell).

¹⁹Agustín Redondo, "El proceso iniciático en el episodio de la cueva de Montesinos," paper read July 7,1978, Primer Congreso Internacional sobre Cervantes, Madrid. Mircea Eliade, *The Quest, History and Meaning in Religión*, (Chicago: University of Chicago Press, 1969), "Initiation," pp. 112-26.

²⁰Diego Ortúñez de Calahorra, *Espejo de príncipes y cavalleros*, ed. D. Eisenberg (Madrid: Espasa-Calpe [Clásicos Castellanos]) vol. 3, ch. 5.

²¹"O Belerma, O Belerma," "Muerto yace Durandarte, " "En Castilla está un castillo," *Cancionero de romances*, (Anvers, 1550). "Por el rastro de la sangre," see notes in my edition, II, 23.

²²*Encyclopedia of World Art* (New York: McGraw-Hill), vol 11, p. 903.

²³*The Oxford Dictionary of the Christian Church*, 2nd ed., eds. F. L. Cross and E. A. Livingston (Oxford: Oxford University Press, 1974). "Sacred Heart."

²⁴Lajos Vargyas, *Researches into the Medieval History of Folk Ballad* (Budapest: Akadémiai Kiado, 1967), p. 34.

²⁵John E. Matzke, "The Legend of the Eaten Heart," *Modern Language Notes*, 26 (1911), 1-8. Antti Amatus Aarne, *The Types of the Folktale*, trans. Stith-Thompson (Helsinki, 1964), n. 992.

²⁶*Diccionario Espasa-Calpe*, v. 15, p. 480.

²⁷W. F. Jackson Knight, *Roman Vergil*, 2nd ed. (London: Faber & Faber, 1954), p. 136.

El *Quijote* a través del prisma de Mikhail Bakhtine: carnaval, disfraces, escatología y locura

Manuel Durán

N sus Meditaciones del Quijote, de 1914, señala Ortega, con su habitual mezcla estilística de elegancia y dramatismo: «¡Cervantes —un paciente hidalgo que escribió un libro— se halla sentado en los elíseos prados hace tres siglos, y aguarda, repartiendo en derredor melancólicas miradas, a que le nazca un nieto capaz de entenderle!»[1]

Creo que no hay palabras que puedan irritar con mayor rapidez a una reunión de cervantistas. Ortega insinúa que, todavía en su época, nadie entiende plenamente a Cervantes. Y extrapolando a nuestra época podemos adivinar que nos desafía a entenderlo. Quizá se trata de una tarea imposible. Quizá, a pesar de todos nuestros esfuerzos, Cervantes aguarda, melancólico, a que alguien consiga por fin desentrañar el sentido de su gran novela. Sin embargo nosotros, cada cual siguiendo su intuición y rigor de crítico investigador, creemos habernos acercado al sentido del *Quijote,* creemos, en nuestros momentos de optimismo, haber entendido el *Quijote.* Cada cual ha aportado algo a una interpretación más inteligente y más sensible de la novela cervantina. Frente al desdeñoso desafío implícito en la frase de Ortega me complazco en rebatirla con otra frase de un escritor también ilustre, Alfonso Reyes, que, refiriéndose a los críticos, investigadores, historiadores, y quizá a la humanidad en general, escribió: «Todo lo sabemos entre todos,»

Creo también que todos estaremos más de acuerdo con las ideas de Ortega cuando sugiere que nos acerquemos a una obra de arte en forma a la vez lenta e indirecta: «. . . el secreto de una genial obra de arte. . . diríase que se resiste a ser tomado por la fuerza, y sólo se entrega a quien quiere. Necesita, cual la verdad científica, que le dediquemos una operosa atención, pero sin que vayamos sobre él rectos, a uso de venadores. No se rinde al arma: se rinde, si acaso, al culto meditativo. Una obra del rango del *Quijote* tiene que ser tomada como Jericó. En amplios giros, nuestros pensamientos y nuestras emociones han de irla estrechando lentamente, dando al aire como sones ideales de trompetas»[2]

En esta ocasión, y para dar, como Jericó, por lo menos una vuelta en torno a las murallas de la novela cervantina, he pedido prestada la trompeta a un gran crítico—crítico formalista ruso—Mikhail Bakhtine.[3] Si queremos cambiar de metáfora, en lugar de trompeta vamos a emplear un prisma. La luz de la novela de Cervantes, refractada en este prisma, nos proporciona un vasto espectro. En rigor toda la experiencia humana, de la más baja a la más elevada, puede identificarse en el espectro resultante. Del infrarrojo al ultravioleta, todo podemos hallarlo en esta gran experiencia vital transformada por el arte cervantino. Pero nos importa mucho identificar ciertas bandas de este espectro, ciertos colores o matices, y relacionarlos entre sí, y situarlos dentro de la totalidad del espectro, ya que las partes ayudan a explicar el todo, y el todo y las partes se relacionan y dialogan incesantemente. Los colores, o más bien los matices del espectro cervantino que quisiera identificar, y si es posible explicar en cuanto a su origen y relacionar con el resto, la totalidad, del espectro creador de Cervantes, son los aspectos del *Quijote* que tienen algo que ver con la visión carnavalesca, medieval y renacentista, del mundo. El mundo como fiesta, como orgía, como explosión y cambio de nuestra personalidad, como disfraz y engaño, como festín y borrachera, pero, también, como locura triunfante, como elogio de la locura, y no únicamente—pero sí también de esta manera—a la usanza y según la visión moral y cósmica de Erasmo, ya que es muy probable que directa e indirectamente la ironía de Erasmo y su sistema de valores haya influido en Cervantes. El Carnaval de la Edad Media culmina en una fiesta orgiástica, en un intercambio de personalidades que es un disfraz y un desafío a los dioses y al destino, un intento encaminado a subvertir las reglas cotidianas y quizá a desafiar la muerte. Es, sobre todo, una fiesta subversiva, y su acto público más notorio es la coronación de un payaso absurdo, un loco, el Rey Momo, bajo cuya guía se colocan los hombres y las mujeres que en la fiesta participan. No quiero forzar los paralelos, sino subrayar los puntos comunes, entre el Carnaval del Medio Evo, tal como ha sido entendido y descrito por Bakhtine en su estudio sobre Rabelais, y la novela de Cervantes. Rabelais y Cervantes elevan sus construcciones artísticas por el aire del Renacimiento, pero no cabe dudar de que los cimientos, en ambos casos, han de hundirse forzosamente en la tradición medieval. Nadie duda de que Shakespeare, por ejemplo, sea un autor renacentista. Lo mismo cabe decir de Rabelais y de Cervantes. Pero sin explorar los cimientos medievales de estas tres obras no podemos apreciar las altas torres edificadas sobre estas bases medievales. El Carnaval, como institución cultural mucho más antigua todavía que la Edad Media, pero, sin embargo, que se ofrece como realidad cultural a nuestros autores revestida de características medievales, es un presupuesto lógico indispensable. Ayuda a explicar el amplio papel de la escatología en Rabelais, presente en innumerables páginas de sus textos. Pensamos también en el Falstaff de Shakespeare, escondido en un cesto de ropa sucia. En Sancho, el Sancho maloliente frente a los batanes, y un Don Quijote desasosegado e incierto ante este desagradable confrontamiento con la vida cotidiana. En la presencia constante de disfraces en la comedia shakespeariana—y, desde luego, no infrecuente en el teatro cervantino y en todo el teatro español de la época. Pensamos también que todo lo que ocurre en torno a Don Quijote y Sancho en la segunda parte de la novela, en el palacio de los Duques, es en el fondo un verdadero carnaval, con sus bromas y disfraces. Y que en este carnaval hay, como lujo extraordinario, como gran aportación de la época moderna, empeñada en superar los siglos antiguos, no uno, sino dos Reyes Momos, Don Quijote y Sancho. Y así entenderemos la necesidad de recurrir a las interpretaciones de Mikhail Bakhtine, cuya interpretación de Rabelais, anclada en una reinterpretación del sentido y la influencia del carnaval medieval, ha venido a renovar numerosos conceptos críticos de nuestra época. Hora es ya de aplicar algunos de estos conceptos a nuestra interpretación del *Quijote*.

El gran mérito de Bakhtine consiste en haber señalado el hilo interno que une las cuentas del collar: la orgía, el desafío, los disfraces, la escatología, la locura. En cuanto juntamos las piezas del rompecabezas todo adquiere nuevo sentido. Pero quizá la pregunta preliminar debiera ser: ¿cómo es posible que hayamos perdido de vista una visión tan importante, tan antigua, tan perdurable? Parece evidente que ha habido una ruptura, una discontinuidad, en la tradición cultural del Occidente. Ello es explicable dado el carácter popular, casi inconsciente o subconsciente, de las fiestas carnavalescas, su falta de codificación, al margen de la Iglesia y de las instituciones culturales oficiales, y finalmente, a lo largo del siglo XVIII, la «superación» y obliteración de ciertos sistemas de valores que habían sobrevivido al Renacimiento y el Barroco pero que tienen que rendirse ante las reglas del «buen gusto» impuestos por un reducido pero poderoso número de críticos y autoridades de la Ilustración y el Rococó. (Nota al margen: no olvidemos que el siglo XVIII está dominado en parte, política, socialmente, culturalmente por las mujeres, en general más opuestas que los hombres a los excesos de la orgía y a las abominaciones de la escatología: solamente el disfraz y su ambigüedad será aceptado.)

En pocas palabras: los elementos carnavalescos, tal como los define e interpreta Mikhail Bakhtine, del *Quijote*, han permanecido invisibles hasta hoy porque hemos leído el *Quijote* a través de una serie de visiones críticas, sobre todo inspiradas en el siglo XVIII y su estética, que tendían a borrarlos o cambiarlos de signo, en nombre de la verosimilitud y del buen gusto. Son, sin embargo, indispensables para una interpretación total de la obra, y ha llegado el momento de subrayarlos.

No es ciertamente Bakhtine el único, ni siquiera el primero, en observar la importancia del fenómeno del carnaval. El carnaval no es simplemente el período de tres días que preceden al miércoles de ceniza y anuncia la cuaresma. No es tampoco, simplemente, la sucesión de desfiles, bailes y mascaradas que anuncian los carteles turísticos invitándonos a acudir a Rio o a Nueva Orleans. Hay en sus orígenes una serie de rituales relacionados con el fin del invierno y la fecundidad restaurada de la tierra que se remontan a épocas muy remotas. Como explica el gran historiador de las religiones, Mircea Eliade, los carnavales y las orgías que suelen acompañarlos representan una restauración simbóloca de la unidad indiferenciada y caótica que precedió la creación del mundo. Mítica y psicológicamente nos permiten una nueva inmersión en el mar de fuerzas ilimitadas que existía antes de la creación, y al renovarnos y renovar con nosotros la naturaleza que nos rodea aseguran el éxito de un nuevo comienzo, de un nuevo ciclo de vitalidad y florecimiento. Pero Eliade señala una clara distinción entre la orgía ritual por una parte y el logro de una fusión total que puede conseguirse mediante técnicas más personales y serias, tales como la meditación, las prácticas del yoga, y las experiencias místicas.[4] El carnaval es, si se quiere, un atajo, un esfuerzo rápido y casi desesperado que reemplaza gracias al entusiasmo colectivo, mediante actividades concretas y fisiológicas, lo que por caminos más arduos se consigue mediante técnicas personales, ascéticas y místicas, de mayor refinamiento. Carl Jung se ha ocupado también en varias ocasiones del carnaval primitivo. Pero es Mihkail Bakhtine quien en su libro sobre Rabelais ha aplicado plenamente el carnaval medieval y renacentista—como sistema de símbolos—a la literatura y específicamente a Rabelais. Podemos preguntarnos cómo un libro de un crítico ruso cuyos temas principales son Rabelais, Dostoyevski, y el carnaval, puede ayudarnos a entender el *Quijote,* donde las fiestas del Carnaval en sí, en rigor, no aparecen. El que el nombre de Bakhtine—que escribió su libro sobre Rabelais en 1940 pero cuya obra está teniendo en estos últimos años un impacto internacional—nos llegue asociado a los nombres prestigiosos de Roman Jakobson y de Julia Kristeva, y a la no menos prestigiosa y muy en boga actividad o escuela de la semiótica y la crítica estructural, no significa que no debamos poner en cuestión la validez de sus interpretaciones y, sobre todo, la posible aplicación de las mismas a Cervantes.

Por suerte para los cervantistas la visión histórica y literaria de Bakhtine es a la vez amplia y profunda. Igual que Eliade y que Jung, concibe su punto de partida—el carnaval—en una forma vasta y coherente: trata de precisar el impacto de una actitud que es a la vez un rito, una fiesta, un sistema de valores, y una filosofía al margen de la filosofía oficial, a veces la imagen al revés, el negativo, de la cultura oficial representada por la iglesia y el Estado. El carnaval ha sido siempre, en forma única y casi imposible de definir, una actividad subversiva. Una gran risa, una risotada a la vez alegre y escéptica frente a la seria y melancólica certidumbre de los dirigentes— medievales, renacentistas, modernos—de nuestras sociedades. Si dejamos a un lado el carnaval de los romanos, las fiestas saturnales, que quizá correspondían bastante bien, en su hilaridad y su pansexualidad, a los ritos más antiguos del carnaval, nos encontramos con el carnaval medieval, que en versiones cada vez más degradadas ha llegado hasta el comercializado carnaval de nuestros días. El carnaval primitivo, incluso en su versión medieval, ya mediatizada por el Estado y la Iglesia, nos recuerda nuestros humildes orígenes y nos dice que, como Anteo, solamente regresando a estos orígenes podemos recuperar nuestras fuerzas. Estos orígenes son el barro, la tierra, incluso substancias más impuras que el barro y la tierra. Nuestras ilusiones de volar muy por encima, de elevarnos hacia las estrellas o las ideas puras platónicas, suelen terminar en fracaso. Como Ícaro, caemos hacia el barro. La risa del pueblo les recuerda a los nobles, los poderosos, que su pretensión y su imperio no duran mucho. En los desfiles romanos que consagraban el triunfo de un general victorioso se incluía simultáneamente y casi en los mismos términos la glorificación y la derisión del vencedor.

Los burócratas, los políticos, los príncipes, los jerarcas de la Iglesia, siempre se han tomado demasiado en serio. Bakhtine señala que todas las formas de lo cómico hubieron de ser transferidas, unas más temprano, otras más tarde, a un nivel no oficial, en el que adquirieron un nuevo sentido, se hicieron más complejas y profundas, hasta convertirse en la expresión de la conciencia y la cultura del pueblo: en las saturnalias romanas y el carnaval medieval. Los rituales cómicos y los espectáculos medievales no son religiosos ni mágicos, no mandan ni piden nada, a diferencia de los rituales mágicos y las plegarias. Muchas de sus formas son parodias de cultos, ritos, ceremonias de la Iglesia. (Pensemos ahora, los hispanistas, en la parodia de las Horas Canónicas en el *Libro de Buen Amor,* y también en la presencia del carnaval en este mismo gran poema, en la lucha entre D. Carnal y Doña Cuaresma: ciertamente que las páginas de Bakhtine arrojan nueva luz sobre el Arcipreste de Hita, y lo mismo podemos decir con respecto a la novela picaresca, en particular el *Buscón,* reinterpretado parcialmente, con gran inteligancia, por Edmond Cros, siguiendo las ideas y las intuiciones de Bakhtine.)

El carnaval es anti-jerárquico. Crea un segundo mundo, una segunda sociedad, al margen del mundo oficial, y todos, en la Edad

Media pueden vivir en este segundo mundo durante una parte del año, por lo menos—y no olvidemos que en muchas regiones el carnaval duraba de dos a tres meses. Frente a los sabios consejeros eclesiásticos del monarca, el espíritu carnavalesco proponía otro tipo de sabiduría, inverso pero no menos decisivo: el bufón, el payaso, el loco, el Rey Momo. Como afirma Bakhtine, «si dejamos de tomar en cuenta esta coexistencia de los dos mundos, el mundo serio y el mundo de la risa, ni la conciencia cultural medieval ni la cultura renacentista pueden ser correctamente interpretadas. Ignorar o subestimar la risa medieval distorsiona nuestra visión del desarrollo cultural de Europa.»[5]

El carnaval subraya la importancia de la materia y de los sentidos que nos ponen en contacto con el mundo material. Las fiestas del carnaval son sensuales, alegres, lúdicas: todo el mundo juega y se divierte, por ello mismo la sociedad entera se transforma en espectáculo. Y a su vez muchos espectáculos medievales se asemejan a las fiestas carnavalescas. Las plazas de pueblos, burgos y ciudades, con sus juglares, sus pequeños teatros, sus cantantes, sus grupos de bailarines, perpetúan el carnaval a lo largo del año. Pero el carnaval no es un espectáculo artístico: es la frontera entre el ritual, el arte, y la vida. No hay propiamente un estrado o un tablado, unas candilejas, un telón, que separen a los actores del pueblo, ya que es esencial que todos, durante el carnaval, sean actores. No vemos el carnaval; lo vivimos, somos parte del mismo. Todo esto resulta difícil de entender hoy porque la mayor parte de nosotros hemos perdido la experiencia personal, vivida, de un carnaval auténtico, no comerciali zado, y, además, porque el más auténtico de los carnavales modernos está separado por un abismo de sensibilidad y de sistemas de valores del auténtico carnaval medieval. Quizá fueron Rabelais, Cer vantes y Shakespeare los últimos grandes escritores modernos que entendieron a fondo el sentido del carnaval medieval, y, cada cual a su manera, supieron darle expresion en sus obras. El racionalismo, la Ilustración, el espíritu del neo-clasicismo y el rococó son hostiles a lo que consideran la risa impura y baja de las masas. El fondo in sobornable de alegre irracionalismo del carnaval tenía que ser rechazado por la nueva estética racionalista. El rococó intimza al carnaval, lo convierte en elegante diversión de salón y alcoba, con lo cual al domesticarlo destruye su esencia.

Resumiendo las diversas manifestiones de la cultura popular relacionada con el carnaval, Bakhtine las define y clasifica en tres formas:

> 1. Los espectáculos rituales: los desfiles carnavalescos, espectáculos cómicos en las plazas de los mercados.
> 2. Composiciones verbales cómicas: parodias orales y escritas, en latín y en las lenguas modernas.
> 3. Distintas clases de «lenguaje grosero»: maldiciones, juramentos, y blasfemias.°

De estas tres categorías las dos de mayor importancia para nuestra interpretación bakhtinana del *Quijote* son la primera y la segunda. Imaginemos ahora la novela de Cervantes como un gran palimpsesto. Por debajo de las palabras con que el autor compone su obra aparecen otros signos de otras realidades que la Historia oculta o enmascara. Cervantes, autor sumamante culto—como más de una vez ha mostrado Américo Castro, si bien la demostración más completa se halla en *El pensamiento de Cervantes*—es también un escritor impregnado de cultura popular, que en Sevilla y otros lugares ha vivido la vida del pueblo y conoce a fondo sus costumbres y sus fiestas. A poco que rasquemos en la superficie del texto cervantino aparecen rasgos, situaciones, descripciones, que solamente adquiere su pleno sentido si las remitimos a sus orígenes en el carnaval. Más que el carnaval mismo aparecen sus consecuencias: los disfraces, las máscaras. Estamos como frente a un rescoldo que nos da indicios de una gran hoguera ya extinguida. Para que esto quede más claro citaré a Octavio Paz, cuya descripción de la Fiesta, en *El laberinto de la soledad*, tiene mucho en común con lo que más arriba he apuntado acerca del carnaval:

> En ciertas fiestas desaparece la noción misma de Orden. El caos regresa y reina la licencia. Todo se permite: desaparecen las jerarquías habituales, las distinciones sociales, los sexos, las clases, los gremios. Los hombres se disfrazan de mujeres, los señores de esclavos, los pobres de ricos. . . Gobiernan los niños o los locos. . . La Fiesta es una revuelta, en el sentido literal de la palabra. En la confusión que engendra, la sociedad se disuelve, se ahoga. . . Pero se ahoga en sí misma, en su caos o libertad original. Todo se comunica; se mezcla el bien con el mal, el día con la noche, lo santo con lo maldito. Todo cohabita, pierde forma, singularidad, y vuelve al amasijo primordial. La Fiesta es una operación cósmica: la

experiencia del Desorden, la reunión de los elementos y principios contrarios para provocar el renacimiento de la vida. La muerte suscita el renacer; el vómito, el apetito; la orgía, estéril en sí misma, la fecundidad de las madres o de la tierra. La Fiesta es un regreso a un estado remoto e indiferenciado, prenatal o presocial, por decirlo así. Regreso que es también un comienzo. . . La sociedad comulga consigo misma en la Fiesta. Todos sus miembros vuelven a la confusion y libertad originales. La estructura social se deshace y se crean nuevas formas de relación, reglas inesperadas, jerarquías caprichosas. En el desorden general, cada quien se abandona y atraviesa por situaciones y lugares que habitualmente le estaban vedados. Las fronteras entre espectadores y actores, entre oficiantes y asistentes, se borran. Todos forman parte de la Fiesta, todos se disuelven en su torbellino.[7]

Es un rasgo común a la Fiesta descrita por Paz y al carnaval de que nos hablan Eliade y Bakhtine que el individuo intenta regresar a un estado original de indiferenciación y libertad, y al intentarlo necesita salir de sí mismo, sobrepasarse. La necesidad de superar sus límites lo obliga a intentar desembarazarse de su personalidad: en ella se sabe limitado, estrecho, encuadrado por las mil restricciones de la vida cotidiana, el trabajo, las obligaciones familiares. Y por ello mismo tiene que disfrazarse. El disfraz oculta a los demás su personalidad normal, y al esconderla la hace desaparecer momentáneamente. La máscara nos hace invisibles: el antifaz, negro como la noche, nos disuelve en tinieblas, Mejor todavía, el disfraz nos convierte en reyes o en policías, en capitán de barco o en Napoleón: todo es posible, ya que a través del disfraz hemos entrado en el reino de la libertad y del desorden. Gracias al disfraz el homosexual se convierte en mujer seductora y vive momentáneamente lo que antes solamente se atrevía a soñar. O la mujer se viste de hombre— cuantas veces acontece eso mismo en la comedia española del Siglo de Oro o en el teatro de Shakespeare—y al hacerlo adquiere la independencia y la libertad del varón, a cambio de innumerables complicaciones y peripecias que convierten ese disfraz en eje de la acción teatral, en resorte de la intriga dramática.

Si ahora dirigimos nuestra atención a la novela cervantina observaremos que el primer incidente de importancia que en la novela ocurre es que alguien se disfraza. Alonso Quijano adopta el disfraz de caballero andante, y con ello disuelve, aniquila, su propia persona lidad. Lo hace con un propósito concreto: al lanzarse al mundo de aventuras que reconoce como propio de los caballeros andantes va a tratar de remontar la corriente del tiempo, devolver la sociedad moderna en la que ha nacido a una edad más primitiva y gloriosa, y, a través de las hazañas que como caballero andante piensa llevar a cabo, regresar a una edad heroica en la que reinará la justicia, y brillarán la hermandad, la caridad, el amor. A través de la búsqueda del Santo Grial todos los caballeros andantes pueden aspirar a una unión perfecta con lo sagrado. Señalemos ahora dos aspectos importantes de esta visión anti-histórica del caballero creado por Cervantes. En primer lugar para entender correctamente la personalidad quijotesca debemos acudir no a la fusión colectiva, el delirio, la risa de carnaval, sino más bien a lo que nos señala Mircea Eliade en la cita anterior: son dos los caminos, las vías que pueden conducirnos a este restablecimiento de la unidad primitiva en que podemos hallar una vida más plena, el camino colectivo y el individual. Don Quijote es un héroe, un asceta, un hombre solitario—si bien la presencia de Sancho le es muy necesaria ya que tiende a recrear cierto equilibrio entre el individuo y la sociedad—y por tanto Don Quijote no intentará adelantarse por el camino colectivo—la fiesta, la orgía, la risa—sino por la vía estrecha del esfuerzo heroico individual, el ascetismo y el sufrimiento. Frente a la risa o la sonrisa tan frecuente en todos los otros personajes de la novela, el rostro de nuestro héroe permanece generalmente grave, serio, melancólico: es, en efecto, el Caballero de la Triste Figura, y el camino del ascetismo y el sufrimiento no le permite casi nunca una visión alegre y regocijada de sus circunstancias.

En segundo lugar cabe señalar que la búsqueda de don Quijote no se limita únicamente a la restauración de la gloriosa edad de la caballería andante. Incluso si tomamos en cuenta que la visión histórica de nuestro caballero no es perfecta ni completa, parece evidente que para él mucho antes de que la caballería aparezca en la escena histórica existe otro período feliz, probablemente mucho más feliz que el de la caballería, ya que en este remoto pasado no hay necesidad de combatir para conseguir la plena libertad y la unión fraternal entre todos los seres humanos. Es el tema de la Edad de Oro, tema favorito, diríase obsesión favorita de la era renacentista, cuidadosamente estudiado por Harry Levin. Para Cervantes el discurso de Don Quijote acerca de esta feliz época, remota en la antigüedad pero presente en la memoria de su héroe, sin dejar de ser un tema común a los literatos de su tiempo se proyecta como algo más profundo: en efecto, la comunidad de intereses, de bienes, de emociones, que queda descrita en este discurso nos permite señalar a nosotros, los críticos modernos de su obra, que existe un lazo, un puente, entre la Edad de Oro tal como fue concebida por el Renacimiento y el Carnaval tradicional transmitido por las costumbres medievales, ya que en ambos casos se trata de una amistosa y—vale la pena subrayarlo—caótica sociedad primitiva. Dichosa edad y siglos dichosos aquellos a quien los antiguos pusieron nombre de dorados, exclama Don Quijote en el capítulo XI de la Primera parte, porque entonces los que en ella vivían ignoraban estas dos palabras de *tuyo* y *mío*. Más que hacernos pensar en el comunismo primitivo, en Rousseau y los primeros socialistas, en las interpretaciones de Fourier y las críticas de Marx, evoquemos el Carnaval en todo su esplendor, que algunos de nosotros hemos vivido, como un momento de alegre promiscuidad, de la que no se halla excluida la promiscuidad sexual, como un intento de supervivencia en la mente colectiva de esta etapa de la historia humana, no sabemos a punto fijo si plenamente validada por la antropología, aunque en todo caso sí respaldada por la tradición cultural.

El placer es fuente de risa. La risa carnavalesca medieval es ya ambigua: hay que reírse de los poderes políticos e ideológicos que dificultan la vieja alegría pánica, el cósmico regocijo frente al paso del tiempo y la presencia constante de la muerte, ya que los que ponen obstáculos a lo que se sabe indispensable son torpes e ignorantes: es, en el fondo, una risa de superioridad, aunque los que se rían sean socialmente inferiores a las clases—y a los individuos—dominantes que han establecido y mantienen las instituciones oficiales de la sociedad. La risa es, con frecuencia, una crítica.

Bakhtine señala (págs. 21-23 de la traducción al inglés) que los procesos de degradación y crítica del medio evo no son puramente negativos. La degradación nos acerca a la tierra. Somos tierra, y como la tierra podemos regenerarnos en un nuevo renacer. La parodia medieval es ambivalente y anuncia una futura regeneración. La parodia moderna no contiene este elemento positivo. La degradación, paródica o de otro tipo, es característica de la literatura renacentista, que en este sentido perpetúa la mejor tradición de la cultura humorística popular, plena y profundamente expresada por Rabelais.

El espíritu de carnaval se halla presente, en forma velada y sutil a veces, más obviamente en otras, a lo largo de la gran novela cervantina. La panza de Sancho evoca la de los grotescos demonios de las ánforas corintias. La risa de los que contemplan las pseudo-hazañas del héroe forma un coro continuo que se propaga a los lectores. El contraste físico mismo entre el caballero y su escudero nos recuerda innumerables parejas cómicas de espectáculos burlescos. El papel de Sancho consiste en ofrecer un constante contraste, una continua parodia crítica, a las altas aspiraciones quijotescas, en la misma forma en que las parodias medievales—pensemos una vez más en el Arcipreste de Hita—contrastan y en cierto modo corrigen las elevadas aspiraciones de la Iglesia medieval. Sancho representa a Don Carnal, en empeñado diálogo ante la Cuaresma ascética del caballero andante.

Dos momentos en la novela, que corresponden a dos importantes secciones de las dos partes, pueden ser subrayados—cosa que Bakhtine no hace—como lo que podríamos denominar dos focos carnavalescos. En la primera parte, todos los sucesos que se relacionan con la venta. Bromas, sorpresas, disfraces, se suceden con toda rapidez. En ambigua pero constante relación con Don Quijote y Sancho, los personajes que llegan a la venta durante los capítulos centrales de la primera parte parecen participar en un baile de disfraces, en que las más extrañas aventuras son posibles ya que no podemos estar seguros de la identidad de los que en ellas participan. Pero son los episodios relacionados con el palacio de los duques, en la segunda parte del libro, los que mejor y más claramente señalan la supervivencia de las fiestas carnavalescas en las páginas cervantinas. Tres son los elementos propios del Carnaval que aparecen en estos capítulos: los desfiles, las bromas, y la elección de un Rey de Carnaval. En este caso es Sancho el elegido, si bien Don Quijote es seleccionado como centro de las burlas en el interior del castillo o palacio, y bien podemos afirmar que la alegre comitiva se disgrega para formar dos grupos, uno que considerará a Don Quijote como su centro y otro que se agrupará en torno a Sancho. Observemos además que la ceremonia de coronación del Rey Momo iba seguida, en el carnaval tradicional, por una ceremonia de signo contrario, una deposición o descoronación, tras un período de reinado que no solía durar más de uno o pocos días. Y esto es lo que ocurre con el asalto a la Ínsula y la consiguiente dimisión de Sancho como gobernador de tan precario reino.

Las bromas, finalmente, no son en caso alguno privadas, sino públicas, y, en especial en el vuelo de Clavileño, que reúne a los dos reyes Momos y parece señalar el final de la fiesta, lo mismo que los fuegos de artificio en muchos carnavales del pasado y el presente. La broma pública se convierte aquí, plenamente, en espectáculo para todos.

En efecto. el Carnaval, fiesta de regeneración, en que los seres humanos afirman su indestructibilidad al ponerse nuevamente en contacto con la tierra, nos ofrece simbólicamente los altibajos de la fortuna: éxitos y fracasos, muertes y renacimientos. El desencanto, el desengaño, la pérdida del trono de la gloria, llegan a Don Quijote en el mismo momento en que más altos triunfos se prometía, como en el caso de los gigantes que resultan ser cueros de vino en la primera parte de la novela. Y la más dolorosa pérdida del trono ocurrirá en los capítulos finales, tras la derrota del caballero a manos de Sansón Carrasco: Don Quijote tendrá que morir para que en las últimas páginas pueda renacer, brevemente, Alonso Quijano el Bueno.

Así, pues, el ritmo de las aventuras del caballero, y las del escudero durante el gobierno de la ínsula, está inspirado por el ritmo de ilusión y desilusión con que los reyes del carnaval—que eran escogidos por su locura y su gracia—podían verse a sí mismos encumbrados un día y destronados al día siguiente. Es precisamente el aceptar que somos parte de una gran rueda cósmica, que nos exalta un día para deprimirnos poco después, lo que convierte al carnaval primitivo en una ceremonia de rejuvenecimiento y supervivencia. Si todo pasa, todo vuelve también, con nuevos rostros, portando nuevos mensajes. Pero para que el mundo pueda renacer es preciso que los hombres desechen sus terrores, sepan reírse, y sepan también acercarse nuevamente a la tierra de la que salieron. Y quien dice tierra dice igualmente otras materias cercanas a la tierra. De ahí la presencia de la escatología en tantas obras medievales, y su supervivencia en el *Quijote*. En las tradiciones carnavalescas la materia fecal y la orina transformaban el terror cósmico en un alegre espantajo de carnaval. Claro está, más adelante, ya en gran parte perdidas con la Ilustración del siglo XVIII las raíces de la cultura medieval que todavía están vivas en la época renacentista, la presencia de elementos escatológicos en el *Quijote*—y en otras obras del Siglo de Oro— será vista como algo desagradable y grosero, algo que hay que leer aprisa y sin comentario. por ser contrario al «buen gusto» y a las normas estéticas del neoclasicismo. Así, por ejemplo, el capítulo de los batanes quedará, entre otros, en el limbo a que son condenados los textos poco limpios. Observemos aquí que no hay en Cervantes verdadera obsesión escatológica comparable, por ejemplo, a la de un Rabelais, un Swift o un Quevedo. Los pocos pasajes que pueden señalarse como escatológicos son, en el fondo, inocentes en su aceptación de las necesidades fisiológicas sin insistir demasiado en ellas, y, como en el caso de Rabelais, se integran en una concepción unitaria de la vida que tiene no pocos puntos de contacto con el mundo del Arcipreste de Hita, Chaucer y Boccaccio. En cambio, la actitud de Quevedo y la de Swift son claramente obsesivas y neuróticas: en parte ello se debe quizá a factores de la personalidad, pero también creo que en parte hay que atribuirlo al proceso de diferenciación y racionalización, mucho más avanzado en ambos casos: el mundo moderno separa y delimita allí donde el mundo medieval integraba y fecundaba. Las suciedades de la prosa y la poesía de Quevedo, a diferencia de las que encontramos en Rabelais, son esencialmente estériles; no ayudan en modo alguno a ponernos en contacto con una naturaleza regeneradora. Están simplemente ahí, frente a nosotros, y su objetivo es arrancarnos una maligna sonrisa de superioridad frente a las víctimas de tan bajos golpes. Y es que la risa misma ha cambiado de sentido a medida que nos alejamos del medio evo. Como señala Bakhtine, «la actitud del siglo XVII en adelante con respecto a la risa puede definirse de la manera siguiente: la risa no puede expresar una concepción universal del mundo, sólo puede abarcar ciertos aspectos *parciales* y *parcialmente típicos* de la vida social, aspectos negativos; lo que es esencial e importante no puede ser cómico.»[8]

Todo lo cual contribuye a explicarnos que después de un claro éxito inicial, éxito de público que muestra que todavía las masas de lectores de principios del siglo XVII comprendían el valor y la importancia de la risa, la novela de Cervantes cayera poco después en relativo descrédito y olvido. Fue preciso que los críticos románticos alemanes la reinterpretaran subrayando todas sus posibilidades serias, dramáticas, patéticas y transcendentes, camino que más tarde seguirá nuestro Miguel de Unamuno en su *Vida de Don Quijote y Sancho,* llegando hasta las últimas consecuencias. El sentido original de la obra tal como fue concebida por Cervantes y entendida por sus contemporáneos quedaba olvidado o soslayado. Podemos comparar este proceso a lo que ocurriría si en un concierto pudiéramos escuchar únicamente el contrapunto, no la melodía. En música el contrapunto es interesante, enriquece la obra, pero no basta por sí solo para proporcionarnos las verdaderas dimensiones sonoras de la composición. Las interpretaciones del *Quijote* como obra seria, filosófica, moral, no son, creo, totalmente erróneas, sí insuficientes para darnos toda la medida de la obra, y en parte están inspiradas por una actitud diversa de la que imperaba cuando Cervantes se educó y aprendió a escribir literatura: pecan, pues, de anacrónicas. Y, como lo ha señalado acertadamente Lucien Febvre, el pecado más grave de un historiador es el pecado de anacronismo.[9]

Y en este momento se impone llegar a una conclusión de esta lectura bakhtiniana del *Quijote,* aunque forzosamente sea una conclusión provisional. Si interpretamos el conjunto de observaciones hechas por el crítico ruso, o que este crítico inspira en nosotros, concluiremos que el *Quijote* es una atrevida tentativa de fusión y simbiosis de dos culturas, la cultura popular y la cultura erudita y aristocrática. Como concesión a la segunda encontramos en la novela cervantina los capítulos de crítica literaria, los comentarios neoaristotélicos del Canónigo, las numerosas alusiones a obras cultas, la presencia de Ariosto, la constante ironía, y el hecho mismo de que el héroe de la novela, el ingenioso hidalgo, sea ante todo un intelectual devorador de libros y buen conocedor de obras literarias. Es Sancho Panza el que representa la influencia siempre latente pero casi siempre oculta de las tradiciones carnavalescas, Sancho con su vientre rotundo, su amor a la comida, sus necesidades fisiológicas insoslayables, sus disparates lingüísticos, su risa robusta y prolongada. Y el diálogo entre el caballero y su escudero, a lo largo de toda la novela, simboliza y sintetiza la posibilidad de interacción de la cultura popular y la culta: a nivel psicológico la quijotización de Sancho y la parcial y esporádica sanchificación del hidalgo apuntan en el mismo sentido. La tentativa de Cervantes, más cuidadosa, mejor integrada artísticamente que la de Rabelais, ya que está sostenida por un argumento coherente y organizada en torno a personajes de tres dimensiones, bien desarrollados y que cambian con el paso de tiempo, estaba, sin embargo, destinada a fracasar a corto plazo: al madurar los estilos del barroco la cultura aristocrática y la popular tienden a separarse cada vez más; el Góngora de los romances paródicos parece ser un poeta distinto del autor de las *Soledades,* y cuando los lectores corrientes tienen que acudir a Pellicer para entender a Góngora y el grueso de los espectadores de autos y comedias mito-lógicas de Calderón apenas si puede seguir las alusiones de dichas obras el divorcio se ha consumado. Gracián, autor culto, despreciará la novela cervantina. Pero por breves años la risa cósmica que surge entre las páginas del *Quijote* simbolizó una reconciliación entre la Edad Media y el Renacimiento maduro, entre la voz del pueblo y la sabiduría de los cultos, una nueva Edad de Oro en que la gran literatura podía ser de todos y para todos.

YALE UNIVERSITY

NOTAS

[1]Cito de la edición original (Madrid, 1914), p. 58.

[2]Ibid., pp. 47-58.

[3]El libro de Bakhtine aparece en su versión original en Moscú, en 1965, con el título de *Tvorchestvo Fransua Rable.* Escrito en parte hacia 1940, revisado más tarde, ya que cita obras de fecha posterior a 1940. La versión al inglés de Hélène Iwolski, por la que cito, apareció en Cambridge, Mass., en la M.I.T. Press, en 1968.

[4]Mircea Eliade, *Mephistopheles and the Androgyne* (Nueva York: Sheed & Ward, 1965), pp. 114-117.

[5]Bakhtine, p. 6.

[6]Ibid., p. 5.

[7]Pp. 45-47 de la edición de 1959 del Fondo de Cultura Económica.

[8]Bakhtine, p. 67. Ver también la p. 115. Y la 66, en que escribe: «The Renaissance conception of laughter can be roughly described as follows: Laughter has a deep philosophical meaning, it is one of the essential forms of the truth concerning the world as a whole, concerning history and man; it is a peculiar point of view relative to the world; the world is seen anew, no less (and perhaps more) profoundly than when seen from the serious standpoint. Therefore, laughter is just as admirable in great literature, posing universal problems, as seriousness. Certain essential aspects of the world are accessible only to laughter.»

[9]En *Le Problème de l'incroyance au XVIe. siècle: La Religion de Rabelais* (Paris, 1942), especialmente la introducción y el capítulo I. Citado por Bakhtine, p. 131.

La locura emblemática
en la segunda parte
del *Quijote*

FRANCISCO MÁRQUEZ VILLANUEVA

A FIGURA DEL «LOCO» o bufón de corte ha constituido en los últimos decenios el centro de
una bibliografía internacional de elevado interés.[1] Brillantes estudios filosóficos, histórico-
literarios y antropológicos han visto en el
tema de la locura bufonesca un mito capaz de
absorber toda la vida intelectual del Norte de
Europa en los siglos XV y XVI. El humanismo
cristiano, con el *Narrenschiff* (1494) de Sebastián Brant y la *Stultitiae
laus* (1509) de Erasmo, ha encontrado en el «loco» de corte la metáfora viviente para su idea de los derechos de la verdad moral y de la
humildad del saber. Medievo y humanismo, Sócrates y San Pablo
podían pisar un terreno de espontánea coincidencia y mutuo enri-
quecimiento bajo la paradoja *De docta ignorantia,* felizmente enunciada
en 1440 por Nicolás de Cusa.

Dicha literatura aparece también en España, con toda puntualidad, a comienzos del XVI, pues puede considerársela iniciada por los
Disparates y piezas de Carnaval de Juan del Encina y proyecta una
fuerte sugestión sobre toda la primera mitad del siglo. Como en casi
todas partes, la bufonería sirvió entonces de disfraz para los más
arriesgados ejercicios de crítica social, política y religiosa y contó con
autores que la encarnan en su más deliberada pureza, como son el
médico Francisco López de Villalobos, el *truhán* de Carlos V don
Francesillo de Zúñiga y el abogado toledano Sebastián de Horozco.
Más aún, había de estampar un sello reconocible en autores de la
fama europea de un fray Antonio de Guevara y hallarse presente
también al nacimiento del relato picaresco en el *Lazarillo de Tormes.*
Con el felicísimo retraso cultural que le caracteriza, y que no hacía
sino dar a su obra aquella exquisita solera, Cervantes lleva a la
cumbre la literatura europea de la locura paradójica con su demente
caballero, no en vano bautizado en ambigua pila como *El ingenioso
hidalgo.* Pero es preciso señalar aquí las dos caras de un mismo lamen-
table fenómeno. Ni los estudios de la literatura del «loco» suelen
prestar atención a sus manifestaciones españolas (ignorando por
completo a una personalidad tan clásica como la de don Francesillo
de Zúñiga), ni los cervantistas madrugaron tampoco para reparar en
tan decisivo nexo europeo del *Quijote* y su arte.

Aunque *El pensamiento de Cervantes* (1925) de Américo Castro había
de recurrir a ilustrarse en muchos puntos con textos de la *Stultitiae
laus,*[2] perduró por demasiado tiempo la creencia de que ni esta ni su
espíritu habían logrado hacer ninguna mella en la península Ibérica.
La muralla de dicha convicción (determinante de aquella otra moro-
sidad crítica) empezó, sin embargo, a resquebrajarse en 1949, al
señalar Antonio Vilanova[3] la nueva luz a que era preciso situar el
problema del erasmismo cervantino en vista del influjo y clara adaptación de muchas páginas de la *Stultitiae laus* en la *Censura de la locura
humana y excelencias della* (Lérida, 1598) por Alonso de Mondragón.
Este jurisconsulto aragonés proclamaba, en vísperas de escribirse el
Quijote, la grande y risueña tesis de la *Moria* erasmiana: «¿I qué rato
se me dará en esta vida que no sea triste, melancólico, desabrido i
lleno de descontento, si no participa algún tanto de locura.?» (p. 179).
Aunque es muy posible que Cervantes leyera el libro de Mondragón, tenía además conocimiento directo de la *Stultitiae laus,* pues el
mismo investigador ha logrado detectar también sus claros ecos en

una pieza tan fundamental como el prólogo de la Primera Parte del *Quijote*.[4]

Si el eco de la *Stultitiae laus* vibraba todavía a fines del siglo XVI, las traducciones españolas de Erasmo habían llevado en su vanguardia otra adaptación de la misma por el bachiller Hernán López de Yanguas,[5] bajo la forma de unos *Triumphos de locura* (Valencia, 1521) cuya relación con la *Moria* fue señalada por Eugenio Asensio en 1968.[6] Ante el peso de tales datos, Marcel Bataillon[7] rectificaba en 1969 uno de los aspectos fundamentales en su idea del erasmismo español para dar plena entrada a los influjos de la *Stultitiae laus* sobre la concepción del *Quijote*. El sabio y llorado hispanista no puede ser más rotundo en sus nuevas conclusiones: «N'hésitons pas à ranger Cervantès dans le sillage d'Érasme, avec Rabelais et Shakespeare, parmi les 'laudateurs de la Folie' qui inaugurent dans la littérature un ton nouveau» (p. 147).

Igual que en el caso de la *Danza de la muerte,* la literatura del «loco» adquirió una inmensa popularidad a través de su iconografía, a la que colaboraron Durero[8] como ilustrador del *Narrenschiff* y Holbein el Viejo de la *Stultitiae laus*. Este aspecto vuelve tanto más importante, para el caso de España, los *Triumphos de locura* de Hernán López de Yanguas, cuyo frontispicio muestra una xilografía con una barca, en cuya proa campea un pavo real en una banderola. En el medio se yergue una doncella que se peina y contempla con coquetería en un espejo. Un «loco» con gorro asnal ayuda a entrar en el esquife a otros colegas con largos gabanes y abundancia de cascabeles.[9] Dicha estampa pregona a voces la ascendencia del *Narrenschiff* de Brant y bastó para ofuscar por algún tiempo la relación de aquel poema, en forma de un debate medieval, con la *Stultitiae laus*. En fecha muy temprana la modesta obra de López de Yanguas capta así por separado los dos temas fundamentales de la literatura del «loco» en el Norte de Europa, al yuxtaponer la nave estultífera de su iconografía (Brant) y la loanza de la locura en su texto (Erasmo).

Si la *Moria* reviste ahora un énfasis simbólico, tan en cabeza de la primera oleada de traducciones españolas de Erasmo, no alcanza menor importancia el gemelo testimonio del eco de Brant y su *Narrenschiff* en la Península. Hay que tomar aquí en cuenta la rareza de su influjo en las literaturas del Sur de Europa y especialmente en Italia,[10] por contraste con el mayor éxito y universal difusión del tema erasmiano de la *Moria*. Más asentado en la moralización exhortatoria del tardío medievo (que hace de sus «locos» típicos pecadores) su nave se mostró poco dispuesta a navegar por el Mediterráneo. Incapaz de acercarse a ningún tema sin iluminarlo de algún modo, Marcel Bataillon identificó la xilografía de López de Yanguas como procedente de las *Stultiferae naves* (París, 1501) de Jodocus Badius Ascensius, [11] breve *additamentum* o resumen latino de la obra de Brant y cuya mayor novedad consiste en embarcar a sus «locos» en barquichuelos correspondientes a cada uno de los sentidos corporales (la estampa de López de Yanguas se inspira en el dedicado al de la vista). Esta «plaquette» de Badius tuvo inmediato eco en España, pues fue impresa en Burgos en 1499 por Fadrique de Basilea.[12] El *Narrenschiff* figuraba en la biblioteca sevillana de don Hernando Colón y Bataillon menciona una cita textual del mismo hecho en 1535 por el obispo de Michoacán don Vasco de Quiroga.[13] Puedo añadir que un nuevo y más extenso resumen de Brant impreso por el mismo Jodocus Badius en 1505 (y diversas veces reeditado hasta 1515)[14] aparece citado por el chantre de la catedral de Plasencia Francisco Miranda Villafañe en sus *Diálogos de la phantástica philosofía* (Salamanca, 1582).[15] Plagia esta insigne rareza de librería los diálogos sobre materias sicológicas de los *Capricci del Bottaio* (1546) del florentino Giambattista Gelli, obra prohibida en Italia desde el año 1554.[16] Al tocar el tema del universal señorío de la locura se amplía que «quien quisiere saber esta verdad, lea en un libro que se llama Nauis stultorum, donde verá todos los estados de los hombres estar tocados de esta enfermedad» (f. 36 v.). Y una nota marginal suplida por Miranda puntualiza aquí: «*Iodocus Badius Ascensis* auctor 1513». Notablemente, tanto Bataillon como Werner Krauss[17] están de acuerdo en incorporar la curiosa obra de Miranda Villafañe al catálogo, cada vez más nutrido, de las fuentes cervantinas.

La nave de la locura se hallaba destinada a la misma fortuna iconográfica en relación con otras dos obras españolas de alto bordo. La portada del *Retrato de la Loçana andaluza* (Venecia, 1528-30) presenta otra xilografía que ilustra a la protagonista en su traslado de Roma a Venecia en la proa de una góndola (bien llamada aquí *cavallo venetiano*) donde hace de timonel y remero el bellacón de Rampín. Figuran a proa y a popa sendas monas (símbolos de lujuria) y la barquilla acomoda a todo un copioso pasaje de cortesanas y alcahuetas. Sobre el pabellón central de la góndola se alza la media figura de San Marcos, con el estandarte del león veneciano. Pero en este mismo toldillo se ve, como en reflexión invertida, una muerte que alza los brazos con gesto amenazador. El carácter alegórico-moral del grabado es indudable y ha sido acertadamente puesto en relación con la iconografía del *Narrenschiff* por el hispanista Francesco A. Ugolini.[18] En opinión del mismo, ha sido, una vez más, Iodocus Badius quien, de entre varias posibilidades, parece haber ofrecido un modelo más cercano para esta inédita transmigración de la Lozana Andaluza, personaje tan poco necio como para saber quitarse a tiempo de aquella Roma tan amenazada por el cielo con el azote del *saco* de 1527.

En vísperas muy inmediatas de la publicación del *Quijote*, un grabado a toda plana de *La Pícara Justina* (Medina del Campo, 1605) va a recoger el mismo tema[19] con una representación mucho más compleja de *La nave de la vida picaresca,* navegando por el río del Olvido hasta el puerto del Desengaño, donde la espera un esqueleto que se levanta del sepulcro. Con el Tiempo como timonel y la Ociosidad adormecida en su bodega, el navío de tres palos (rebosante de símbolos alusivos a la vida disipada) lleva a su bordo la más insigne *trimurti* literaria, compuesta por el Pícaro Alfarache, la protagonista Justina y la madre Celestina, maliciosamente ataviada esta última con un gran capelo cardenalicio. En un diminuto chinchorro los sigue, a fuerza de remo, Lazarillo de Tormes en compañía del toro de Salamanca.

Esta meditadísima estampa de *La pícara Justina* equivale a toda una tesis sobre el itinerario del género picaresco, en su periplo desde el humanismo cristiano hasta el espíritu barroco. La dilatada vigencia del tema iconográfico demuestra que la ideología del *Narrenschiff* no ha permanecido inoperante ni ajena al desarrollo de dicho género. Y es solo a su luz como adquiere todo su sarcástico relieve la alusión del prólogo del *Lazarillo,* con su loanza de sí mismo (igual que la *Moria* erasmiana) y de cuantos «con fuerza y maña remando salieron a buen puerto». Se reconoce la misma huella[20] en el *Relox de príncipes* (1529) de fray Antonio de Guevara, cuyo buen emperador Marco Aurelio envía a una isla del Helesponto tres barcos cargados de «locos» que representan solo una fracción de los muchos que sobran en Roma. Las *Navicula fatuorum* (1510) y *Navicula penitentie* (1511) del imitador de Brant Johann Geiler de Kaysersberg han sido incorporadas también a la genealogía de las *Barcas* vicentinas.[21] Tampoco hay que perder en esto de vista las recientes investigaciones que apuntan el probable influjo de Brant y de la literatura nórdica sobre vagabundos en la picaresca y en Mateo Alemán.[22]

Con tales antecedentes, «la famosa aventura del barco encantado» (II, 29) se perfila no solo como parodia de un tipo particular de aventura caballeresca, sino también como cita con un motivo ya tradicional. La crónica de tan catastrófico periplo es pura bufonada sin redención de contrapesos heroicos. Don Quijote, tan fiero mientras se trata de dar tajos al aire en la proa del barquichuelo, renuncia ante las aceñas a proseguir la aventura y da media vuelta con su primer y único «yo no puedo más». La nave estultífera ha encontrado su previsible destino, rodeada de un grotesco coro de molineros enharinados[23] que «representaban una mala vista» y terminan por reintegrarse a sus tareas «teniéndolos por locos». Como ha sido ya observado,[24] la fatídica navegación por el Ebro conduce a don Quijote y Sancho a la región infernal que para ellos ha de resultar el palacio de los duques aragoneses. Solo que ese orco aristocrático no es el *Hades* clásico, ni la *Malabolgia* dantesca, sino la más endiablada y perfecta *Narragonia* que Sebastián Brant hubiera alcanzado a soñar.

Unos capítulos atrás (II,11) don Quijote ha tenido ya un mal encuentro con la misma locura emblemática, personificada por el actor de *Las cortes de la Muerte* que, en traje de «bojiganga» o «moharracho», turbó con sus cabriolas, con sus vejigas y con sus cascabeles el proverbial sosiego de Rocinante. Los principales personajes y aventuras de la Segunda Parte toman ya como supuesto previo la locura lúcida de don Quijote y la discreta simpleza de su escudero, tan pregonadas por la fama literaria de la Primera. En vista de tal planteamiento, era lógico y casi obligado que Cervantes se aplicara en su segundo *Quijote* a un plan de agotar las posibilidades narrativas de la locura paradójica, con su peculiar juego de ambigüedades y de inversiones dialécticas. Y por lo mismo es allí donde, como enjuicia Marcel Batailllon, el sabio autor «se montre disciple à la fois fidèle et génial de la *Moria*».[25]

He expuesto en otro lugar cómo Cervantes parece haber dado máxima consideración a la paradoja de la locura sabia y de la cordura indiscreta en los capítulos dedicados al caballero del Verde Gabán. La locura de don Quijote se muestra allí sabia y dispuesta a predicar sensatez a don Diego de Miranda, también otro «loco», solo que orate de la vida prudente y dosificada con la que se imagina esquivar los riesgos que a todo hombre acechan en la tarea de vivir. Cervantes se planta con ello en una de las encrucijadas más características de la locura paradójica, pues como advierte Enrico Castelli, «la sagesse n'est pas suffisante: elle *n'assure* pas. L'Humanisme a montré

le 'savoir du risque', ou mieux: la sagesse du risque».[26] El loco cuerdo
de la vida como arrojo y el cuerdo loco de la vida como renuncia a la
acción, no dejan de ser un buen par de «locos» asentados en los
respectivos cuernos de un dilema ético. Con lógica correlativa, la
técnica cervantina recurre, además, a la emblemática de la locura
bufonesca para proclamar esa coincidencia en la oposición. A punto
de comenzar la aventura de los leones, donde la temeridad de don
Quijote alcanza su cénit, se le rodea a éste la burla de los requesones
que fortuitamente fueron a parar a su yelmo. El oloroso lacticinio
alcanza también aquí un carácter emblemático, por cuanto el queso
se consideraba como alimento más propio y adecuado para el loco, al
que solía ponérsele en el capillo de su ropón. Don Diego de Miranda
reniega a su vez, de las modernadas costumbres y amor al anonimato
en su desmedido gusto por la indumentaria de color verde, que tan
mal cuadra con su edad e inclinaciones. El efecto es todavía más
incongruo y chillón, porque su gabán se adorna con apliques «jirona-
dos» (esto es, triángulos o rombos) de terciopelo leonado, material
del que también está hecha su montera. Don Diego de Miranda viste
así de un modo arlequinesco, lo cual significa su ingreso en el mismo
terreno emblemático, pues los «locos», tanto naturales como fingidos, solían vestir amplias ropas talares, *sayos* o *gabanes* de colores
chillones, de preferencia verde y con apliques de diversas pieles ani-
males. Así viste oficialmente (grabados de Holbein) la avispada *Moria*
erasmiana. Y todos recordaríamos en este punto el aria *Vesti la giubba*
de la ópera *Pagliacci*.

El atuendo de don Diego de Miranda, tan cuidadosamente descrito en el *Quijote*, tiene dicha explicación fácil y constructiva para el
lector de la época, aunque haya constituido después un espinoso
problema para la crítica moderna.[27] Sobre el rastro de algún posible
simbolismo, nuestra colega Helena Percas[28] ha hecho inventario de
la frecuente aparición en el *Quijote* de este ubicuo color verde. La
clave, en efecto, no se halla demasiado recóndita, pues en cuanto
color emblemático de la locura bufonesca, el verde realza (a modo de
marbete) el acento hilarante de muchas situaciones y personajes,
como ocurre, por ejemplo, con el color de las cintas de la celada en la
Primera Parte y con el de la seda para los puntos de las medias en la
Segunda. El verde se menciona también en asociación característica
con los momentos y personajes aparejados para jugar algún engaño
más o menos grotesco: el Cura se viste «unos corpiños de terciopelo

verde guarnecidos con unos ribetes de raso blanco» (I, 27) para hacer ante don Quijote la doncella menesterosa. Pero cuando se halla mejor actriz para el desempeño de este papel, Dorotea se engalana también de saya y mantellina «de otra vistosa tela verde» (I, 29) en preparación para *dar el mico* a que alude su nombre de «princesa Micomicona». La hermosa Quiteria, objeto de tan pesada burla para el rico Camacho, y sobre cuya complicidad quedan siempre sospechas, se atavía precisamente de terciopelo verde. Ginés de Pasamonte, paradigma de personaje huidizo, surgirá reencarnado en el titiritero Maese Pedro y «traía cubierto el ojo izquierdo y casi medio carrillo con un parche de tafetán verde» (II, 25), semiantifaz que ofusca una de las más dolosas realidades de todo el libro.

Al centrarse más de intento sobre los temas de la locura paradójica, la Segunda Parte confía al simbolismo del color verde la misión caracterizadora que, de un modo analógico, llega a asumir en el abigarrado gabán de don Diego de Miranda. El lector, ya avisado por un prólogo muy denso en historias de locos, se topa con otro de lo más emblemático nada más poner pie en el capítulo primero: «Visitáronle, en fin, y halláronle sentado en la cama, vestida una almilla de bayeta verde, con un bonete colorado toledano; y estaba tan seco y amojamado, que no parecía sino hecho de carne momia» (II, 1). Don Quijote, con una media chilaba verde (que eso venía a ser la *almilla*)[29] y el bonete rojo (exactamente lo que hoy se llama un *fez*) presenta, no ya una inconfundible facha bufonesca, sino una sugerencia de fantasmón oriental muy acorde con la costumbre de vestir a los hombres de placer en trajes de moros, judíos o turcos (recuérdese a Pernía como *Barbarroja*, entre los retratados por Velázquez).

La indumentaria emblemática del «loco» se hallaba también predestinada a brillar en la corte de los duques, donde tan altos señores pretenden hacer grotescos juguetes del andante y su escudero. Don Quijote echa mano de toda su prosopopeya para desfilar ante la enamorada Altisidora y salir al encuentro de los duques, envuelto en un «mantón de escarlata» y cubierto con «una montera de terciopelo verde, guarnecida de pasamanos de plata» (II, 46), ricas prendas de corte que sin duda forman parte de la malévola hospitalidad de los ociosos aristócratas. Capítulos atrás, amo y criado habían sido ya blanco de una asechanza similar, pues antes de acudir a la caza de montería:

Diéronle a don Quijote un vestido de monte y a Sancho otro
verde, de finísimo paño; pero don Quijote no se le quiso poner,
diciendo que otro día había de volver al duro ejercicio de las
armas y que no podía llevar consigo guardarropas ni reposte-
rías. Sancho sí tomó el que le dieron, con intención de venderle
en la primera ocasión que pudiere (II, 34).

Tales *sayos*[30] o sobrevestes encubren venenosas intenciones,
sobre todo (por su inconfundible color) el reservado para Sancho. La
negativa de don Quijote a aceptar el dudoso favor significa, en su
inocencia, una decepción para sus anfitriones y hasta un conato de
repudio hacia estos, es decir, uno de los primeros síntomas del curso
de enfrentamiento a que se halla destinada la relación entre el
andante y el aristócrata, entre la Caballería y la Corte. Sancho, en
cambio, traga todo el anzuelo y adornará el venatorio ejercicio con
su gran *intermezzo* cómico, al quedar colgado de un árbol por los
faldones del sayo infamante, que lo exponen así como en una picota.
Sancho lleva en esto cierto merecido, no tanto por su codicia como
por su gustosa entrada en el prominente papel de hombre de placer
y en la característica seudointimidad entre príncipe y bufón. No hay
que perder de vista que, apenas pisar el castillo ducal, don Quijote
llama a su escudero «truhán moderno y majadero antiguo», previ-
niéndole contra el riesgo profesional de que «quien tropieza en hablador y en gracioso, al primer puntapié cae y da en truhán desgraciado»
(II, 31). El sayo verde de la cacería ha de dar todavía más juego, al ser
enviado a la aldea como especial regalo para la hija Sanchica,
cubriendo con su sombra a la familia que ha quedado atrás. Sancho
hace después la entrada solemne a su gobierno «vestido a lo letrado,
y encima, un gabán muy ancho de chamelote de aguas leonado, con
una montera de lo mesmo» (II, 44). Lleva, pues, una indumentaria no
muy distante de la de don Diego de Miranda, salvo que su gabán es
todo *leonado* y en tejido de pelo de camello, esto es, con un significativo desarrollo del elemento de comparación animal.[31]

Quedan todavía en la Segunda Parte otros casos de intención no
menos clara. Don Quijote encuentra a Montesinos arropado en una
demencial indumentaria, sin estilo o época reconocible y que es, a la
vez, de joven y de viejo, de caballero y de religioso, de luto y de
risotada:

. . . y hacia mí se venía un venerable anciano, vestido con un

capuz de bayeta morada, que por el suelo le arrastraba; ceñíale
los hombros y los pechos una beca de colegial, de raso verde;
cubríale la cabeza una gorra milanesa negra, y la barba, can-
ísima, le pasaba de la cintura; no traía arma ninguna, sino un
rosario de cuentas en la mano mayores que medianas nueces, y
los dieces asimismo como huevos medianos de avestruz. (II,
23).

Centrada por la intensa nota verde de la beca colegial, estas ropas
del barbas carolingio, con su veste talar y su capuchón, ofrecen
marcado carácter bufonesco y no andan muy lejos de los violentos
contrastes de policromía que distinguen a don Diego de Miranda y a
su cabalgadura, enjaezada también de verde y de morado.

Vestida de hombre, «de damasco verde, con pasamanos de oro»
(II, 60), irrumpe en el *Quijote* Claudia Jerónima, que acaba de tomar
cruenta y sumarísima venganza por sus infundados celos. El proceder de la joven catalana es paradigmático de los desmanes acarrea-
dos por una pasión cegadora del entendimiento y causante por ello
de otra modalidad muy real de «locura», anunciada también por el
color de su brillante vestido.

Caso aparte es el planteado por la misma Duquesa, cuyo encuentro en traje de bella cazadora sobreabunda igualmente en color
verde:

Llegóse más, y entre ellos vio una gallarda señora sobre un
palafrén o hacanea blanquísima, adornada de guarniciones
verdes y con un sillón de plata. Venía la señora asimismo vestida de verde, tan bizarra y ricamente, que la misma bizarría
venía transformada en ella (II, 30).

En principio, dicha indumentaria se hallaría justificada a secas por
tratarse de un vestido de caza, que por razones de elemental *camouflage* solía ser con frecuencia de dicho color. Se repite así la misma
ambigüedad implícita en el vestido de Quiteria, pues también las
novias solían vestir de verde en sus desposorios. Pero no hay que
olvidar tampoco la censura de que los duques son objeto por su
participación en las innúmeras burlas a don Quijote: «Y dice más
Cide Hamete: que tiene para sí ser tan locos los burladores como los
burlados, y que no estaban los Duques dos dedos de parecer tontos,
pues tanto ahínco ponían en burlarse de dos tontos» (II, 70). El texto
es inequívoco y se sitúa en una de las encrucijadas conceptuales de la
comicidad bufonesca. Lo mismo que el moderno payaso de circo

aprovecha y saca a flote las candideces del público, entre príncipe y
bufón mediaba un juego de mutuo peligro, imposible de disfrutar sin
episódicos trueques de papeles ni, más aún, sin que ambas partes
aceptaran de antemano el rasero nivelador de la «locura». Las burlas
de los duques revisten un aspecto como de dilatada *sottie*,[32] donde
estos se ven obligados a hacer también de bufones, y aun de
bufones-comparsas, en entretenimientos planeados por su servi-
dumbre o que se salen del curso previsto. La bella Duquesa recibe de
Teresa Panza no solo las solicitadas bellotas, sino por añadidura un
queso «por ser muy bueno, que se aventajaba a los de Tronchón» (II,
52). Pocas páginas atrás había descendido tan alta señora al plano de
protagonista en una escena de *slapstick*, cuyo foco eran los miembros
pellizcados de don Quijote y las nalgas de doña Rodríguez.

Pero mi principal afán hoy no es el de extenderme en tareas de
hermenéutica, sino el de probar que los simbolismos emblemáticos
de la locura bufonesca eran harto bien conocidos y moneda aceptada
y corriente en la literatura de la época. Los textos comprobantes se
localizan sin dificultad en obras coetáneas del *Quijote* y escritas por
plumas de primera fila. Puede servirnos como ejemplo insigne y
precoz, pues se hallaba ya divulgado en 1591,[33] la conocida parodia
por don Luis de Góngora del romance morisco *Ensíllenme el potro rucio*,
uno de los más famosos de Lope de Vega, y que por cierto, figura
también en el *Entremés de los romances*. Lope había escrito:

> Ensíllenme el potro rucio
> del alcalde de los Vélez;
> denme la adarga de Fez
> y la jacerina fuerte.

Puesto a zaherir, Góngora transforma al moro enamorado y heroico
en lo que Emilio Orozco[34] ha llamado «una figura bufonesca», y lo
hace justo en estos términos:

> Ensíllenme el asno rucio
> de el alcalde Antonio Llorente,
> denme el tapador de corcho
> y el gabán de paño verde.

Aquí tenemos, pues, a nuestro viejo conocido, el *verde gabán* como
pieza clave en este proceso de parodización en un sentido bufonesco.
En los versos que siguen se acentúa dicho propósito hasta un punto

de máxima transparencia alusiva:

> El lanzón en cuyo hierro
> se han orinado los meses,
> el casco de calabaza
> y el vizcaíno machete,
>   y para mi caperuza
> las plumas del tordo denme
> que por ser Martín el tordo,.
> servirá de martinetes.[35]

En sustitución homóloga del espléndido atavío caballeresco del moro Azarque desfilan aquí, puntuales, los símbolos más característicos de la locura emblemática. Su lanza se acorta en *lanzón*, similar a la pértiga o cetro ridículo que distinguía a los bufones de corte (y a don Quijote tras la aventura de los molinos de viento). El villanesco *machete* se despega del adalid lo mismo que cualquier cosa *vizcaína* lo hace de un moro, y no deja de ser curioso que don Diego de Miranda lleve, con la misma incongruencia, un magnífico alfanje morisco. El casco no es ahora de acero, sino una solemne *calabaza*, jeroglífico de todo lo huero y casquivano: luce una de ellas en el mástil del navío de *La pícara Justina* y rodeado de cucúrbitas aparece el idiota Calabacillas en la serie de los bufones velazqueños.[36] Pero, sobre todo, figura allí la *caperuza*, jeroglífico rey de la «locura» y prenda distintiva o *de rigueur* para el «loco» de corte. Cuando se pronunciaba aquel vocablo no era preciso aclarar intenciones ni ofrecer más detalles, como ilustra la misma Urganda la Desconocida en los «cabos rotos» de los preliminares del *Quijote*:

> Que suelen en caperu—
> Darles a los que grace—

Y esta infamante caperuza reservada para Azarque-Lope era de las más clásicas y pomposas, con ridículo adorno de plumas, alusivas en su origen a la tópica lujuria del gallo y de otras aves,[37] y por lo mismo harto adecuadas como distintivo para un poema del ardiente ciclo de Elena Osorio. Por lo demás, es interesante comprobar cómo Lope hace también uso de este simbolismo, cuando en su comedia *La locura por la honra* saca a escena a un imitador fingido de la locura de Orlando «metidas muchas plumas en la cabeza».[38] Caso idéntico es el del cetro o lanzón del «loco» en *Belardo el furioso*, donde «sale Belardo armado graciosamente con una caña por lanza»,[39] de la cual se sirve para mantener un ridículo duelo con Siralbo, pastor dispuesto a seguirle su «tema» en una pelea a cañazos. A la hora de presentar en escena cierto galán «loco» de amor, una acotación de *La cortesía de España* puntualiza: «Sale don Juan con un gabán, medio desnudo».[40]

El popularismo de la comedia lopesca, a la vez que la frecuencia con que en ella se trata el tema de la locura,[41] ofrecen una oportunidad privilegiada para comprobar la divulgación de la emblemática que venimos estudiando. El público del corral de comedias entendía perfectamente aquel lenguaje simbólico (herencia viva de la Edad Media) y no había olvidado, como nosotros, la vieja identidad del color verde como el más propio de la «locura». Por eso debían de reír cuando en *Belardo el furioso* el enloquecido protagonista se dispone a quemar los billetes y demás amorosas reliquias de la infiel pastora Jacinta:

> SIRALBO: Una bandilla está aquí.
> BELARDO: ¿Qué color?
> SIRALBO: Verde.
> BELARDO: ¡A buen tiempo! (p. 677)

A la misma clase de chiste recurre, por cierto, el entremés de Salas Barbadillo *El caprichoso en su gusto y la dama setentona,* donde sale esta última muy compuesta para su boda en traje cuyo color es interpretado de muy distinta manera por la añeja novia y por las dueñas que con asombro la contemplan:

> LUCRECIA: ¿Y el vestido?
> DUEÑA 2:   Es peregrino.
> LUCRECIA: El color verde me aumenta
>   más donaire y hermosura.
> DUEÑA 1:   Ésta con tanta locura
>   nuestros oídos afrenta.[42]

En Lope reviste especial importancia el tema de los hospitales de locos. Fue precisamente en España donde, ya a principios del XV y en ruptura significativa con la actitud medieval hacia las enfermedades mentales, se fundaron los primeros manicomios de Occidente. Su exilio en Valencia familiarizó a Lope con el más antiguo y progresista de éstos,[43] tenido entonces por maravilla de buen gobierno y lugar de obligada visita turística. Incluso *El peregrino en su patria* (1604), que no deja de incluir una trasnochada aventura sentimental en este famoso manicomio, hace un juego conceptista con el *sayo* verde de los «locos» en unas redondillas puestas a describir el hospital alegórico en que Amor recogió a sus más desdichadas víctimas:

> Puso un sayo verde y blanco
> a la esperanza en amar,
> porque tras largo esperar
> entretiene y deja en blanco.[44]

En la comedia *El loco por fuerza*, que es una especie de «documental» sobre el manicomio de Zaragoza, escenifica el recibimiento de un nuevo «loco» (cuerdo como de costumbre), cuando el Maestro de locos y ciertos alienados subalternos, bien provistos de palos y de odiosos modales, desnudan al recién llegado y lo fuerzan a vestir el infamante *sayo* de inconfundible color:

> NICOLÁS: Viste, borracho, este sayo.
> GONZALO: No ha trocado mal la capa,
> pues yo dije que era Papa
> y él viene a ser papagayo.[45]

El *sayo* de «loco» podía ser también de otros colores y en el hospital valenciano parece ser que se usaba para tal el «paño pardo»,[46] según testimonio de *Los locos de Valencia*, que es una divertida pintura de la vida intramuros de aquella Meca de la locura. En esta comedia la heroína Erífila ha de vestir también el clásico atuendo, con sus obligados pingajos y caperuza, «con su sayo de jirones y una caperucilla de loco» (p. 424). Pero aún más curiosa resulta allí otra alusión, hasta ahora indescifrable, al queso emblemático de la «locura», según una respuesta del falso demente Floriano a la sobrina del administrador del hospital, importunamente «loca» de amor por él:

> FLORIANO: ¿Sabéis desto que perdí?
> y os daré en hallazgo un queso?
> FEDRA: ¡Pluguiera a Dios que supiera,
> como sé lo que has perdido,
> adónde está tu sentido
> porque yo te lo trujera! (p. 423)

En mi estudio sobre el caballero del Verde Gabán traté de recoger algunos testimonios de urgencia en torno al uso y conocimiento de la locura emblemática en España,[47] claramente reconocible ya en el siglo XV. Tratándose de una realidad tan común y admitida, tales datos arqueológicos pueden ampliarse igual que los literarios, sobre todo en lo relativo a la indumentaria del «loco». Ejemplo insigne de ella debió ser el gran don Francesillo de Zúñiga, que se autorretrata asistiendo a las bodas del Emperador en Sevilla (1526) «hecho un veinticuatro, con una ropa muy rozagante, de terciopelo morado, forrado de damasco naranjado, con que la ciudad [de Sevilla] le sirvió».[48]

Pero tal vez no haya mejor indicio de la respetabilidad alcanzada por la institución del «loco» de corte como su rastro entre los bienes de la infanta doña Juana, hija de Carlos V y ex-reina de Portugal, inventariados a su muerte en 1573. Su refinada colección de joyas, objetos de arte y libros (principalmente devotos) son testimonio del gusto y estilo de vida más severos. En su galería de efigies de la casa imperial, pontífices y hombres como el canonista Azpilcueta o el Padre Ignacio de Loyola, no se desdeñaba incluir también «un retrato de pincel, en tabla, de un chocarrero húngaro».[49] Más aún, la prócer testamentaría conservaba asimismo parte del vestuario usado en entretenimientos y farsas palaciegas, con «un sayo de bobo de paño pardo gironado con pestañas de paño amarillo» y hasta «tres caperuzas de paño pardo para bobos» (p. 378). Hemos de hacernos, pues, a la idea de que los innumerables *bobos* del teatro primitivo y prelopista debieron de vestir una versión algo atenuada en lujo y vistosidad del traje de *bugigangu* o «loco» de farándula.

El útil libro en que Martine Bigeard reconstruye las líneas esquemáticas del tema de la «locura» en España ofrece datos sobre los manicomios, cuyos asilados marchaban en procesión a la iglesia, en días de fiesta, ataviados con sus ropones verdes y amarillos.[50] No es de extrañar que la simple mención de *sayo* o *gabán* llegase a bastar como alusión y hasta como nombre sustantivo de la «locura» bufonesca. Un toledano, el licenciado Gutiérrez, se sirve de este nuevo y antonomástico lenguaje para reprochar a Sebastián de Horozco su excesiva e impropia afición al trovar chocarrero:

> Con esto ved que dirán
> que andáis ancho más que un odre
> con capa y con balandrán
> y bonete de un jayán,
> que no ay cosa que no os sobre.

Y después, por otra parte
presumís de muy galán
en los meneos y arte,
y las mangas del gabán
colgándoos a cada parte.

El grande y olvidado Horozco le devuelve la pelota, tachando de
locura aún mayor el recurrir para semejante fraterna a estilo no
menos chocarrero y propio del *mester* del gabán:

E aun según las cosas van
no es poco que el paño sobre,
mas burlar de mi gabán
ni me da pena el afán,
ni haze rico ni pobre.
Lo que falta en otra parte
bien pareçe en el gabán,
mas va el mundo de tal arte
que donde ruines están
no bastará baluarte.[51]

El estudio de Sebastián de Horozco dentro de los parámetros de la
literatura bufonesca es un gran tema todavía en espera de su investigador. Aquel Toledo, tan especial y aún tan desconocido, del siglo
XVI fue también uno de los ambientes más trabajados por la obsesión de la «locura», amplia y ruidosamente albergada en su Casa del
Nuncio. El mismo Horozco ha sido puntual cronista de las regocija-
das fiestas públicas con que la ciudad celebró en 1555, con excesivo
optimismo, «la reductión del reyno de Yngalaterra al gremio de la
Sancta Madre Yglesia», es decir, el reinado de María Tudor y su
matrimonio con Felipe II. Desde el 9 de febrero hasta el 26 del
mismo, martes de carnestolendas, los toledanos se dieron un torbellino de espectáculos, danzas y mascaradas que sin duda representan
una de las pleamares europeas de la más clásica bufonería carnavalesca. La participación colectiva en los solemnes actos religiosos se
prolongaba de un modo espontáneo en las más desenfadadas danzas
y máscaras

de moros, judíos, doctores, médicos, deçeplinantes, salva-
jes, locos, triperos, melcocheros, buñoleros, cornudos,
romeros, diablos, correos, porteros de cofardías, caçado-
res, hermitaños, negros, negras, portugueses, amazonas,

ninfas, cardenales, monjas, biudas, Celestina con su cuchillada y su canastillo de olores, lenceras vizcaýnas, rreyes, pastores y aun frayles salieron al prinçipio, aunque la justicia se lo prohibió. Y otros muchos disfrazes así a cavallo como a pie.[52]

Como nada de cuanto significaba vida corporativa había de quedar al margen de la alegría proclamada en la ciudad, el 10 de febrero «especialmente salieron las mujeres de la mançebía en hábitos de hombres en una dança a pie baylando con panderos» (p. 169). Y dos días después no pudo quedarse atrás «una quadrilla de ynoçentes con las mismas rropas de los locos de casa del Nunçio, y con su baçín pidiendo como ellos andauan» (p. 170). Pero, sobre todo,

> este día en la noche salió una máxcara de una quadrilla de hombres de a cavallo, hijos de vezinos y mercaderes, con rropas contrahechas de los mismos locos, unas de rrasos y otras de bocasís amarillos y verdes, y con sus hachas y mucha música de trompetas y atabales y ministriles, y anduvieron rregozijando toda la çibdad y así se fueron estas fiestas callentando (p. 170).

En su moderna edición, el conde de Cedillo recurrió a los puntos suspensivos al toparse con párrafos como el que sigue, testimonios extremados de un espíritu de *Fastnachtspiele* en desacuerdo con la idea de severidad que solía atribuirse a aquel pasado español:

> Este día entre los otros entremeses estropajosos salió un sacamuelas con todo su herramental y una muger a quien sacava la muela, y sentávala en una silla y descarnávala con un cuerno y después sacava unas tenazas de herrador y, ella dando gritos, sacávale un miembro de hombre tan grande que dava no poco plazer y risa a toda la gente. La qual como es natural más se huelga y ríe con estas cosas que con las buenas. A este tenor salieron un tripero y una tripera caballeros en sus bestias y llevaban su mal cozinado. Ella llevaba dos ollas delante en un serón y con un garabato sacava dél unas tripas, y de la otra muchas naturas de hombres. Con que tampoco llorava la gente, ni aun las damas que los veýan.[53]

Pasaron cincuenta años y el espíritu de la «locura» resurgió intacto con la desaparición física de Felipe II. En la primavera de 1599, el mismo Lope de Vega no tuvo remilgos (con tal de llamar la atención) en hacer el *botarga*[54] delante del rey y de toda la corte, congregada en Valencia para festejar las bodas del nuevo joven soberano. El texto de la relación contemporánea no necesita de ninguna glosa:

> Consequitivamente despés por su horden yvan delanteras dos máscaras ridículas quel huno dellas fue conoscida ser el poheta Lope de Vega, el qual venía vestido de botarga, ábito italiano que era todo de colorado, con calsas y ropilla seguidos y ropa larga de levantar de chomelote negro, con una gorra de terciopello llano en la cabesa, y éste yva a cauallo, con huna mula ensillada a la gineta y petral de cascaueles, y por el vestido que traýa y arsones de la silla leuaua colgando diferentes animales de carne para comer, representando el tiempo del carnal como fueron muchos conexos, perdisses y gallinas y otras aves colgadas por el cuello y cintura de su cuerpo que avía mucho que mirar en éll.[55]

Su compañero de mojiganga era un truhán del rey, vestido de *ganassa* y no menos en carácter, pertrechado de pescados frescos y ceciales, para hacerle la contrafigura de la Cuaresma.

El *Quijote* ha de verse también como producto inmediato de ese mismo deshielo nacional y literario, iniciado con el advenimiento del nuevo rey y con la publicación (1599) del *Guzmán de Alfarache*. Se necesita meditar el testimonio de la *Fastiginia*[56] o crónica extraoficial de la corte vallisoletana por el portugués Tomé Pinheiro da Veiga para comprender la magnitud del cambio. Tras una represión y luto de medio siglo, ha vuelto a haber en España monarcas jóvenes, una corte alegre y un respiro de paz exterior. En Valladolid, alejado del maleficio madrileño, se redescubren la risa, la diversión y el galanteo justo al mismo tiempo que Cervantes da postrera lima a su *Ingenioso hidalgo*. De no ser por esta espléndida y veraz *Fastiginia*, no podríamos documentar hasta qué punto la «locura» había recuperado sus fueros de carcajada liberadora en el aire de la flamante corte. Burlas y discreteos restallan a diario en máscaras, saraos y fiestas públicas donde se comentan las últimas ocurrencias de los bufones reales Rebello y Vinorex, famosos como cualquier otra estrella del momento. Y aun como los mismos don Quijote, Sancho y Dulcinea del Toboso, ya en labios de todos y pasto común para el juego de las comparaciones chocarreras, a lo Francesillo de Zúñiga.[57] Un orbe donde la inmemorial tradición carnavalesca se remoza con unos puntillos de redicho conceptismo que se filtra hasta las más bajas capas del pueblo.

Si la «locura» emblemática es objeto en la Segunda Parte del cuidadoso tratamiento que he venido esbozando, no quiere decir que ésta haya sido menos cierta ni fundamental como concepto determinante para la totalidad de la obra. Lejos de hallarse agotado, el campo solo acaba de ser abierto y no ha rendido todavía la plenitud de su cosecha. Como ejemplo y a título de avance me permitiré sugerir que la iconografía de la «locura» incluía también el emblema del molinillo de viento, juguete apropiado para expresar la inestabilidad de la demencia. La *Iconologia* de Cesare Ripa (Roma, 1603) prescribe representar a la *Pazzia* como un hombre «a cavallo sopra una canna, nella destra mano una girella di carta istromento piaceuole, & trastullo de fanciulli, li quali con gran studio lo fanno girare al vento». En el retrato de la antigua colección Cook, hoy en el Museum of Art de Cleveland, Velázquez retrata al bufón Calabacillas[58] con lo que el Diccionario Académico exactamente define por *molinete:*«3 Juguete de niños: consiste en una varilla en cuya punta hay una cruz o una estrella de papel que giran movidos por el viento». Los andaluces decimos *estar como un molinillo* o *tener la cabeza como un molino* para describir a una persona alocada. No es así de extrañar que el lenguaje de la comparación chocarrera ascendiera el frágil *molinillo* o *molinete* a la formidable masa del *molino* de viento, a la hora de encarecer una locura de lo más desaforado, y dicho paso lo ilustra con toda puntualidad Sebastián de Horozco, en un poemita de su *Cancionero* que parece casi una profecía:

El auctor, motejando a uno de loco y vano

Es lo que yo de vos siento,
que pisáis tan de liviano
que podéis dar bastimento
a dos molinos de viento,
aunque fuese en el verano.
Y aun según las cosas van,
aunque digáis abernunçio
determinados están
de hazeros su capitán
los que están en Cas del Nunçio.[59]

Este botarate padece locura suficiente para dar «bastimiento» u ocasión de moler a un par de molinos de viento. Pero las quintillas de Horozco usan la imagen del *viento*, complementaria e implícita en la del *molino* (grande o pequeño) como signo del empuje ingobernable de la locura. Igual que el infeliz motejado, don Quijote no podía faltar a la cita de su enfrentamiento con el simbolismo adecuado a su gigantesca demencia, dando paso con ello a la aventura más famosa de todo el libro, al pie de un molino de viento. Es solo al acercarse el caballero cuando las aspas comienzan a girar bajo el soplo de «un poco de viento» muy impropio de la estación («aunque fuese en el verano»). Cuando su lanza nada más toca el aspa, «la volvió el viento con tanta furia, que hizo la lanza pedazos, llevándose tras sí al caballo y al caballero, que fue rodando muy maltrecho por el campo.». Tan fuerte ventolera viene causada, como es lógico, por el torbellino de la locura caballeresca en el cerebro enfermo del andante, como enseguida ayuda a entender el certero comentario de Sancho Panza:

> —¡Válame Dios!—dijo Sancho— ¿No le dije yo a vuestra merced que mirase bien lo que hacía, que no eran sino molinos de viento, y no lo podía ignorar sino quien llevase otros tales en la cabeza? (I, 8)

El núcleo genético de la aventura de los molinos de vientos aparece ligado de esta forma a una lexicalización de la emblemática de la «locura». Según Góngora, Lope tenía algún *viento*, pero no tanto como el requerido por las diecinueve torres del escudo de *La Arcadia* (1598), es decir, tenía su ramo de «loco», pero no tan amplio como para hacerse perdonar aquella bufonada monumental.

Futuras investigaciones podrán sin duda ampliar y matizar todavía mucho más esta presencia en el *Quijote* de la literatura europea del «loco». Como explica Joel Lefebvre,[60] era esta el filo cortante del humanismo nórdico, comprometido por Erasmo a una revolución copernicana de la literatura culta, por primera vez autónoma y devota del entretenimiento y de la risa como valor estético, legitimado con independencia de ningún estrecho didactismo. En rigor, se trataba del ideal de la *relaxatio animorum* que define el *De sermone* de Pontano, antes de la escisión del humanismo en el siglo XVI y de su cautividad por el aristotelismo académico y contrarreformista. Debemos, pues, de comprender la noble satisfacción de Cervantes, apreciar el peso de sus palabras y darles todo su crédito cuando, en el

ocaso de su vida, se enorgullecía de la perfección y constancia con
que su obra había servido a dicho ideal:

> Yo he dado en don Quijote pasatiempo
> al pecho melancólico y mohino,
> en cualquiera sazón, en todo tiempo.
>
> (*Viaje del Parnaso*, IV)

Había realizado ciertamente todo cuanto el arte podía dar de sí para
hacer realidad el *anxiis illis curis animum liberare* prometido por la *Moria*
erasmiana. Pero hemos de advertir también cómo el *Quijote*, dentro
de un planteamiento más que nunca paradójico, significaba también
el punto final y acta de defunción de toda aquella literatura del
«loco». Porque no es menos evidente que don Quijote, Sancho y don
Diego de Miranda no quedan circunscritos por el moralismo alegórico de la nave estultífera, y que hasta parece a primera vista deni-
grante el relacionarlos con la literatura bufonesca o la dislocada
temática de carnaval o *Fastnachtspiel*. Concebido dentro de supuestos
que eran tesis polémicas para *Das Narrenschiff*, la *Stultitiae laus* o las
«prouesses gigantales» de Rabelais, el *Quijote* no es una obra revolu-
cionaria, sino el programa de trabajo para el día siguiente a la revolución, amanecido con la tarea de construir un mundo nuevo, cuya faz
nadie conoce. Puesto ante la responsabilidad de esa situación límite,
el *Quijote* inicia entonces, con su lugar de la Mancha y sus personajes
de carne y hueso, la infinita complejidad autorregulada y fáustica de
la modernidad literaria.

Una última consideración por hacer. Y es que al mismo tiempo
que la Segunda Parte del *Quijote* agotaba la estética literaria del
humanismo nórdico, Cervantes pulía también el *Persiles* y llevaba a
su perfección (pero una perfección muy distinta y totalmente suya)
el ideal del último humanismo italiano y de sus directrices clasicis-
tas.[61] Uno y otro humanismo convivieron en España como en ninguna otra parte y Cervantes sabe sacarles todo su partido, lo mismo
dentro de la estética italianizante, orientada hacia un pasado arquetí-
pico, que construyendo el futuro posibilista entrevisto desde el púl-
pito de la *Moria* erasmiana. Aun amargado y puesto en trance de
autoelogiarse por la ausencia de reconocimiento colectivo,[62] Cervantes sentía la satisfacción de contemplar a la hora de su muerte el
buque de una obra que era *summa* integral y cualitativa (no mera-
mente numérica como la de Lope) del pensamiento y quehacer litera-

rio de una gran época. Occidente no había conocido dicho fenómeno desde los días de *La Divina Commedia*.

Harvard University

[1] Me remito a la bibliografía ofrecida en mi ponencia «Un aspect de la littérature du 'fou' en Espagne», para el Coloquio Internacional *L'Humanisme dans les lettres espagnoles* (julio, 1976) patrocinado por el «Centre d'Études Supérieures de la Renaissance» de la Universidad de Tours (actas en curso de publicación).

[2] Nueva edición (Barcelona: Noguer, 1972), pp. 88, 120, 217, 222, 299, 313, 331. Castro considera probable que Cervantes conociera la traducción italiana de 1539, pero no descarta la posibilidad de que hubiese leído tanto el original latino como alguna traducción española hoy perdida y cuyos indicios fueron ya apuntados por Menéndez Pelayo (p. 114, n. 62 y p. 170). Sobre huellas de la misma en los índices inquisitoriales españoles, M. Bataillon, *Erasmo y España* (México: Fondo de Cultura, 1966), p. 178.

[3] *Erasmo y Cervantes* (Barcelona: CSIC, 1949). La *Censura* fue publicada con prólogo y notas del mismo estudioso en 1953 (Barcelona: Selecciones Bibliográficas). El carácter de la misma y sus relaciones con Erasmo son puntualizados por R. Surtz, «En torno a la *Censura de la locura humana* de Jerónimo de Mondragón», *Nueva Revista de Filología Hispánica*, 25 (1976), 352-63.

[4] «La *Moria* de Erasmo y el prólogo del *Quijote*», *Collected Studies in Honour of Américo Castro's Eightieth Year* (Oxford: 1965), 423-33.

[5] En *Cuatro obras del bachiller Hernán López de Yanguas*, ed. A. Pérez Gómez (Cieza: 1960).

[6] «Heterodoxos españoles en el XVI. Los estudios sobre Erasmo de Marcel Bataillon», *Revista de Occidente*, n. 63 (junio, 1968), p. 315.

[7] «Un Problème d'influence d'Érasme en Espagne. L'*Éloge de la Folie*», *Actes du Congrès Érasme, 1969* (Amsterdam: Académie Royale Néerlandais, 1971), pp. 136-47. El *Erasmo en España* en su segunda edición de 1966 insistía, por contraste, en que, a pesar de haberse formado Cervantes muy cercano al humanismo de Erasmo, «su ironía, su humor, suenan a algo completamente nuevo» (P. 801).

[8] E. H. Zeydel, *Sebastian Brant* (New York:Twayne, 1967), p. 86.

[9] Sobre la asociación entre cascabeles y locura, W. Willeford, *The Fool and his Scepter. A Study in Clowns and Jesters and their Audiences* (Northwestern University Press, 1969), p. 22. La protagonista de la *Pícara Justina* se intitula (a lo oriental) «hija de cascabeles» por hallarse su linaje tan saturado de titiriteros, gaiteros y demás oficios truhanescos.

[10] Aunque se advierten en ella bastantes ecos del tema de la locura o *Moria* erasmiana, no se registra el de la nave estultífera ni el de Niemand (característicos de Brant), según conclusiones de C. Ossola, «Métaphore et inventaire de la folie dans la littérature du XVIe siècle», *Folie et déraison à la Renaissance* (Bruxelles: Université Libre, 1976), p. 171. J. Lefebvre observa cómo no se ha conservado un solo ejemplar de Brant en bibliotecas italianas; *Les Fols et la folie. Étude sur les genres du comique et la création littéraire en Allemagne pendant la Renaissance* (Paris: Klincksieck, 1968), p. 163. El caso de España se perfila así como intermedio entre la gran receptividad nórdica y la completa cerrazón italiana.

[11]«Un Problème d'influence d'Érasme en Espagne», p. 137. Sobre el importante papel de Badius como difusor en latín y en francés del *Narranschiff*, J. Lefebvre, *Les Fols et la folie*, p. 162, nota. A. Gerlo, «Badius Ascenscius' *Stultiferae Naves* (1501), a Latin Addendum to Sebastian Brant's *Narrenschiff* (1494), *Folie et déraison à la Renaissance*. pps. 110-127. Y en especial Ph. Renouard, *Bibliographie des impressions et des oeuvres de Josse Badius Ascenscius, imprimeur et humaniste* (Paris, 1908), 3 vols.

[12]Descrita por K. Haebler, *The Early Printers of Spain and Portugal* (London: Bibliographical Society, 1896-1897), p. 111. Recientemente estudiada en su aspecto iconográfico (idéntico al de las ediciones francesas en Renouard) por I. Mateo, «La temática de la nave de los locos en una edición española del siglo XV», *Traza y Baza* (Palma de Mallorca), n. 3 (1973), 45-51. No se comprende cómo Renouard, conocedor de esta edición burgalesa del original latino de Badius, reserva sin embargo la categoria de *princeps* para la de París, 1501.

[13]Datos comunicados por Bataillon a J. Lefebvre, *Les Fols et la folie*, p. 163, n. 354. Refiriéndose al ejemplar de la Colombina insistía allí Bataillon en el detalle de que este figure como adquirido en la misma Sevilla, pues la pérdida de otros ejemplares no supondría entonces sino el final reservado a los libros de mucha circulación y uso. Surtz detecta asimismo la pervivencia del concepto negativo de la locura, propio y característico de Brant, en algunas secciones del libro de Mondragón («En torno a la *Censura de la locura humana*», p. 363).

[14]Su título era *Nauis Stultifera*. Concentra allí los principales temas de Brant en versos latinos de su cosecha y reproduce también buena parte de la iconografía original del *Narrenschiff*, clásica desde el momento de su aparición. Las intervenciones de Badius en traducciones latinas y francesas de Brant, complicadas por las distintas versiones con título muy similar, son felizmente elucidadas por Renouard, *Bibliographie*, I, p. 158 y ss. y c. IV.

[15]Descrito por Nicolás Antonio, Salvá y Paláu. He manejado el ejemplar de la Hispanic Society of America (Nueva York).

[16]Cuestiones bien estudiadas por A. L. De Gaetano, «The Plagiarism of Giambattista Gelli's *Capricci del Bottaio* by Francisco Miranda Villafañe», *Italica*, 32 (1955), 226-241.

[17]M. Bataillon, «Exégesis esotérica y análisis de intenciones del *Quijote*», *Beiträge zur Romanische Philologie* (Sonderheft 1967), pp. 22-26 y 102. W. Krauss, *Miguel de Cervantes. Leben und Werk* (Berlin: Luchterhand, 1966), pp. 26-28 (ideas similares acerca del tema de Armas y Letras, en que Miranda Villafañe introduce, por cierto, materiales propios en independencia de Gelli).

[18]«Nuovi dati intorno alla bibliografia di Francisco Delicado desunti da una sua sconosciuta operetta», *Annali della Facoltà di Lettere e Filosofia della Università degli Studi di Perugia*, 12 (1974-1975), p. 475.

[19]Reproducido en la edición de J. Puyol(Madrid: Bibliófilos Madrileños, 1912). Más asequible en B. M. Damiani, *Francisco López de Úbeda* (Boston: Twayne, 1977). El grabado es también reproducido y descrito por A. A. Parker, *Los pícaros en la literatura* (Madrid: Gredos, 1971), p. 32.

[20]E. Grey, *Guevara, a Forgotten Renaissance Author* (The Hague: Nijhoff, 1973), p. 31.

[21]S. Reckert, «Bajo el signo del latín (Cultura literaria de Gil Vicente)», *Studia hispanica in honorem R. Lapesa* (Madrid: Gredos, 1972), III, p. 394.

[22]E. Cros observa el relieve que el tema de los pobres (auténticos o fingidos) y de su policía y asistencia reviste en Brant y en el *Liber Vagatorum*, significativamente reeditado este último por Lutero; *Mateo Alemán: introducción a su vida y a su obra* (Salamanca: Anaya, 1971), pp. 127 y 164. El posible eco de esta literatura nórdica de mendigos y vagabundos sobre la picaresca fue ya señalada por J. E. Gillet, «A Note on

the *Lazarillo de Tormes»*, *Modern Language Notes*, 55 (1940), 133. Idea renovada también por M. Molho, *Romans picaresques espagnols* (Paris: Gallimard, 1968), p. xvi.

23Sobre la consustancialidad intemporal de la figura del «loco» con diversos géneros de máscaras ridículas, tizne, bermellón, harina, corcho quemado, etc., Willeford, *The Fool and his Scepter*, p. 52. Sobre el enharinamiento en las fiestas populares de Carnaval, J. Caro Baroja, *El carnaval (análisis histórico-cultural)* (Madrid: Taurus, 1965), pp. 67-69.

24Según D. Gitlitz, con el barco encantado «se sugiere ser el que cruza el río Estigio y que conduce al Infierno», en este caso el palacio ducal; «La ruta alegórica del segundo *Quijote*», *Romanische Forschungen*, 84 (1972), 116.

25«Un problème d'influence d'Érasme en Espagne», p. 114.

26«Quelques considérations sue le Niemand et. . . Personne», *Folie et déraison à la Renaissance*, p. 111. En el mismo sentido, P. Jacerme recuerda la afirmación de Nietzsche en su último libro (*Ecce homo*) y según la cual: «c'est la certitude qui rend fou»; *La Folie, de Sophocle à l'antipsychiatrie* (Paris: Bordas, 1974), p. 17.

27Y en especial para el coloquio internacional sobre «Das literarische Werk von Miguel de Cervantes», convocado por la Academia de Ciencias de Berlín y donde el caballero del Verde Gabán fue amplia y perplejamente discutido. Bataillon trató de explicarlo como atavío propio de «caballero labrador rico» y consideraba «notas de buen gusto» la yuxtaposición de verde, leonado, morado y oro («Exégesis esotérica», pp. 24-25). En otro momento opinó, sin embargo, que dicho color ocultaba «un cierto simbolismo» relacionado con la esperanza de don Quijote. El gran hispanista terminaba por aconsejar a los participantes deseosos de resolver el enigma, estar muy atentos a estudios de histórica económica, en los cuales podría surgir la clave de aquella asociación o emparejamiento entre los diversos colores y prendas del vestido; *Beitrage zur Romanische Philologie* (Sonderheft, 1967), 75.

28*Cervantes y su concepto del arte* (Madrid: Gredos, 1975), p. 387 y ss. («El verde como símbolo»). El verde significaba en Cervantes «la profunda autodecepción del hombre cuando se aparta de lo propio o lo natural» (p. 394).

29M. Herrero García, «Estudios de indumentaria española de la época de los Austrias», *Hispania*, 13 (1953), 200.

30Sobre la veste más o menos talar del loco «natural» y sus razones, Willeford, *The Fool and his Scepter*, p. 242, n. 28. Un fresco de Giotto en la Capella dell'Arena de Padua (1303-06) representa ya a la *Stultitia* como un hombre panzudo, con sayo hasta la rodilla, festoneado y con cola, y un tocado de plumas terminadas en cascabeles; E, Tietze-Conrat, *Dwarfs and Jesters in Art* (London: Phaidon Press, 1957), p. 58. Lo habitual en España de este *habitum fatui* como signo parlante se aprecia, por ejemplo, en ciertas redondillas *Contra los mozos de monjas* fechables entre 1591 y 1594: «La que no sabe hilar,/o el bobo de largo sayo/vienen en esto a parar,/y luego saben hablar/como tordo o papagayo»; *Cancionero de la Academia de los Nocturnos de Valencia*, ed. P. Salvá y F. Martí Grajales (Valencia, 1906), IV, p. 105.

31El chamelote era tela de uso típico en atavíos carnavalescos. Cuando a cierto galán de comedia lopesca lo obligan a enmascararse con un capirote «de loco», el disfrazado rezonga: «¡Aun de bayeta lo hicistes!/¿No fuera de chamelote?»; *La viuda valenciana*, ed. J. L. Aguirre (Madrid: Aguilar, 1967), p. 100. El gabán de chamelote de Sancho encaja en la acumulación de elementos carnavalescos en el episodio de su gobierno, estudiada por A. Redondo en el VI Congreso de la Asociación Internacional de Hispanistas (Toronto, 1977).

32Sobre su carácter de forma extrema de la literatura bufonesca, E. Welsford, *The Fool: His Social and Literary History* (London, 1935), p. 220 y B. Swain, *Fools and Folly During the Middle Ages and the Renaissance* (New York: Columbia University Press,

1932), p. 64. Willeford define la *sottie* como el jolgorio «in which those of high social station are debased to the level of fools or in which fools even take the places the great ones have vacated» (*The Fool and his Scepter*, p. 217). Sobre el inevitable intercambio o equivalencia entre príncipe y bufón, «The Sovereign Fool: The Tragedy of King Lear» (*Ibid.*, pp. 208-225). Para la afinidad radical de Rey, Sacerdote y Bufón en cuanto figuras necesarias y típicas de una sociedad basada en normación divina, Swain, *Fools and Folly*, p. 195. En todo ello cabe considerar también la validez específica de la regla enunciada por *Das Narrenschiff:* «Ser ist eyn Narr der nit verstot-/Wann er mit eynem Narren red» (n. 68, «Schympf nit verston»). Trotaconventos, excelente conocedora, encarecía cómo don Melón «con los locos fázes' loco, los cuerdos dél bien dixieron» (728b).

³³E. Orozco Días, *Lope y Góngora frente a frente* (Madrid: Gredos, 1973), p. 31. La parodia de Góngora es también estudiada por J. García Soriano, *Los dos Don Quijotes* (Toledo, 1944), p. 55 y ss.

³⁴*Lope y Góngora frente a frente,* p. 37.

³⁵Dada la insistencia con que los textos españoles reservan para locos el nombre de *Martín,* se impone deducir que tan grotescos *martinetes* conllevan aquí una alusión el mismo sentido.

³⁶J. J. Martínez González, «Algunas sugerencias acerca de los 'bufones' de Velázquez», *Varia velazqueña* (Madrid: Dirección General de Bellas Artes, 1960), p. 253.

³⁷Willeford, *The Fool and his Scepter,* p. 4. Mateo, *La temática de la nave de los locos*, p. 48.

³⁸*Obras dramáticas* (Madrid: Academia Española, 1930), VII, p. 313.

³⁹*Obras de Lope de Vega* (Madrid: Academia Española, 1895), V, p. 686.

⁴⁰*Obras dramáticas* (Madrid: Academia Española, 1917), IV, p. 356.

⁴¹A. Albarracín Teulón, *La medicina en el teatro de Lope de Vega* (Madrid, CSIC, 1954), p. 42 y ss. y 122 y ss.

⁴²*Ramillete de entremeses y bailes*, ed. H. E. Bergman (Madrid: Castalia, 1970), p. 79.

⁴³J. R. Pertegás, *Hospitales de Valencia en el siglo XV* (Madrid, 1927). J. R. Zaragoza Rubira, «Breve historia de los hospitales valencianos», *Medicina Española,* 47 (1962), pp. 152-160 y 237-246. Este *Hospital de Inocentes,* fundado en 1409, fue el primer manicomio abierto en la Europa cristiana y su organización y fines fueron modelo de institutos similares que le siguieron en Zaragoza y Sevilla, J. Delgado Roig, «Historia del hospital de Inocentes de Sevilla», *Actas Españolas de Neurología y Psiquiatría* (abril, 1941), pp. 143-152. Estos manicomios españoles del siglo XV suelen basarse sobre organizaciones preexistentes para el cuidado de leprosos, en perfecta comprobación de las ideas de M. Foucault, *Historia de la locura en la época clásica* (México: Fondo de Cultura, 1967).

⁴⁴Ed. J. B. Avalle-Arce (Madrid: Castalia, 1973), p. 346.

⁴⁵*Obras dramáticas* (Madrid: Academia Española, 1916), II, p. 265.

⁴⁶*Obras dramáticas* (Madrid. Academia Española, 1930), XII, p. 424. Pero según unos inventarios de 1512 en los *sayos* y *robes* de los hospitalizados predominaba el azul: «blau» mezclado con «vermell», «rosat» y «groch» (Pertegás, *Hospitales de Valencia*, p. 22). Claramente se seguía en esto la moda nórdica, que a principios del siglo XV consideraba el azul como el color más propio de la locura y tituló *De Blauwe Schuit* a un antecedente de *Das Narrenschiff;* R. H. Marijnissen, «Bosch and Bruegel on Human Folly», *Folie et déraison à la Renaissance,* p. 41.

⁴⁷Principalmente del libro de J. Moreno Villa, *Locos, enanos, negros y niños palaciegos. Gente de placer que tuvieron los Austrias en la corte española desde 1563 a 1700* (México, 1939). Sobre el Verde Gabán, F. Márquez Villanueva, «El caballero del Verde Gabán y su reino de paradoja», en *Personajes y temas del Quijote* (Madrid: Taurus, 1975).

[48]*Crónica*, ed. Adolfo de Castro en *Curiosidades bibliográficas* (Madrid: BAE, 1855), p. 40.

[49]C. Pérez Pastor, «Noticias y documentos relativos a la historia y literatura españolas», *Memorias de la Real Academia Española*, XI (Madrid, 1914), p. 373.

[50]M. Bigeard, *La Folie et les fous littéraires en Espagne 1500-1650*, (París: Centre de Recherches Hispaniques, 1972), p. 33.

[51]*Cancionero*, ed. J. Weiner (Bern und Frankfurt/M: Lang, 1975), pp. 85-86;

[52]Conde de Cedillo, «Algunas relaciones toledanas que en el siglo XVI escribía el licenciado Sebastián de Horozco», *Boletín de la Sociedad Española de Excursiones*, 13 (1905), p. 169.

[53]Biblioteca Nacional, MS. 9175, f. 153 r.

[54]Por el cómico italiano Stefanello Botarga. Como en el presente ejemplo, su fama estaba ligada a la de Alberto Naselli, el famoso Zan Ganassa, tan importante para los orígenes del teatro español. En 1584 Botarga debió desgajar de la compañía de Ganassa la suya propia, pues sin duda debieron representar juntos por bastante tiempo (probablemente en memorable pareja de gordo y flaco) como acredita la conservación de cierto bufo *Lamento di Giovanni Ganassa con M. Stefanello Botarga suo padrone sopra la morte di un pidochio*; J. V. Falconieri, «Historia de la *commedia dell'arte* en España», *Revista de Literatura*, XI (1957), 3-37, XII (1957), 69-90. El tipo e indumentaria de Botarga perduran, adaptados, en algunas fiestas rurales; S. García Sanz, «Botargas y enmascarados alcarreños», *Revista de Dialectología y Tradiciones Populares*, IX (1953),. 471-76.

[55]Según la relación de las fiestas nupciales por el vecino de Valencia Felipe de Gaona; E. Juliá Martínez, «Lope de Vega en Valencia en 1599», *Boletín de la Real Academia Española*, III (1916), 542-543.

[56]*Fastiginia o fastos geniales*, trad. N. Alonso Cortés (Valladolid, 1916). Su título completo ostenta un humor de burla caballeresca no muy alejado del de la Academia de la Argamasilla: *Fastiginia ou Fastos Geniales tirados da tumba de Merlin, onde forão achados com a Demanda do Santo Brial, pello Arcebispo Turpim. Descubertos e tirados a luz pelo famoso lusitano Fr. Pantaleão, que os achou em hum Mosteyro de Calouros.*

[57]«Fue el caso que pasando un Don Quijote, vestido de verde, muy desmazalado y alto de cuerpo, vio a unas mujeres al pie de un álamo y se puso de rodillas a enamorarlas» (p. 121). Del embajador de Portugal de dice que parecía otro don Quijote por su empeño en lucirse públicamente con sus anteojos, su ostentosa orden de Cristo sobre el pecho y un escudero Sancho Panza siempre por delante. Una dama del acompañamiento de la reina, en el que salió a caballo, es comparada con Dulcinea del Toboso (p. 71). El jocundísimo Pinheiro mantenía, bien informado, que «hacer reír es costumbre de truhanes, y reír mucho, de locos» (p. 177).

[58]J. Guidol, *Velázquez* (Barcelona: Ediciones Polígrafa, 1973), n. 95. Tietze-Conrat menciona también un ejemplo italo-hebreo de la misma iconografía («man with a fan-blower») de 1511 (*Dwarfs and Jesters in Art*, p. 104, n. 54.).

[59]*Cancionero*, p. 73.

[60]Lefebvre, *Les Fols et la folie*, p. 227, nota. Al cabo de medio milenio, la validez de los mismos principios es brillantemente defendida por un maestro de la novela ante la Academia Sueca. «The storyteller of our time, as in any other time, must be an entertainer of the spirit in the full sense of the word, not just a preacher of social and political ideals. There is no excuse for tedious literature that does not intrigue the reader, uplift his spirit, give him the joy and the escape that true art always grants»; Isaac Bashevis Singer, *New York Times*, 9 diciembre, 1978.

[61]De acuerdo en esto con las matizadas páginas finales de A. K. Forcione, *Cervantes, Aristotle and the 'Persiles'* (Princeton: Princeton University Press, 1970).

[62]E. L. Rivers, «Cervantes' 'Journey to Parnassus'», *MLN*, 85 (1970), 243-48.

Sancho Panza y Gandalín, escuderos

Eduardo Urbina

A APARICIÓN DEL AMADÍS DE GAULA en 1508 refundido por Montalvo cristaliza en España el interés por lo caballeresco nacido a raíz de las últimas etapas de la reconquista y del descubrimiento del Nuevo Mundo.[1] El éxito e influencia del *Amadís* se mide en la proliferación inmediata de continuaciones durante el siglo dieciséis que conducen a la parodia cervantina.[2] Esta literatura surge para dar reflejo a una situación vital y llega a ser a su vez motivo de imitación e inspiración en las cortes de Europa, donde *Amadís de Gaula* rivaliza con la obra de Castiglione como manual de cortesía.[3]

A pesar de sus raíces medievales en la materia artúrica el espíritu que habita y promueve la obra de Montalvo resulta característico del renacimiento.[4] Amadís se muestra a lo largo de su historia como el completo y perfecto caballero, cortés y guerrero, virtuoso y valiente, mesurado y fiel en extremo. Su amor por Oriana, depurado, íntimo y honesto, se ve acompañado de un propósito doble, moral y político: la reafirmación de la monarquía en un marco cristiano.[5]

El hecho de que Cervantes tomara como modelo principal a Amadís de Gaula ha dado lugar a afirmar que don Quijote es también héroe y figura culminante del género, revitalizándose en él el ideal caballeresco como arquetipo de reforma, y que en este sentido depurador el *Amadís de Gaula* y el *Quijote* son obras no sólo afines sino paralelas.[6] Con todo, el gran hallazgo de Cervantes, como se señala con frecuencia, está en la yuxtaposición del mundo literario ideal de la caballería andante y del mundo real, histórico de un hidalgo de aldea empobrecido y cincuentón en la España de finales del siglo dieciséis.[7] Esta yuxtaposición ocurre en el héroe Alonso Quijano-don Quijote, pero se encarna vitalmente en la creación de la pareja don Quijote-Sancho Panza. ¿Añora Cervantes los valores expuestos en *Amadís de Gaula* o se propone en cambio la superación del género planteándose la cuestión de la imitación a un nivel eminentemente burlesco y literario? A fin de explorar la deuda de Cervantes, el sentido de su parodia, quisiera adelantar el presente tema: Sancho Panza y los libros de caballerías.[8] En el contexto del tema de la fidelidad en los triángulos Oriana-Amadís-Gandalín y Dulcinea-don Quijote-Sancho nos proponemos mostrar cómo Sancho y Gandalín actúan paralelamente en lo que se refiere al interés amoroso del caballero, cómo Cervantes realiza al dar mayor relevancia a Sancho la parodia del caballero enamorado y, finalmente, cómo en sus relaciones con don Quijote el sin par escudero resulta parodia del leal Gandalín.

La tensión dramática del *Amadís de Gaula*, resultado de su herencia artúrica, se centra en el conflicto entre el deber del caballero como vasallo del rey y su interés amoroso, individual y juvenil, hacia su señora.[9] Sus acciones como caballero, según la orden que profesa, han de ser realizadas desinteresadamente, aunque, subrayando el conflicto, puedan beneficiar a su vez al rey. En cualquier caso, tales acciones guerreras reafirman su valor como caballero y sustentan su honra y fama. Ahora bien, inicialmente y por designio, Amadís está bajo el control de la pasión amorosa suscitada por su señora Oriana. El esfuerzo realizado en batallas y encuentros tiene su origen y fin en ella, en la esperanza de verse definitivamente en su compañía, en su posesión. Sin embargo, y de manera irónica, las demandas que este interés amoroso originan en el caballero pueden poner en peligro su fama y hasta ser contrarias a la caballería que sigue y mantiene. Este conflicto, consecuencia de la evolución del género, fue ya anticipado y criticado por Chrétien de Troyes,[10] y es el que hace necesaria la eliminación de Amadís y el nacimiento de un nuevo tipo de caballero, Esplandián, más en acuerdo con las circunstancias del siglo dieciséis.[11]

El papel del escudero en el conflicto entre el deber y la pasión del caballero y su continuada presencia en la historia son los puntos claves en que se centra nuestro análisis. El escudero, compañero y amigo, descendiente e inversión de la figura del ayo guardián, apoya inicialmente a Amadís en el ejercicio de su deber y profesión frente a la influencia debilitadora de su señora.[12] Más tarde, actúa como mensajero y medianero facilitando encuentros y manteniendo el secreto. Finalmente, pasa a acentuar el sentido social de la aventura sirviendo al tiempo de sustituto de la dama ausente; diluyendo así el conflicto inicial y anticipando su final resolución con la domesticación de Amadís.

Gandalín constituye como escudero un avance significativo con respecto a personajes similares en la tradición caballeresca. El escudero de Amadís ha abandonado el anonimato propio de su oficio y figura junto al héroe desde sus comienzos, unido a él por fraternal lazo. Sin embargo, la posibilidad de adquirir relieve se ve frustrada a causa de la solución que Montalvo decide dar al conflicto entre deber y pasión. Esforzándose en reconciliar extremos, Amadís será enamorado ejemplar y perfecto caballero cristiano, y en su matrimonio con Oriana coincidirán la culminación de sus propios intereses con los del rey, padre de su señora, y representante del orden monárquico.

Dadas las premisas paródicas de las que parte la concepción de don Quijote, no sólo se desfigura el conflicto apuntado haciendo de Dulcinea un objeto ilusorio e inalcanzable, sino que, simultáneamente, se hace posible el desarrollo del escudero como sustituto inevitable en la narrativa de la dama. Su prolongada y necesaria presencia será núcleo de críticas y burlas, señalando la ridícula existencia de su atrevido señor.

A fin de hacer evidente la parodia del escudero que tiene lugar en la creación de Sancho Panza procedemos a aislar, someramente, las diversas intervenciones de Gandalín en las que, motivado por su fidelidad y gracias a la proximidad que siempre guarda con Amadís, llega a entrar en conflicto con los intereses de su amo, delineándose en el proceso como modelo paródico.

La dependencia de Gandalín con respecto a Amadís, un tanto femenina y siempre basada en un íntimo afecto, se hace patente desde bien temprano. Siendo todavía niños Amadís ha de socorrerle cuando otro doncel le arrebata al arco. Gandalín, que ya es compañero si no guardián, al dejar constancia de su inferioridad física en el juego prefigura en este episodio su posterior impotencia. Gandalín simplemente no puede concebir en ningún momento su vida sino en compañía de su hermano y señor: «Señor, yo os digo que a mi grado nunca de vos seré partido» (I, 45). Su fidelidad es constante, su afecto invariable. Una vez armado caballero Amadís, Gandalín siempre tendrá todo dispuesto para la aventura sin necesidad de instrucciones o educación alguna. Como compañero y guardián de Amadís sus conversaciones tratarán invariablemente de la ausente Oriana y del secreto amor entre ambos.

Sancho Panza, dadas las imposiciones de la parodia, habrá de conversar constantemente con su señor don Quijote, quien intentará instruirle sobre la caballería y sus deberes de escudero. Sin embargo, y aun dentro de los fines burlescos a los que debe su existencia, la fidelidad de Sancho como compañero y guardián no es menos admirable o constante. Si cuando Amadís decide dejarse morir, conocidas las órdenes de Oriana, Gandalín adelanta su promesa de lealtad, «si vos murierdes yo no quiero biuir» (II, 376), Sancho, viendo morir a su amo exclamará: «No se muera vuestra merced, señor mío, sino tome mi consejo, y viva muchos años; porque la mayor locura que puede hacer un hombre en esta vida es dejarse morir, sin más ni más, sin que nadie le mate, ni otras manos le acaben que las de la melancolía» (II, 74). Esta voluntad de vida, de ser y hacer a pesar de todo y de todos, equiparada aquí al ejercicio de la libertad, es evidencia en Sancho de una nueva actitud, independiente y personal en contraste con el fatalismo tipificado de Gandalín. En *Amadís de Gaula* se trata de la fama puesta en peligro por el desánimo. La vida de Amadís no parece estar en sus manos sino en la voluntad de Oriana. Gandalín, dependiendo del amor entre ambos, carece de voluntad propia; hecho que causará su fracaso como guardián de Amadís y su consiguiente abandono. Sancho, aun ignorando la parodia que sirve, determina con sus acciones, en el ejercicio de su voluntad, la dirección de la historia y el destino de su enamorado pero ineficaz señor.

Gandalín se niega a aceptar la ínsula que Amadís le deja en su testamento como pago por sus servicios ya que su único premio o fin, reconoce, es la existencia junto a su amo. Sancho, que en virtud de la parodia se hace escudero con la promesa de la ínsula, la aceptará de buena gana, si bien una vez obtenida y gobernada en circuns-

tancias doblemente burlescas reconocerá su verdadero interés: «A-
brid camino, señores míos, y dejadme volver a mi antigua libertad;
dejadme que vaya a buscar la vida pasada, para que resucite de esta
muerte presente» (II,53). Sancho aquí, sin renunciar a su oficio o a su
quimera, renuncia a la recompensa y a la fama obtenida en favor de
su independencia, a fin de recuperar el control de su vida. En el
marco de la ficción que ejecuta tal voluntad se manifiesta en su
realización como individuo y personaje, permaneciendo ajeno y aun
sobrepasando gracias a su ignorancia de simple la parodia de que es
vehículo y objeto.

El fracaso y abandono de Gandalín como guardián y escudero al
que hemos aludido tiene lugar en varias etapas. La primera crisis
ocurre cuando la desolación de Amadís, presenciando el panorama
de la ciudad donde se halla su amada, alcanza su apogeo: «¡Ay, villa,
cómo eres agora en gran alteza por ser en ti aquella señora que
entre todas las del mundo no ha par en bondad y hermosura. . . » (I,
114). Viendo como su señor se consume en lamentos, Gandalín
intenta primero confortarle con el atractivo del mundo físico, con
la aventura inminente. Intenta luego reanimarle tomándole de la
mano como testimonio de su presencia y fidelidad. Pero no consi-
guiendo suscitar la reacción deseada termina confrontándole verbalmente con su deber de caballero: «Assí me ayude Dios, señor, mucho
me pesa de vuestro pensar que tomýs mal cuidado qual otro cauallero del mundo no tomaría, y deuríades hauer duelo de vos y tomar
esfuerzo como en las otras cosas tomáys» (I, 115). Como se pone de
manifiesto, Gandalín no es un ser transformado por el amor como
resulta con su amo, y todavía puede apreciar el contraste entre los
otros caballeros y el proceder de Amadís. Estas palabras de Gandalín
tienen un eco en las que Sancho dirige a su señor tras la burla del
encantamiento de Dulcinea. «. . . vuestra merced se reporte, y vuelva
en sí, y coja las riendas a Rocinante, y avive y despierte, y muestre
aquella gallardía que conviene que tengan los caballeros andantes»
(II,11).

Vemos, pues, como Gandalín no puede aceptar el destino de su
señor, la subordinación del espíritu «esforçado» ál interés amoroso.
Su fidelidad y su interés como escudero en la caballería de las armas
están en conflicto con el destino de un Amadís enamorado. Las palabras que Gandalín logra sacar de su amo—«. . . si tú me amas sé que
antes me consejarías muerte que biuir en tan gran cuyta deseando lo

que no veo»—no podrían estar más lejos de la mente del escudero. Implican éstas una contradicción que no puede sufrir, por lo que termina declarando la supremacía de Amadís, a quien él sirve como señor y bien supremo: «Yo creo que no hay tan buena ni tan hermosa que vuestra bondad ygual sea» (I, 115). Sancho en la parodia también cree que «no hay mayor locura que la que toca en querer desesperarse como vuestra merced...» (II, 59). Y sobre su señora Dulcinea, y el daño que le causa a su amo, se muestra igualmente parcial: «Mas que se lleve Satanás a cuantas Dulcineas hay en el mundo, pues vale más la salud de un solo caballero andante que todos los encantos y transformaciones de la tierra.» (II, 11).

La tensión acumulada durante la escena se disipa una vez que el discreto Gandalín, tras sacar a su señor de su estado «estordeçido», logra volver su atención al mundo de la aventura. Sin embargo, el conflicto de intereses expuesto no desaparece; la semilla del abandono queda sembrada. Si el interés amoroso de Amadís está en conflicto con su deber de caballero, también lo está, dado el lazo entre ambos, con el interés de Gandalín, escudero, compañero y guardián. La resolución del primer conflicto precluye la del segundo, y de ahí el fracaso de Gandalín, su abandono y su transformación final.

Más adelante Gandalín volverá a situarse en un primer plano, esta vez como mensajero, pero todavía en relación con los amores secretos entre Amadís y Oriana. Lo que Gandalín dice a Oriana serán los sentimientos de su señor expresados en sus propias palabras, y según sus deseos. (Recuérdese la carta de don Quijote a Dulcinea y la versión y respuesta de Sancho.) Gandalín actúa en tal ocasión como intermediario, ejerciendo un papel propio de doncella, y encareciendo sobre todo las privaciones de su amo. Aun sin inventar nada, las palabras del escudero encierran cierta ambivalencia. Su interés, claramente, es Amadís y no Oriana, y como Sancho, aunque sin su interés personal, tan sólo desea que su amo llegue « a ser el mejor cauallero que nunca armas traxo» (I, 124).

Aunque la nota cómica y el sentido malicioso, como es frecuente en la literatura caballeresca, pertenecen en *Amadís de Gaula* al enano Ardián, encontramos en Gandalín elementos propios del escudero cervantino. Así, estando los tres reunidos en un campo entrega Oriana su anillo a Gandalín para que éste consiga provisiones en la villa cercana. Amadís y Oriana habrán de quedarse solos en su ausencia. He aquí las palabras con que se despide Gandalín: «Y quando él se yua, dixo a passo contra Amadís: Señor, quien buen tiempo tiene y lo pierde, tarde lo cobra» (I, 285). Estas palabras un tanto pícaras de Gandalín parecen contradecir la imagen del escudero celoso y guardián que hasta aquí hemos tratado de presentar. Sin embargo, expresa en ellas Gandalín su complicidad y su consentimiento. En su ausencia Oriana será dueña. Ve Gandalín a su amo en acción, venciendo con la posesión el interés amoroso que le debilita.

De gran importancia es la siguiente intervención de Gandalín. Llega un mensajero de Oriana con la carta en la que por error acusa a Amadís de infidelidad en el momento preciso en que éste se dispone a llevar a cabo la prueba del arco de los fieles amadores. Sin conocer aún su contenido, Gandalín impide que su señor reciba la carta hasta que haya puesto feliz término a la prueba. Gandalín actúa «temiendo lo que en ella venir podría, hora que fuese alegre o triste. . . que bien era cierto él que no solamente aquella, mas el mundo que suyo fuesse dexaría luego por cumplir lo que por ella le fuesse mandado. . .» (II, 372-73). Gandalín protege así a Amadís del mundo conflictivo del interés amoroso, del que a su pesar no ha logrado librarle con la posesión de Oriana efectuada en su ausencia.

Gandalín, a pesar de su celo, no es capaz de alterar el destino de su señor. Al contrario, es la decisión de Gandalín con respecto a la carta lo que permite que más tarde Amadís pueda probar a Oriana su condición de «leal enamorado». La noticia de la prueba del arco llegará a oídos de Oriana y le enviará una segunda carta de perdón.

La segunda y definitiva crisis entre Amadís y su escudero, en conexión siempre con el conflicto entre espíritu «esforçado» e interés amoroso debilitador, se produce al dejar Amadís desconsolado la Insula Firme tras conocer el contenido de la primera carta de su señora. Como hiciera antes, Gandalín intenta de nuevo resucitar el interés por la aventura en su señor, devolverle la vida; si bien esta vez parece conformarse con que su amo acepte un pacto entre lo épico y lo amoroso. Razona Gandalín sobre lo que dijera Oriana en su carta y adelanta la posibilidad de un error por su parte. Amadís se niega a aceptar culpa alguna en su señora, irrumpe en cólera y, finalmente, abandona al fiel escudero mientras éste duerme (II, 392).

A pesar de su fidelidad y constancia y de su continuada presencia, Gandalín no recobrará ya nunca su antigua posición. Al regreso de

Amadís, y con la consiguiente reconciliación de los enamorados, Gandalín entra al servicio de Oriana y hasta, por conveniencia o por lealtad, admite su error; haberse atrevido a sospechar falta alguna en ella (II, 440). El Gandalín que abre y cierra puertas, trae y lleva mensajes, proporciona llaves y arregla encuentros nocturnos no es sino un ser rebajado, medianero forzado y guardián impotente. No sorprende, pues, que el Gandalín de los libros III y IV, en parte, creemos, debido a la labor de Montalvo, desarrolle a fin de perpetuar su existencia una dimensión contraria a su concepción original. Revela allí sus ocultos deseos de independencia y, una vez que su función de acompañar y consolar a Amadís, que de continuo padece la ausencia de Oriana, deja de ser necesaria ante su definitiva unión, se despierta en él un poderoso e insospechado interés por profesar la caballería. Así, es armado caballero y, aunque viejo, sale como caballero novel en busca de aventuras, parcialmente reemplazando al jubilado señor.

Aunque de manera breve esperamos haber establecido en nuestro análisis los siguientes puntos: 1) que cuando Gandalín deja la anonimidad y el silencio propios del escudero para adoptar una posición prominente en la historia lo hace con motivo del interés amoroso de Amadís; 2) que Gandalín ve este interés debilitador y el espíritu «esforçado» de los caballeros como dos aspectos en conflicto en la vida de su señor; 3) que Gandalín, intentando resolver el conflicto en favor de la aventura, ocasiona la ira de Amadís, lo cual resulta en su abandono, entrando en conflicto a su vez la fidelidad Amadís-Oriana con la fidelidad Amadís-Gandalín.

Sancho Panza, como anotara Clemencín, guarda inevitablemente estrecha relación con Gandalín; primero, en virtud de su presencia constante junto a don Quijote y luego, como parte de sus funciones de escudero en la parodia, sirviendo de mensajero a Dulcinea. Es en su quehacer como intermediario forzado entre don Quijote y Dulcinea de donde arranca su creación que, como solución insospechada del conflicto entre deber y pasión en la parodia, origina su definitivo despegue como personaje.

En contraste con lo expuesto en el caso de *Amadís de Gaula* la situación que tenemos en el *Quijote* es totalmente inversa. Sancho apoya en todo momento al débil e ineficaz hidalgo hecho caballero en el plano físico, reforzando la parodia, actúa como mensajero ante Dulcinea sin llegar a facilitar el encuentro deseado, y si sirve al final como su sustituto, apoderándose de su lugar e imponiendo su ficción, es a consecuencia de su burlesco e inocente deseo de preservar su cuerpo y mejorar de estado. Paradójicamente, tal acción precipita el fin de su señor don Quijote como caballero andante promoviendo su fatal melancolía ante la imposibilidad de verse reunido con su señora, clave de su auténtica realización en imitación de su modelo. He aquí la gracia suprema de Sancho Panza como escudero, simple de natural discreto.

Cabe, pues, recordar cómo el propio Cervantes, orgulloso y consciente de su creación, concluye el prólogo a la Primera Parte:

> Yo no quiero encarecerte el servicio que te hago en darte a conocer tan noble y tan honrado caballero; pero quiero que me agradezcas el conocimiento que tendrás del famoso Sancho Panza, su escudero, en quien, a mi parecer, te doy cifradas todas las gracias escuderiles que en la caterva de los libros vanos de caballerías están esparcidas.

Ahora bien, ¿qué gracias escuderiles son estas? ¿Se trata, quizás, de una síntesis depuradora de elementos cómicos y folklóricos? Sin duda algo hay de ironía en estas palabras. Por muy esparcidas que estén resulta difícil creer que de ser así tales gracias hayan desafiado a los anotadores más rigurosos y a la crítica mís exacta y pertinaz.[13] En lugar de buscar el rastro de las gracias escuderiles de Sancho en tipos cómicos previos se propone aquí que su verdadero sentido radica en el desplazamiento de Dulcinea y lo que tal acción supone como núcleo generador de la parodia llevada a cabo creativamente por Cervantes en el *Quijote*.

Al analizar al Gandalín escudero buscando lo que Cervantes pudo haber incorporado en la génesis de Sancho vimos que, en cuanto al interés amoroso del caballero y el conflicto que representa, se dan en éste las gracias escuderiles de su modelo en grado sumo, y por razón de la parodia, con burlesca desmesura.

La fidelidad de Amadís hacia Oriana es superior al lazo afectivo que une a Amadís y Gandalín. Por otro lado, el carácter primordial en la historia del interés amoroso no deja lugar sino incipientemente para que se desarrollen las relaciones entre la pareja Amadís-Gandalín o para explorar las posibilidades narrativas de la interferencia causada por la constante presencia del escudero. En el *Quijote*, ante la ausencia de un interés amoroso real y la negación de la aventura caballeresca tales posibilidades son exploradas con industria e invención únicas. Sancho, que conoce bien la identidad de Dulcinea, aunque declare no haberla visto nunca, da pie al comienzo de la Segunda Parte a la burla del encantamiento, trasladando a su persona el interés de don Quijote. Gandalín, incapaz de controlar la pasión amorosa de su señor, revierte al fondo de la acción menoscabando así su incipiente identidad. Aunque intenta persuadirle de que tal interés causará su perdición como caballero no consigue superar el poder de Oriana y es abandonado, para después ser relegado a tercero. Sancho, viviendo su presente y viendo en peligro su herencia y existencia, precipitará la melancolía de don Quijote al desposeerle de su interés amoroso e impidiendo en su favor la realización paródica de su amo como caballero.

En *Amadís de Gaula* el conflicto entre deber y pasión, entre la vida hazañosa del caballero, social y reparadora, y su interés amoroso, individual, queda debilitado al ser el amor entre Amadís y Oriana un amor, aunque secreto, honesto y posible en último término. De este modo, y a expensas de gran parte de la tensión dramática, queda resuelto el conflicto entre el rey, el caballero y la dama, a su vez reina y esposa del rey, todavía presente en *Tristán de Leonís*. Paralelamente, la figura del escudero, hasta entonces anónima e insignificante, toma posesión del lugar y atributos del guardián y surge como el tercer miembro del triángulo. Su presencia y sus relaciones con Amadís reemplazan parte del interés sacrificado a la solución más cristiana de los amores entre el caballero y su dama.

En el *Quijote*, donde la voluntad vital y creadora del individuo cuenta más que la sumisión a una tradición o a un deber, el hidalgo cincuentón apenas puede concebir o llevar a cabo interés amoroso alguno. Sancho entra en la historia para reforzar paródicamente la ineficacia y anacronismo del caballero en el plano de la aventura, pero pasa pronto a tomar posesión del lugar de su señora Dulcinea, tanto por designio de su modelo como por el ejercicio de su voluntad. Don Quijote, por su parte, socavado su control creador se ve necesaria e inevitablemente desposeído. La ausencia de un interés amoroso verdadero precipita su pasividad en cuanto al desarrollo de la aventura como fuente de su devenir y, con ello, consolida su fatal melancolía.

En conclusión, al asalto individual que Sancho realiza desde su propia ignorancia, sobrepasando las funciones heredadas de su modelo y los límites impuestos por la parodia, facilita el proceso burlesco por el cual se lleva a cabo el ataque contra los libros de caballerías: la imitación frustrada del valiente y enamorado Amadís de Gaula por parte del viejo e ingenioso don Quijote de la Mancha.

UNIVERSITY OF CALIFORNIA, BERKELEY

NOTAS

[1] *Amadís de Gaula* (texto de 1508 refundido por) Garci Rodríguez de Montalvo, ed. Edwin B. Place, 4 vols. (Madrid: C.S.I.C, 1959-1969). Citamos por esta edición tomo y página. Para el *Quijote* citamos por la edición de Luis A. Murillo, 3 vols. (Madrid: Castalia, 1978), parte y capítulo.

[2] Pedro Bohigos Balaguer, «Los libros de caballerías en el siglo XVI», en *Historia general de las literaturas hispánicas,* vol. II, ed. Guillermo Díaz-Plaja) Barcelona,1963), pps. 213-225. Véase también William J. Entwistle, *The Arthurian Legend in the Literatures of the Spanish Peninsula* (London y Toronto: J. M. Dent & Sons, 1925), pps. 213-224 y María Rosa Lida de Malkiel, «Arthurian Literature in Spain and Portugal», en *Arthurian Literature in the Middle Ages, a Collaborative History (ALMA),* ed. Roger S. Loomis (Oxford. Clarendon Press, 1959), pps. 406-418.

[3] E. B. Place, «El *Amadís* de Montalvo, como manual de cortesanía en Francia, *RFE,* 38 (1954), 151-169. Véase asimismo John J. O'Connor,«*'Amadis de Gaule' and its influence on Elizabethan Literature* (New Brunswick: Rutgers University Press, 1970).

[4] Henry Thomas, *Las novelas de caballerías españolas y portuguesas* (1920), trad, Esteban Pujals (Madrid: C.S.I.C., 1952), p. 41 y ss. Véase también Frank Pierce, *Amadís de Gaula* (Boston: Twayne, 1976), pps. 89 y 105.

[5] Véase el estudio literario de Place en su edición del *Amadís de Gaula,* III, pps. 929-930.

[6] Marcelino Menéndez y Pelayo, «Interpretaciones del *Quijote*» (1905), en *Edición nacional, Obras Completas, Estudios y discursos de crítica histórica y literaria,* vol. I (Santander: Aldus, C.S.I.C., 1941), pps. 302-322. Menéndez y Pelayo consideró el *Quijote* no como antítesis de los libros de caballerías sino como ejemplo de obra nueva, depuradora, donde el ideal caballeresco queda nuevamente ennoblecido. Véase al respecto Anthony J. Close, *The Romantic Approach to 'Don Quixote'* (Cambridge: Cambridge University Press, 1978). Sobre la relación entre el *Amadís* y el *Quijote* véase, en particular, E. B. Place, «Cervantes and the *Amadis*», en *Hispanic Studies in Honor of Nicholson B. Adams,* ed. J. E. Keller y K.-Ludwig Selig (Chapel Hill: University of North Carolina Press, 1966), pps. 131-140. Tanto el *Amadís* primitivo como Montalvo y Cervantes parecen tener motivaciones afines. Sobre Montalvo, por ejemplo, indica Place que «se proponía explotar la popularidad de lo artúrico y del amor cortés a fin de popularizar lo antiartúrico» (IV, 1346). Sobre el *Amadís* primitivo observa Place: «parece evidente que su intento principal fue acabar con la caballería a lo artúrico motivada por el amor cortés—intento realizado mucho más plenamente por Moltavo en su *Esplandián*» (III, 932). De Cervantes podría afirmarse que lleva el ataque de Montalvo a sus últimas consecuencias, parodiando el género abiertamente, haciendo uso extenso de las incongruencias introducidas por adaptadores y refundidores y, a su vez, arremetiendo contra la literatura anti-idealista y anti-caballeresca representada por el *Guzmán de Alfarache.*

[7] Véase, por ejemplo, Américo Castro, «Cervantes y el *Quijote* a nueva luz», en *Cervantes y los casticismos españoles* (Madrid: Alianza, 1974), pps. 57-58.

[8]Sobre el *Quijote* y los libros de caballerías véase Martín de Riquer, «La technique parodique du roman médiéval dans le *Quichotte*», en *La Littérature narrative d'imitation, des genres littéraires aux techniques d'expression* (Paris: Presses Universitaires de France, 1961), pps. 55-69 y «Cervantes y la caballeresca», en *Suma Cervantina*, eds. J. Avalle-Arce y E. C. Riley (London: Támesis, 1973), pps. 273-292. Cf. Federico Sánchez y Escribano, «El sentido cervantino del ataque contra los libros de caballerías», *Anales Cervantinos*, 5 (1955-1956), pps. 19-40. Para un estudio más detallado del tema de este trabajo, véase nuestra tesis doctoral *Sancho Panza, 'escudero sin par'. Parodia y creación en* Don Quijote *(1605, 1615)*, University of California, Berkeley, 1979.

[9]Sobre el conflicto amor-deber, véase Joan M. Ferrante, *The Conflict of Love and Honor; The Medieval Tristan Legend in France, Germany and Italy* (The Hague/Paris: Mouton, 1973); Eugène Vinaver, *The Rise of Romance* (Oxford: Clarendon Press, 1971), pps. 123-139: Jean Frappier, «Chrétien de Troyes», en *ALMA*, p. 161.; Georg Lukács, *The Theory of the Novel* (1920), trad. Anna Bostock (Cambridge: MIT Press, 1971), pps. 97-111.

[10]Frappier, p. 170; E. Vinaver, «The Prose *Tristan*», en *ALMA* p. 340; D. D. R. Owen, «Introduction», Chrétien de Troyes, *Arthurian Romances*, trad. W. W. Comfort (1941; reimpreso London: Dent, y New York: Dutton, 1975), pps. vii-xvi.

[11]Samuel Gili-Gaya, «*Las Sergas de Esplandián* como crítica de la caballería bretona», *BBMP*, 23 (1947, 103-111; E. B. Place, «Montalvo's Outrageous Recantation», *HR*, 37 (1969), 192-198. Cf. Eloy R. González y Jennifer T. Roberts, «Montalvo's Rencantation Revisited», *BHS*, 55 (1978), 203-210. Véase asimismo María Rosa Lida de Malkiel, «El desenlace del *Amadís* primitivo», *RPh*, 6 (1952, 1953), 283-289 y E. B. Place, «Fictional Evolution: The Old French Romances and the Primitive *Amadís* Reworked by Montalvo», *PMLA*, 71 (1956), 521-529.

[12]Gandalín resulta inversión de Gorvalán, ayo guardián de Tristán de Leonís. Sobre Gorvalán (Gouvernal) como tipo fundamental del tutor-acompañante encargado de la educación del héroe, véase Madeleine P. Cosman, *The Education of the Hero in Arthurian Romances* (Chapel Hill: University of North Carolina Press, 1965), pps. 3-48, 139 y 198.

[13]W.S. Hendrix, «Sancho Panza and the Comic Types of the Sixteenth Century», en *Homenaje a Menéndez Pidal* (Madrid: Hernando, 1925), II, pps. 485-494; Salvador de Madariaga, *Guía del lector del* Quijote, *ensayo psicológico. . .* (Madrid: Espasa, 1926), pps. 151 y ss; Dámaso Alonso, «Sancho-Quijote, Sancho-Sancho», *Del siglo de oro a este siglo de siglas* (Madrid: Gredos, 1962). pps. 9-19; Francisco Márquez Villanueva, «Sobre la génesis literaria de Sancho Panza», *Anales Cervantinos*, 7 (1958), 123-155. y en *Fuentes literarias cervantinas* (Madrid: Gredos, 1973), pps. 20-94; Leif Sletsjoe, *Sancho Panza, hombre de bien*, (Madrid: Ínsula, 1961); Anthony J. Close, «Sancho Panza: Wise Fool», *MLR*, 68 (1973) pp. 344-357; Mauricio Molho, «Raíz folklórica de Sancho Panza» en *Cervantes: raíces folklóricas* (Madrid: Gredos, 1976), pps. 217-355.

Don Quixote and the Origins of the Novel

JOHN J. ALLEN

 LTHOUGH IT IS generally agreed that *Don Quixote* is one of the world's great novels, one can scarcely find critics who agree as to precisely where that greatness lies. Similarly, although it is widely held that *Don Quixote* is the first modern novel, each critic or theorist sees the central "novelty" of the novel differently. Lionel Trilling's phrase is often quoted: "All prose fiction is a variation on the theme of *Don Quixote*."[1] According to Trilling, Cervantes set for the novel "the problem of appearance and reality." Perhaps Harry Levin's characterization, in *The Gates of Horn* (New York: Oxford University Press, 1963), of Cervantes' masterpiece as "the prototype of all realistic novels" is based upon a view rather close to that of Trilling, since Mr. Levin finds the originality in what he calls "the literary technique of systematic disillusionment" (pp. 47-48). René Girard begins his sweeping study of the modern novel as the exposure of the inauthenticity of mediated desire with *Don Quixote* as a whole and "The Tale of Foolish Curiosity" from Part I in particular.[2] Both Wayne Booth and Marthe

Robert, though subsequently proceeding in quite different directions, consider central to the development of modern fiction the self-conscious narrator as used by Cervantes. As Mme. Robert says: "Le *Don Quichotte* est sans aucune doute le premier roman 'moderne', si on entend par modernité le mouvement d'une littérature qui, perpétuellement en quête d'elle même, s'interroge, se met en cause, fait de ses doutes et de sa foi à l'égard de son propre message le sujet même de ses récits."[3]

Alejo Carpentier affirmed last spring on receiving the Cervantes prize in Alcalá de Henares that Cervantes, "con el *Quijote*, instala la dimensión imaginaria dentro del hombre, con todas sus implicaciones terribles o magníficas, destructoras o poéticas, novedosas o inventivas, haciendo de ese nuevo *yo* un medio de indagación y conocimiento del hombre."[4] This, as Carpentier sees it, was the dimension lacking in the picaresque, the foundation, in other respects, of the modern novel. Finally, we might look at the words of another contemporary novelist, Robert Coover, who acknowledges in very sugestive terms the debt of the modern novel to Cervantes, terms which I will recall a little later in dealing with genre and countergenre. He speaks directly to Cervantes:

> Your stories. . . exemplified the dual nature of all good narrative art: they struggled against the unconscious mythic residue in human life and sought to synthesize the unsynthesizable, sallied forth against adolescent thought-modes and exhausted art forms, and returned home with new complexities. In fact your creation of a synthesis between poetic analogy and literal history (not to mention reality and illusion, sanity and madness, the erotic and the ludicrous, the visionary and the scatological) gave birth to the Novel—perhaps above all else your works were exemplars of a revolution in narrative fiction, a revolution which governs us—not unlike the way you found yourself abused by the conventions of the Romance—to this very day.[5]

Even those historians and critics who conceive of the realistic novel as a creation of the eighteenth century can scarcely afford to exclude *Don Quixote* explicitly from their conception of the genre. The following are Ian Watt's criteria for characterizing the modern novel: (a) originality of plot, (b) realistic particularity of detail, (c) individual identity of characters, (d) and (e) particularized time and space, and (f) an authentic account of the actual experiences of individuals, achieved through referential (as opposed to strictly stylized) language.[6] Which of these characteristics is lacking in *Don Quixote*? None, obviously.

The novelists themselves have consistently been the most enthusiastic admirers of this "paradigmatic novel of novels."[7] "Defoe was proud to acknowledge 'the Quixoticism of R. Crusoe'. Marivaux's first novel, *Pharsamond*, was subtitled *Le Don Quichotte français*. Fielding brought out a comedy, *Don Quixote in England*, before announcing—on the title-page of *Joseph Andrews*—that his first novel had been 'written in the manner of Cervantes.' " William Faulkner read *Don Quixote* every year, "as some do the Bible." Stendhal and Flaubert both admit it was their original stimulus, and Turgenev wrote one of the classic essays on the book.[8] Of course, I do not mean to imply that their admiration for the book is restricted to an appreciation of its technique; Flaubert, Turgenev, Dostoevsky, do not speak of technique when they praise the work, and André Malraux said, after World War II, that "only three books, *Robinson Crusoe, Don Quixote* and *The Idiot*, retained their truth for those who had seen prisons and concentration camps."[9]

I

My interest here today, however, *is* technique and the origins of a genre, *the* genre of the post-Renaissance West, the most important literary creation of that immensely fertile period in European history. One must begin, I believe, with an attempt to characterize the relationship between the novel and its prose rivals. One can say, with Harry Levin, that "the romance—from verse to prose, from manuscript to print—was a transitional form, standing somewhere between the idealism of the epic and the realism of the novel."[10] But this view introduces two distortions, or at least it predisposes us to introduce them: first, the idea that the novel supersedes the romance, historically, and second, the idea that the novel is, strictly speaking, a countergenre to the romance—an anti-romance.

Having indicated these reservations, with which I will deal directly in a moment, I would like to pursue briefly this historical, generic perspective. "A primary function of art and thought," says Lionel Trilling, "is to liberate the individual from the tyranny of his culture in an environmental sense and to permit him to stand

beyond it in an autonomy of perception and judgment."[11] To
achieve this, art makes us see new things, previously unnoticed, and
makes us see old things in a new way, through association and
dissociation. It tries to break up blinding habitual preconceptions
and prejudices. As Victor Shklovsky has put it: "The object must be
extracted from its envelope of habitual associations."[12] "Art in general and fiction in particular can be seen as a dialectic of *defamiliariza-
tion* in which new techniques of representation ultimately generate
countertechniques which expose them to ridicule, and this dialectic
is at the center of the history of fiction," in the words of Robert
Scholes.[13] This is precisely what Coover was talking about, in the
passage quoted earlier.

Now, as we move from these general comments about the history of fiction to the more specific considerations of genre which
they suggest, we may first of all see the reception of *Don Quixote* by
its earliest readers in a somewhat different light. The context in
which we read a work of literature, according to E. D. Hirsch, is
generic. As we begin reading a work, we assign it tentatively to a
genre, which we specify more precisely as we read, approaching the
unique nature of the individual work through its affinities with
other works from our literary experience.[14] My point in bringing
this up here is that early readers of *Don Quixote* could only assimilate
it to the existing genres of romance or satire, and with this choice,
of course, it had to be the latter, a fully anti-romance genre.

As Claudio Guillén points out, Cervantes is in "active dialogue
with the generic models of his time and culture. This dialogue is
active in the sense that the poet does not merely choose among the
standards that are accessible to him—he makes possible their survi-
val; and he determines *which* are the preferable or the pertinent or
the potentially 'new' norms."[15] Thus far Guillén, but I would add,
parenthetically, that the dialogue is, in Cervantes, "active" also in
the sense of an ongoing, unresolved dialogue still being debated in
the course of the novel, such as that between the Canon and Don
Quixote in I, 47, as explicated by Alban Forcione.[16]

At this point Robert Scholes' theory of fictional modes, developed out of Northrup Frye's initial formulation, can be helpful.[17]
The three modes with which Scholes begins embrace at one
extreme the heroic, superior world of romance, and at the other the
degraded world of satire, with the mimetic world of history at the

center. These three modes encompass in a general way all of the possible relations between the fictional world and the world of existence. From history toward the pole of romance on the spectrum fall sentiment and tragedy; toward the pole of satire fall comedy and picaresque.

In this scheme it is clear that although the picaresque emerges as anti-chivalric, modally, as well as (perhaps) historically, the novel—that is, *Don Quixote*—is something else. In Scholes' words, "we can. . . see the rise of the novel as a result of a flow of fictional impulses from both romance and satire, attracted toward history by a growing historical consciousness in the later Renaissance" (p. 135). Again, Guillén is helpful here: "The novel as it emerges in the sixteenth century, after the great Florentine historians and the chronicles of the conquest of America, owes much to this crucial *rapprochement* between literature and history—to the organization and detailed recreation and tolerant understanding of the concrete wealth of experience by a 'third' person." Guillén stresses that "the saturation of the picaresque with the narrator's individual and willfully limited point of view is most remote from history." (p. 156). "The novel," then, in Scholes' and Kellogg's formulation, "is not the opposite of romance, as is usually maintained, but a product of the reunion of the empirical and fictional elements."[18]

If we can see *Don Quixote* as the culmination of this historical development, see it in its generic *and* modal context, we must see it as involving a parody of the excesses of a literary form, a historical genre (the books of chivalry), but not a criticism of the fictional mode of romance. When Byron said that Cervantes "smiled Spain's chivalry away," he was confusing parody of a fictional genre with rejection or devaluation of the heroic embodied in the mode of romance. There is, of course, ample evidence of this apart from the theoretical construct whose utility I am suggesting: *Amadís* is not burned, the Canon specifically indicates that there is a "right" way to write romance, and Cervantes' *Persiles* is in fact a romance written according to the Canon's prescription.

So, although Cervantes obviously did not reject the mode of romance with its superior hero, he created *Don Quixote* with a set of parodic counter-techniques ridiculing those books of chivalry, and moved the reader towards the realization that there is a kind of heroism which involves a victory over oneself, and not over the environment. To the façade of pseudo-history of the books of chivalry is opposed the unreliable Cide Hamete Benengeli, about whom more in a moment, to the fantastic and supernatural is opposed the commonplace and verisimilar, to mythical past time and legendary place is opposed contemporary Spain, to the single lofty style is opposed a multiplicity of stylistic levels ironically juxtaposed, to exemplary deeds are opposed failures and inconsequential meetings, and so forth.

I might speculate, in closing these considerations of the modal aspect of *Don Quixote*, that the picaresque novel may have taught Cervantes that the reader is engaged at a more meaningful level when the protagonist struggles with his *inadequacies* in dealing with his environment, rather than simply seeking occasions to demonstrate or confirm his superiority over it. Don Quixote, who began as a figure from the world of satire, inferior to his environment, the anti-type of Amadís, moves through a process of self-purification to a position of superiority through humility and self-knowledge.

II

I would like now to talk about three aspects of Cervantes' achievement which overlap with and include most of what has been brought out by the critics whose formulations I have been presenting, and which seem to me to clarify the nature of his innovation. In *Don Quixote* Cervantes accomplishes three fundamental movements: (1) the movement from an established genre to generic compendium and confrontation, which provided the answer to the respective limitations of chivalric, pastoral and picaresque, (2) the movement from the miraculous to the providential, which provided the solution to the problem of achieving the goal of *admiratio* without sacrificing verisimilitude, and (3) the movement from the classical preoccupation with establishing the authority of a narrative to an exploration of the fertile possibilities in the management and manipulation of point of view.

The generic move is the one most successfully elucidated in the criticism just reviewed. The "active dialogue" which, according to Guillén (p. 127), Cervantes sustains with the written and unwritten norms of his day is embodied in *Don Quixote* in the encounter with Ginés de Pasamonte, who represents not so much the *pícaro* as the picaresque genre; in the juxtaposition of the rustic goatherds on the one hand, and Rocinante's "pastoral" adventure with the Yangue-sans' mares, on the other, and the episodes of Marcela and Gris-óstomo; in the persistent "literary" evaluations of interpolated stories ranging from Sancho's tales through "The Tale of the Foolish Curiosity" and the Captive's tale, and, as noted above, in the inconclusive dialogue between Don Quixote and the Canon. The whole elaborate process is heavily involved in the manipulations by Cervantes of a multiplicity of stylistic levels ironically juxtaposed as mentioned above. Cervantes is cognizant as no one before him of the inseparability of style and genre, and manages to distinguish between at least five different levels of style, as I would characterize them, with characters passing at times from one to another, both straight and parodied. The whole thing is a marvelous sustained *tour de force*. The best concrete example of a modulation from one level to another is Pedro the goatherd's introduction to the episode of Marcela and Grisóstomo in I, 12.[19]

In the second movement which I have listed, Cervantes consciously opposes the consistently providential world of his fiction to the miraculous world of the books of chivalry. Certainly the esthetic principle most persistently invoked in the *Quixote* is verisimilitude.[20] Cervantes' problem was to achieve the effects of *admiratio*—to provoke wonder in the reader—within these self-imposed bounds of verisimilitude. One of the solutions to this Aristotelian dilemma lay in the providential arrangement of events, which is the mildest conceivable use of the Christian supernatural—a domain on the frontiers of the verisimilar explicitly permitted by the literary theorists of Cervantes' day.[21] I have spoken recently at length of the providential world of Cervantes' fiction,[22] and so today I want simply to indicate the link between Providence and the marvelous with a few quotations from the works.

In *Las dos doncellas*, the narrator comments upon Marco Antonio's astonishing recovery:

> Dios, que así lo tenía ordenado, tomando por medio e instrumento de sus obras—cuando a nuestros ojos quiere hacer una maravilla—lo que la misma Naturaleza no alcanza, ordenó que la alegría y poco silencio. . . fuesen parte para mejorarle. (966a)

In the *Persiles*, the association between the marvelous and the operation of Providence is mentioned by the characters and the narrator in quite similar terms; Sinforosa says to Auristela:

> Creo que los Cielos te han traído por tan extraño rodeo, que parece milagro, a esta tierra. (1580b)

The narrator informs the reader, at another point:

> Y en esta sazón tan confusa, no se olvidó el Cielo de socorrerle, por tan extraña novedad, que le tuvieron por milagro. (1537a)

So preoccupied is Cervantes with the issue of verisimilitude and the distinction between miracle and mystery, that the narrator digresses to specify the difference:

> Los milagros suceden fuera del orden de la naturaleza, y los misterios son aquellos que parecen milagros y no lo son, sino casos que acontecen raras veces. (1577a)

Thus it is clear that Cervantes expects, or at least hopes, that his "misterios," the coincidences, chance encounters, prodigious feats and eleventh-hour rescues and recognitions with which his works are filled, will be plausible, where outright miracle would not, as manifestations of the operation of Providence in the world.

Juan Bautista Avalle-Arce has pointed out the rejection of the supernatural solutions of the problems of the characters in *La Diana* implicit in the resolution of the tangled affair of Cardenio, Luscinda, Fernando and Dorotea, in Part I of *Don Quixote*, in which Cervantes is at pains to work out the complications "dentro del ámbito de las existencias en juego".[23] In the examination of the books in Don Quixote's library, in Chapter 6 of Part I, the priest had spared *La Diana*, but called for the elimination of "todo aquello que trata de la sabia Felicia y de la agua encantada" (1053b), or, in other words, everything involved in the supernatural solution of the characters' dilemmas. In his own *Galatea*, which, as the priest says, "propone algo, y no concluye nada," the resolution of the problems of the central characters is left for the promised second part, but in one *caso de amor* which is brought to its conclusion—that of Timbrio, Silerio, Nísida and Blanca—the providential resolution is unabashedly applied. The authoritative characters expect it:

> Damón y Tirsi. . . con muchas razones le persuadieron [a Silverio] a no perder la esperanza de ver a su amigo Timbrio con

más contento que él sabría imaginar, pues no era posible sino
que tras tanta fortuna serenase el Cielo, del cual se debía
esperar que no consentiría que la falsa nueva de la muerte de
Nísida a noticia de Timbrio. . . no viniese. . . (666a)

In due course God provides:

El cielo ahora con tantas ventajas ha dado remedio a nuestras
calamidades. (721b)

Something similar happens in connection with the books of chivalry, with respect to which the element most insistently criticized
is inverisimilitude. But Cervantes' rectification does not take us
from the *deus ex machina* to a world without God, and one of the
fundamental reasons for the inclusion of the interpolated stories in
Don Quixote is precisely the reiterated confirmation of the operation
of divine Providence in the world in which Don Quixote and Sancho
live. It is not the world of *La Diana* nor that of *Amadís*, but that of
Fielding, for example.

Some years ago I looked at *la Fuerza de la sangre* as a verisimilar
recasting of the legend of *El Cristo de la Vega*.[24] Leocadia, abducted
and raped by the insolent young Rodolfo, raises their son, Luis, for
seven years before a providential accident brings about the restitu-
tion of her honor through marriage to the rapist. This solution,
repugnant as it may be to the modern reader, is explicitly presented
as an example of the operation of Providence. At the time of the
offense, Leocadia's parents "se pidieron venganzas y desearon mila-
grosos castigos," a clear allusion, in the context, to the legend of *El
Cristo de la Vega*, but the solution is less spectacular, and it comes not
as vengeance, but as a reward for Leocadia's virtue: "permisión fue
del Cielo el haber atropellado [a Luis], para que, trayéndole a vuestra casa, hallase yo en ella. . . el remedio." (896a)

The operation of Providence in *Don Quixote* is not quite so much
on the surface of events, nor is it usually so specifically identified in
commentary, but it continues to underlie the basic trajectories of
the characters and thus to define the world of Don Quixote and
Sancho.

This brings me to my third and final point: the movement away
from the classical preoccupation with establishing the authority of a
narrative to an exploration of the fertile possibilities in the manage-

ment and manipulation of point of view. Several aspects of this third and final movement are interesting to me: (a) the juxtaposition, in *Don Quixote*, of all of the classical possibilities for establishing the authority of a narrative in such a way that each is undercut by the others, just as the juxtaposition of stylistic levels deflates and the confrontation of genres undermines, (b) the implications of Cervantes' adoption, in *Don Quixote*, of the narrative paradigm of *Lazarillo*, rather than that of *Guzmán de Alfarache*, i.e., of distance, rather than identity, between author and narrator, and (c) the transformation, achieved by the careful management and manipulation of point of view, of *events* into *experience*.

As for the first of these aspects, the subversive juxtaposition of all of the classical possibilities for establisihing the authority of a narrative, the following are the classical possibilities, as enumerated by Scholes and Kellogg, in *The Nature of Narrative:*

(1) *histor* (Tacitus): "The *histor* as narrator is not a recorder or recounter but an investigator. He examines the past with an eye toward separating out actuality from myth."[25]

> Quieren decir que tenía el sobrenombre de Quijada, o Quesada, que en esto hay alguna diferencia en los autores que deste caso escriben; aunque por conjeturas verosímiles se deja entender que se llamaba Quejana. (1037-38)

(2) inspired bard (Virgil, Ovid):

> ¡Oh perpetuo descubridor de los antípodes, hacha del mundo, ojo del cielo, meneo dulce de las cantimploras, Timbrio aquí, Febo allí, tirador acá, médico acullá, padre de la Poesía, inventor de la Música, tú que siempre sales y, aunque lo parece, nunca te pones! A ti digo, oh Sol,. . . que me favorezcas, y alumbres la oscuridad de mi ingenio.; . . (1424ab)

(3) personal eyewitness account in his own name (Augustine):

> dice [Cide Hamete] que pocas veces vio al rucio sin Sancho ni a Sancho sin el rucio. (1393a)

(4) fictional account in a character's name (Petronius, Achilles Tatius):

> el autor desta historia, que deste harriero hace particular

mención, porque le conocía muy bien, y aun quieren decir que era algo pariente suyo. . . (1085a)

The bulk of the novel is, of course, presented as an account in a character's name: Cide Hamete's shifting indentity and incompatible attributes may make him a very strange character in the world of Don Quixote, but a character, nonetheless. This proliferation of mutually exclusive bases for authority in the narrative ends by throwing all of it in doubt and thus combines with other aspects of unreliability to achieve the same effect.

In regard to the second aspect, it must be noted that the narrative paradigm for *Don Quixote*, with respect to the relationship between the narrator and the author, is that of *Lazarillo*, and not that of *Guzmán*. I will be dealing with this point at somewhat greater length in San Diego next month at the AATSP meeting. Suffice it to say here that just as Lazarillo and the anonymous author do not share the same vision of the world, Cervantes does not share the view of his obtuse and insensitive narrator, Cide Hamete, who remains unaware of the spiritual development of the protagonist in Part II.

The last of these three aspects of the movement from the classical preoccupation with establishing the authority of a narrative—the transformation of events into experience through the management and manipulation of point of view—is my primary interest today, and the final point of this presentation.

In Book III of the *Galatea*, Cervantes presents in great detail the lavish country wedding of Silveria and the wealthy Daranio, with the lament of the unfortunate, rejected Mireno, whose suit found less favor than that of his richer rival. The parallel with Camacho's wedding, in *Don Quixote*, Part II, is obvious. Basilio wins Quiteria, as Mireno does not win Silveria, but this is not the essential difference between the two tales. The difference is nothing less than one of the essential differences between romance and novel, between the old and the new, between, as Cervantes put it, those stories in which the interest lies in what is told, and those in which it lies in the way in which the story is told (999b).

Tirsi and Damón come to the wedding, their curiosity piqued by what they hear of the affair:

— . . . mañana se desposa Daranio con la pastora Silveria, con

quien [Mireno] pensaba casarse. Pero, en fin, han podido más
con los padres de Silveria las riquezas de Daranio que las habilidades de Mireno.

—Verdad dices—replicó Elicio—; pero con Silveria más
había de poder la voluntad que de Mireno tenía conocida que
otro tesoro alguno; cuanto más que no es Mireno tan pobre
que, aunque Silveria se casara con él, fuera su necesidad not-
ada. (663a)

Similarly, Sancho and Don Quixote are drawn to Camacho's
wedding by the account of the student:

. . . —Basilio se enamoró de Quiteria desde sus tiernos y primeros años, y ella fue correspondiendo a su deseo con mil hones-
tos favores. . . El padre de Quiteria. . . ordenó de casar a su hija
con el rico Camacho, no pareciéndole ser bien casarla con Basilio, que no tiene tantos bienes de fortuna como de naturaleza.
(1336b)

To the lament of the "triste y desdichado Mireno" corresponds
the description of Basilio: "siempre anda pensativo y triste, hablando
entre sí mismo, con que da ciertas y claras señales de que se le ha
vuelto el juicio."

The presentation of both weddings begins with a standard classical dawn description. In *La Galatea:*

. . . Apenas había dejado la blanca aurora el enfadoso
lecho del celoso marido cuando dejaron los suyos todos los
más pastores de la aldea. . . (666b)

In *Don Quixote:*

Apenas la blanca aurora había dado lugar a que el luciente
Febo con el ardor de sus calientes rayos las líquidas perlas de
sus cabellos de oro enjugase, cuando don Quijote, sacu-
diendo la pereza de sus miembros, se puso en pie y llamó a
su escudero Sancho, que aun todavía roncaba. (1339a)

A clue to the revolutionary difference between the accounts of the
two weddings can be found here, in the technique of Cervantes'
parody. The dawn description from *Don Quixote* is not in itself ridiculous nor is it significantly different from others in *La Galatea:* it is the
juxtaposition with Sancho's snores which brings it down, the intrusion of vulgar reality into the classical stylistic stratosphere. Com-

pare lines 3 and 4 from Quevedo's "Romance de los infantes de Carrión":

> Medio día era por filo,
> que rapar podía la barba,
> *cuando, después de mascar,*
> *el Cid sosiega la panza.*[26]

In an entirely different way, it is the presence and function of Don Quixote and Sancho in the rest of the presentation—an almost Jamesian function—which transforms the material which follows.

The account of the wedding of Daranio and Silveria proceeds through a straightforward omniscient description of the decorations and the music, the lament of the rejected Mireno, the large number of guests and the sumptuous feast, and the fine wedding attire of the bride and groom. The third-person objective account is varied only by the interjection of an exchange between Mireno and Elicio and the reading of the stanzas of the former's lament, and the irruption of Erastro in praise of the beauty of Galatea as she appears in the wedding party, praise which, though it is wholly conventional in content and though it degenerates into an extended neoplatonic discourse between Erastro and Elicio, is nevertheless a clear antecedent of the brilliant *tour de force* of Sancho's rustic praise of Quiteria in the later passage.

The dawn description in *Don Quixote* is followed by some very subtle and complex insights into both Don Quixote and Sancho. First comes Don Quixote's well-known speech on the burdens of his class and chosen profession:

> —¡Oh tú, bienaventurado sobre cuantos viven sobre la haz de la Tierra, pues sin tener envidia ni ser envidiado, duermes con sosegado espíritu, ni te persiguen encantadores no sobresaltan encantamientos! Duerme, digo otra vez, y lo diré otras ciento. . . (1339a)

As usual, the context deflates the overblown rhetoric of magnanimity. Though he tells Sancho to sleep on, Don Quixote rudely awakens him immediately with the butt of his lance. Comparable passages—though with important differences—are the invitation to Sancho to join him in the meal with the goatherds (I, 11), with its hollow protestation of a desire for equality between master and man, and the congratulations on Sancho's receipt of the governorship (II, 42), with its mixture of genuine satisfaction and envy.

Sancho, for his part, provides on awakening one of the most damning revelations of his propensity toward egocentric rationalization. He had initially favored the suit of Basilio for Quiteria's hand, identifying with him against his wife's obstinate opposition to Sanchica's marrying "up":

> —Lo que quisiera es que ese buen Basilio, que ya me le voy aficionando, se casara son esa señora Quiteria. . . (1336b)

But now a whiff of Camacho's banquet is sufficient to make him change sides:

> —Mas que haga lo que quisiere [Basilio]—respondió Sancho—; no fuera él pobre, y casárase con Quiteria. ¿No hay más sino no tener un cuarto y querer casarse por las nubes? (1339b)

Castro was certainly correct in stressing that it is not what happens in *Don Quixote* that matters, but the reactions of the characters to what happens and how they assimilate their experience and shape themselves out of it. The presentation of the wedding of Camacho with which the rest of Chapter 20 occupies itself is evidence of how deeply true this is, and it illustrates well, I think, the fundamental justification for the perspectivist school of criticism. In contrast to the parallel presentation of the wedding in *La Galatea*, Cervantes makes us see it through the eyes of his characters, deepening our involvement with and understanding of them at the same time that he advances his narrative. *Events* become *experiences*, and therein lies the modernity of the passage:

> Hizo Sancho lo que su señor le mandaba, y, poniendo la silla a Rocinante y la albarda al rucio, subieron los dos, y paso ante paso se fueron entrando por la enramada. *Lo primero que se le ofreció a la vista de Sancho* fue, espetado en su asador de un olmo entero, un entero novillo. . . *Contó Sancho* más de sesenta zaques de más de dos arrobas cada uno. . .
> *Todo lo miraba Sancho Panza, y de todo se aficionaba.* Primero le cautivaron y rindieron el deseo de las ollas, de quien él tomara de bonísima gana un mediano puchero. . .(1340 ab)

And where is Don Quixote, who had arrived together with Sancho, all this time?

> En tanto, pues, que esto pasaba Sancho, estaba don Qui-
> jote mirando como por una parte de la enramada entraban
> hasta doce labradores sobre doce hermosísimas yeguas, con
> ricos y vistosos jaeces de campo. . .

There follows the description of the dances, executed "con tantas vueltas y con tanta destreza, que aunque don Quijote estaba hecho a ver semejantes danzas, ninguna le había parecido tan bien como aquélla. . . También le pareció bien otra que entró de doncellas hermosísimas. . ." The dances give way to allegorical figures and elaborate recitations, "algunos elegantes y algunos ridículos, y sólo tomó de memoria don Quijote—que la tenía grande—los ya referidos." By this point in the account Don Quixote seems actually to have become our source for the description, so focused through his eyes has the narrative become. Both at the same party, Sancho counts wineskins and Don Quixote memorizes verses, and their eyes are ours. This is the world of the modern novel, and Sancho's rustic praise of Quiteria is simply the centerpiece in this revolutionary recreation of what had been among the commonplace and conventional set pieces in Renaissance literature—the lavish country wedding.

I have tried to give you some idea of the range of innovation which *Don Quixote* represents: the movement away from the established genres of his time, the movement from magic and miracle to providential verisimilitude, and finally, the movement away from all the bother about narrative authority to spectacular advances in the management and manipulation of point of view. So great were the advances achieved by Cervantes that novelists and critics alike are still engaged in discovering and exploring the endless subtleties of his technique.

UNIVERSITY OF FLORIDA

NOTES

1"Manners, Morals, and the Novel," in *The Liberal Imagination* (New York: Viking Press, 1950), p. 203.

2*Mensonge romantique et vérité romanesque* (Paris: Grasset, 1961).

3*Roman des origines et origines du roman* (Paris: Grasset, 1972), p. 11.

4*Literatura y filología,* Fundación Juan March, 60 (May 1978), p. 2.

5*Pricksongs and Descants* (New York: E. P. Dutton, 1969), p. 77.

⁶*The Rise of the Novel* (Berkeley: University of California Press, 1962).

⁷Robert Alter, in his Foreword to the English translation of Marthe Robert, *The Old and the New* (Berkeley: University of California Press, 1977), p. ix.

⁸Harry Levin, *The Gates of Horn*, pp. 44-48.

⁹*Les Noyers de l'Altenburg* (Paris, 1948), pp. 119-21. Cited in Watt, p. 133.

¹⁰*The Gates of Horn*, p. 40

¹¹*Beyond Culture*, (New York, Viking Press, 1955), p. xiii.

¹²Victor Shklovsky (Chklovski), "La Construction de la nouvelle et du roman," from *Sur la théorie de la prose*, in *Théorie de la littérature. Textes des Formalistes russes réunis, présentés et traduits par Tzvetan Todorov* (Paris: Éditions du Seuil, 1965), p. 184.

¹³*Structuralism in Literature* (New Haven: Yale University Press, 1974), p. 85.

¹⁴*Validity in Interpretation* (New Haven: Yale University Press, 1967), p. 74.

¹⁵*Literature as System* (Princeton: Princeton University Press, 1971), p. 128.

¹⁶*Cervantes, Aristotle and the 'Persiles'* (Princeton: Princeton University Press, 1970), pp. 91-130.

¹⁷*Structuralism in Literature*, pp. 132-38.

¹⁸Robert Scholes and Robert Kellogg, *The Nature of Narrative* (New York: Oxford University Press, 1966), p. 15.

¹⁹ *Don Quijote de la Mancha*, ed. John Jay Allen (Madrid: Cátedra, 1977), I, 168n.

²⁰See E. C. Riley, *Cervantes's Theory of the Novel* (Oxford: Clarendon Press, 1962), Chapter V.

²¹Forcione, pp. 40-41.

²²The Fordham Cervantes Lecture, October 27, 1978. The following five paragraphs are excerpts from that lecture. Subsequent citations to Cervantes' works are to page and column in *Obras Completas* (Madrid: Aguilar, 1964).

²³*La novela pastoril española* (Madrid: Revista de Occidente, 1959), p. 76.

²⁴"El Cristo de la Vega and La fuerza de la sangre" in *MLN* 83 (1968), 271-75.

²⁵pp. 242-47.

²⁶Francisco de Quevedo, *Obras Completas*, I, ed. José Manuel Blecua, 2nd edition (Barcelona: Planeta, 1968), 1029.

Cervantes

and the Games of Illusion

RUTH EL SAFFAR

EO SPITZER'S well known essay on *Don Quixote* places Cervantes at the very brink of the world of certitude, at a moment when the order which linked word to referent, and sense perception to objective data teetered precariously, with only the hand of God preventing its fall into chaos.[1]

Many modern critics have tapped the vein in Cervantes' work that leads us to the perplexing epistemological questions it seems to pose. Unlike our seventeenth and eighteenth century counterparts, who thought they *knew*, nineteenth and twentieth century readers find themselves wondering who *is* really mad in *Don Quixote*, and what is the nature of the reality the novel presents.[2]

To work through these questions critics have focused on a number of conflicting elements in *Don Quixote*. Some, the most extreme examples being provided by Unamuno, have pitted Don Quixote against an uncomprehending author and world.[3] Others have chosen to view Don Quixote's posture in the world through the eyes of the many in the novel who find him utterly mad.[4] To break out of this seeming deadlock, interest has turned to the novelistic techniques through which Cervantes created the illusion of reality in his work, most notably to the device of the fictional narrator. The obviously flawed narrator in *Don Quixote*, as many have pointed out, both calls into question the truth of his story and heightens our impression that the character he is presenting is real. Although Cervantes undoubtedly had the Turpins of the romances of chivalry in mind when he created *Don Quixote*, his exploitations of Cide Hamete and his use of the technique of stories within stories align him with the Renaissance development of point of view.

Whether or not we choose to ascribe to Cervantes the epistemological preoccupations that modern critics have found in his work, the fact is that the perspectivism that Américo Castro and Leo Spitzer find as characteristic of *Don Quixote* is part of a Renaissance phenomenon which we traditionally see first manifested in the paintings of Giotto in the fourteenth century. Stephen Gilman's studies of *La Celestina* and *Lazarillo de Tormes* show the presence in Spain in the sixteenth century of an approach to art grounded in the sense that reality, or at least what appears to be reality, is the product of a particular character's version of it.[5]

The location of the perceiving subject in a specific time and place recreates our own experiences with reality at the same time that it reveals the limited nature of our view of it. Necessarily, the abandoning of the univocal sense of order turns attention away from the objects described and toward the subject who is viewing them. The reader or viewer is asked to take into account not only the world the character experiences, but the history of the character that explains why he views the world as he does.

Like the author of *Lazarillo de Tormes*, Cervantes interposes between himself and his story a fictional narrator whose peculiar limitations must color the truth he promises to present. This stepping aside of the author that gives a sense of perspectivism to the work also creates an atmosphere of irony, and again we are in the presence of a phenomenon characteristic of Renaissance art and letters. The author purposely does not identify, nor does he want the reader to identify, with the values expressed by the characters in the work. This disjunction between author and character allows us to appreciate both the character's shortcomings, and those of the literary world that informs his actions and attitudes. In a period of tremendous intellectual and artistic activity, works designed to undermine earlier masterpieces are bound to be generated.

Along with perspectivism and irony, and arising out of the attitudes they spawn, is a tendency in some Renaissance art—I think not only of Shakespeare and Ariosto, but also of Velázquez—to create a multiplicity of levels of fiction within a work. Characters tell stories and create plays for one another, and the reader thus finds, duplicated within the text, the relationship between author, character and audience in which he, on another level, participates.

The reduction of truth to personality, the challenge to previous literary models, and the creation of levels of fiction calls into question, inevitably, the status of the Absolute. In its absence, words would lose their power to evoke things and would become objects themselves, opaque and non-referential. Góngora and Calderón veer in that direction, their sources, references, and productions being inspired from other works of art, and their ornate verbiage calling us to admire the poetic structure apart from the rather simple ground to which it ostensibly refers. For Calderón, at least, God continues to have a role, but it is one absolutely severed from the world his characters inhabit. In the mutable world of time and space, the characters are subject to the most extreme awareness of the limits of their ability to reason, to perceive, and to understand.

This is the situation that Spitzer anticipates in the essay mentioned above, and the situation that Michel Foucault finds in Cervantes: the intuition of a threatened severance of world and word that would indeed plunge us into chaos.[6]

And yet we protest in the case of Cervantes. Surely, without taking sides, without declaring Don Quixote mad or misunderstood, Cide Hamete reliable or deceptive, we can sense that Cervantes ultimately did not consider the human condition such that we are severed from all possibility of perceiving Truth. What I think becomes increasingly clear in Cervantes' works, when viewed chronologically, is that it is precisely as the sense Truth as something available to human intuition becomes more fully appreciated that the games of illusion come more fully into play.

What I will be proposing here is a model for understanding Cervantes' works which allows for perspectivism, irony, and the story-within-a-story structure while offering a view of Cervantes not weighed down by epistemological puzzles, but capable of enjoying the immense freedom that a sense of Truth provides. The illusions which I will discuss, especially as they appear in Part II of *Don Quixote*, are ones that many of the characters consciously employ. When they turn illusion to their own purposes, they experience delight and success. They are limited only by the limits of their ability to disengage themselves from what they are presenting. Don Quixote, to the extent that he identifies with the self he has invented, is incapable of manipulating illusion and becomes its victim. His liberation occurs when he dissociates his being from the mirage he has created.

I see Cervantes sharing with other major writers of his period—Ariosto, Tasso, Calderón, Góngora—the crisis of consciousness that develops when, for all sorts of reasons, the sense of unity between self and community, man and woman, perceiver and perceived, signifier and signified is called into question. What interests me, however, and what I think distinguishes Cervantes from the authors of *La Celestina* and *Lazarillo* and certainly from Calderón, is his working into and back out of the problems that arise when the dominant consciousness is one of separation. Because such consciousness inevitably calls into question the reality of experience, I have chosen the word "illusion" to express the epistemological dilemma facing Cervantes and writers of his age. At a time when the substantiality of the material world was being questioned overtly by major philosophers, Cervantes was digging through the series of novels that stretch from his release from captivity in Algiers to his death-bed in Madrid, for solid ground on which to rest his imagined universe. To give a quick overview of what I am about to unfold in more detail, I would say that *La Galatea* and *Don Quixote* Part I reflect, in their unresolved ending, the persistence of a split in Cervantes' consciousness that is healed in *Don Quixote* Part II and the *Persiles*. In all four long novels we find main characters suffering separation from home, family, and loved-ones, and undergoing struggles that tax their sense of security. What changes, from novel to novel, is the range of things we are invited to see as illusory. In *La Galatea*, though some effort to present various viewpoints is made, the material world is by and large taken very seriously. It is heavy, almost oppressive, and certainly insurmountable for Elicio and the

other characters. There is little play or make-believe, and the interpolated tales told are all first-person accounts of events experienced
by the narrators. In *Don Quixote* Part I, though there is some clumsy
effort at game-playing and disguise, the material world still remains
to all intents and purposes obdurate, and the one character who
presumes to overleap objectives is clearly intended to be seen as
mad. By Part II, however, illusion and invention take on a major
role, and we begin to see a merging of the material and the imaginative, as characters skilled in deception become successful in control-
ling reality. In the *Persiles*, finally, we find a main character who
achieves conscious control over the material world by identifying
not with it but with its intangible creative source. Everything tangi-
ble is rendered illusory and subject to the manipulation of those
who realize that.

Both in the history of Western lyric poetry and in Cervantes'
own history as a novelist, the first expression of the severance of
self and others comes through the experience of unfulfilled love.
Denis de Rougemont has shown us how the tradition of courtly
love was based precisely on unfulfillment and on a renunciation of
social norms.[7] The poetry such a position generates is one that
sharpens the lover's self-perception but does not further his integra-
tion either with his loved-one, or with the church, the family, and
the community. The pastoral novel, that enjoyed a vogue in the
Renaissance and that Cervantes chose as the frame on which to
build his first work, continues the anti social attitude of the courtly
lover, moving the setting out of the city, the girl away from her
family, and the men away from their occupations. Love and the
lover's frustrations become the sole topic of conversation and the
basis for whatever action takes place.

For Elicio, in *La Galatea*, there is no hope and Cervantes brings
the novel to an abrupt end with the lovers still suspended in their
separation and unfulfilled desire. Twenty years elapsed between the
publication of Cervantes' pastoral novel and Part I of *Don Quixote*.
What remains of the pastoral hero Elicio in Cervantes' next novel is
the isolation, the unfulfillment, and the separation of the main character from his community. These problems afflict not only Don
Quixote but all the secondary characters worth naming. Love drops
out as the apparent motivating factor in this new hero's quest as
Don Quixote bursts past the bonds of his nameless village inflamed

with the desire to reform the world. A large part of the uncertainty we sense when confronting Part I of *Don Quixote* comes from the even balance Cervantes maintains throughout between Don Quixote and the host of antagonists who constitute his experience in Part I. A gulf persists from beginning to end between the mad gentleman and the corrupt but solid world that surrounds him. Both seem to lay equal claim to Cervantes' attention, and so he ends Part I allowing society a temporary victory, which he makes clear will erode again before the undiminished power of Don Quixote's madness, and anticipating a second part in which his hero will continue his career undaunted.

What Cervantes does in Part II is to probe to its extreme the experience of isolation, creating a character out of phase not only with his time and place but with his own self. In the process he has created a novel that bears all earmarks of the modern novel as Edward Said has described it: the hero is celibate, literate, and combative.[8] He sets out to fill a void in his own life by creating an alternate one in conflict with his origins. It is interesting that Don Quixote's two major speeches in Part I would deal with the Golden Age and with Arms and Letters. For it all shows how intimately linked are a rejection of the here and now, the development of intellect, and the need to resort to force to settle differences. More interesting still is that this combination of abstraction and force emerges from a character incapable of a relationship with women. In another study I have shown that Don Quixote's inability to deal with women is echoed throughout Part I, where Cervantes seems to go out of his way to expunge mothers from even the smallest sub-stories. Don Quixote inhabits a world in which the feminine as symbol of nurture and stability is totally absent.

In *Don Quixote* Part II a major change seems to have taken place that allows finally for a resolution. In the first two novels Cervantes seems to have ridden two horses, insisting on the truth of apparently inalterable but equally justifiable positions on any number of terms in opposition. In *La Galatea*, Elicio and Galatea were both attended to, the reactions of each justified, yet their desired union barred. In *Don Quixote* Part I Don Quixote and those he encounters earn equal right to a position, and yet each position denies the other so that again no resolution is possible. In *Don Quixote* Part II, and this is where I really want to probe the question of illusion in the works of Cervantes, Don Quixote returns to his village and home and trades in all his inventions—from Rocinante to Dulcinea—after a momentary vision of Truth. The vision allows the defeated Don Quixote to be transformed into the glorified Alosno Quijano "The Good", as resistance gives over to acceptance, not only of home and origin, but of death.

Were this the last of Cervantes' novels we might take little comfort in this "victory", since it seems to proclaim that all of life is vain role-playing and that only at death are we—with luck—vouchsafed a glimpse of the Divine. The *Persiles*, which Cervantes worked on while writing Part II of *Don Quixote* and completed on his own death-bed, offers finally a hero whose fortunes in *this* life are governed by the presence of the Divine, and who lives to enjoy *here* the rewards of a harmonious interaction between himself and others, symbolized now most clearly by his marriage to Sigismunda.

But before showing how the *Persiles* completes the cycle of novels that began with *La Galatea*, we must look at some crucial episodes in Part II of *Don Quixote* that illustrate how Cervantes has altered his vision of the world so as to embrace the terms which had been irreconcilable in earlier works. What emerges very clearly is that the world Don Quixote meets in Part II is literally he himself, at every turn.

It is not just that Don Quixote invented himself. Chapter 2 of Part I makes it clear that Don Quixote is also responsible for the creation of his scribe, Cide Hamete, and for the book that has been written about him. Don Quixote's criticisms of his author at the beginning of Part II and Sancho's comments reveal a sense on the part of both characters that they have the last word on what the book about them says. What we as critics have failed to do, once having enjoyed the enormous literary joke of having a character criticize the author's version of him, is to carry the implications of that situation into the heart of the novel.

If Don Quixote is in fact responsible for the world his author has presented, then Cide Hamete is in some sense Don Quixote himself and everything they jointly create, successes as well as failures, benefactors as well as ill-wishers, reflects the being whose name in the novel is Don Quixote. The confusion Don Quixote experiences in Part II comes from the fact that each item he has created has come into manifestation, but not in the form that he consciously

intended it. Yes, there is a book written about him, but no, it is not
the book he had expected; yes, there is a woman whom Sancho calls
Dulcinea, but no, she is not as he saw her in his mind's eye; yes,
there are knights wandering about in the woods, but no, they are
wearing masks and saying they are Sansón Carrasco and Tomé
Cecial; and yes, there is a chivalric knight called Don Quixote in the
world, but no, the character by that name is ill-at-ease with the
image he has generated. Behind all the bravado, especially in Part II,
hides a strong current of melancholy and self doubt which makes
understandable the otherwise surprising comment of Cide Hamete
on Don Quixote's reception by the Duke and Duchess in chapter 31:
"y aquel fue el primer día que de todo en todo conoció y creyó ser
caballero andante verdadero, y no fantástico."

What we come to understand, in pondering these things, is that
the experience of separation that was envisioned in Part I as a split
between Don Quixote and his material surroundings is envisioned
in Part II as a split between parts of the main character himself. The
identity of the hero and his self-creation as Don Quixote is loosened
in Part II, producing a character prone to contemplation and melancholy, slow to jump into his knightly image, and sensitive to his
bodily hunger and fatigue as never in Part I.

Having removed himself, ever so slightly, from the inverted
image, Don Quixote often looks on in amazement at the world
which reflects back on him more than he had intended, and much
that he does not recognize as his. If it takes Don Quixote the entire
novel to release as false the invented self, the author makes it clear
early in the work that *he* now perceives his character as the inhabit-
ant of a world entirely of his own making. This is the only way to
understand the ending. It is not that there *is* no origin, no destiny,
no Truth, but that between beginning and end stretches a vast
wonderland of illusion, generated out of everyone's letter-bound
imaginations, and often, though not necessarily, divorced from the
source of reality out of which everything springs. But what we
must examine here is the degree to which Cervantes shows us that
Don Quixote is responsible for the enchanters which plague him.
Close examination of the episode of the enchantment of Dulcinea,
the first of Don Quixote's adventures once on the road in Part II,
reveals that Sancho did *not* in fact enchant Dulcinea. We laugh at
Sancho's later readiness to agree in Chapter 34 when the Duchess

suggests that Dulcinea really is enchanted but there is more wisdom there than we generally appreciate.

Sancho tried several times in Chapter 9 to tell Don Quixote that they would not find Dulcinea in El Toboso because, like his master, Sancho himself had never been there and had never seen her. Don Quixote refused to hear Sancho's protestations, however, and reminded Sancho that he *had* described a peasant girl to him in detail after his return from her village in Part I. Sancho, then, simply took the script that Don Quixote, in his attachment to the illusion he had created, gave him, and produced the peasant girl Don Quixote asked for.

Throughout the first part of Part II we find discussions, characters, and episodes that reflect a preoccupation with the question of illusion. The key to the new atmosphere is available in a simple contrast in the opening settings of the two novels. In Part I Don Quixote sets out at dawn and seems perpetually to be awake. We envision a sun-drenched Manchegan plain and a hero whose vigils sustain the flame of consciousness through the night. In Part II Don Quixote and Sancho are concerned more with arriving than with setting out. They have a series of destinations that regularly determine their direction—El Toboso, Camacho's wedding, Montesinos' cave, Zaragoza, Barcelona—something not characteristic of their peregrinations in Part I.

The first goal is El Toboso, they arrive at midnight. The braying of donkeys and other farm animals fills the air. Absent is consciousness of human activity. Throughout Part II we will see increased attention paid to those elements which suggest the unconscious world: sleep, darkness, and animals. Monkeys, wild boars, pigs and bulls figure in Part II as creatures independent of Don Quixote's consciousness. The sea is also there, later in the novel, and along the way a surcease from travel is offered in the refuge of a number of quiet enclosures: Don Diego de Miranda's home, the hut of Basilio and Quiteria, the cave, the palace of the Duke and Duchess, and Don Antonio's home in Barcelona. The Knight of the Mirrors who challenged Don Quixote toward the beginning of his adventures in Part II defeats him as the Knight of the White Moon at the end. Both present images of reflection, of passivity, of the world in its material manifestation. That the first effort of Don Quixote in Part II would be to seek the lady in her place of origin and to find in her

absence a town locked in silence and asleep except for the disquiet-
ing sounds of animals suggests a turning in a new direction that will
be consistent with the entire second part of Don Quixote. Throughout Part II Don Quixote is being asked to look beneath appearances,
to expand his identifications of himself to include his entire experience and not just that part of it that he believes is he.

I suggest that the series of episodes that begins with the trip to
El Toboso in Chapter 8 and ends with the meeting of the Duke and
Duchess in Chapter 30 constitutes a persistent effort on Don Quixote's part to catch a glimpse of the hidden world of the unconscious
and to break the strangle-hold of ego-consciousness that allows the
enchanters to romp through his world unchecked.

Intellectually, Don Quixote knows that appearance is a sham,
and that reality is elsewhere. After leaving El Toboso, the first thing
he and Sancho meet is a chariot carrying actors. Don Quixote,
though he calls them by the figures their costumes represent, recognizes their masks as such, and later discourses to Sancho on the
vanity of appearances: "Pues lo mismo. . . acontece en la comedia y
trato de este mundo, donde unos hacen los emperadores, otros los
pontífices, y finalmente, todas cuantas figuras se pueden introducir
en una comedia; pero en llegando al fin, que es cuando se acaba la
vida, a todos les quita la muerte las ropas que los diferenciaban, y
quedan iguales en la sepultura." And yet, in the next episode, when
he meets the Knight of the Mirrors, he refuses to see Tomé Cecial
and Sansón Carrasco beneath the grotesque costumes the false
knight and squire have assumed.

When Don Quixote meets the Knight of the Green Coat, he
shows clearly the difference between knowledge and wisdom.
Before the single totally undisguised figure in Part II, and the one
whose life style most closely resembles that of Alonso Quijano, he
demonstrates both unbelievable folly—thinking cheese curds to be
his melting brain, and challenging a lion to fight—and great intelligence, speaking knowledgeably of literature, child rearing, and
sundry other matters.

Taken all together, we see that what Don Quixote lacks is not
knowledge of the world but knowledge of self. Though he has
created his scribe, he cannot see himself in the picture the scribe
presents of him. He recognizes that everyone is an actor yet cannot
dissociate himself from the role he himself has chosen; he unmasks

the Knight of the Mirrors yet clings to the mirage Sansón has created. Don Quixote's world is ridden with enchanters and illusion because he insists on taking as real an image of himself that is of his own creation.

In the next several episodes after leaving Don Diego's home, Don Quixote will encounter characters who are successful because they have learned that only by understanding themselves can they master the world. The student fencers demonstrate the superiority of training over force. The one who wins does so because he has studied and learned to control the thrusts and parries of his sword. The opponent, who lacks such control, is roundly defeated. Basilio performs an identical feat on a different terrain in the next episode. Unlike earlier Cervantine characters faced with the parental decision of the loved one to marry her to someone richer or more noble, Basilio does not collapse in despair when he learns that Quiteria is to be wed to the rich Camacho. What he does do is to behave *as if* he had collapsed in despair. By consciously playing a role that others unconsciously expect of him, he is able to exploit their automatic responses to his benefit. Rather than losing, he wins the girl.

Don Quixote will show in the Cave of Montesinos episode that he is unable to see himself in others, and Cervantes will show at the same time that those others—Durandarte, Montesinos, Belerma, Dulcinea, the crystal palace—are what Don Quixote is. The brave knight is a tiny portion of his whole being, and all the pinchings, beatings, scratchings, tramplings, and humiliations that follow the visit to Montesinos' cave are designed to dislodge the hero from the knight with whom he is identified so that everything else can be recognized.

The final major episode before the period of torment that extends from chapter 30 to the end is that of Master Peter. Master Peter is truly a master, and Don Quixote is right in throwing himself finally upon the puppet stage. For Master Peter has worked him as surely as he has worked any of the knights and ladies on his tableau, pressing insistently on Don Quixote's self-image until he has eroded whatever distance Don Quixote had begun to establish between himself and it. Master Peter's true mastery comes from his extension of the "all the world's a stage" homily that Don Quixote thought he understood in Chapter 12 to include himself. It is not just puppets he controls, but himself as puppeteer. The real master is Ginés de Pasamonte, whose stage is everywhere, and whose self is whatever role the situation calls for.

The limited consciousness that Don Quixote finally transcends at the end of the novel is one from which Cide Hamete had also suffered. That is why Don Quixote's transfiguration would have remained incomplete had Cide Hamete not also entered the final pages with his famous comment that he and Don Quixote are one. All of Part II thus traces a circle. End touches beginning, antagonists recognize their mutual dependence, and illusion is dissolved in truth.

But figures such as Ginés de Pasamonte and the Captain in Part I, and Basilio and Master Peter in Part II point out what the *Persiles* will make unmistakably clear: illusion and truth do not have to be mutually exclusive terms. Cervantes ultimately does not inhabit the universe Calderón depicted. Spirit and matter are not forever consigned to non-tangential spheres for Cervantes. Illusion is simply the result of taking the part for the whole. The thief, the magician, the puppeteer and the actor all demonstrate the control over appearances that the skillful possess. In all cases the control results from careful attention to the automatic responses and unconscious roles those around them assume. By anticipating these responses and roles, the trickster can as easily control his acquaintances as a puppeteer the marionettes on his strings.

Kerenyi, Jung and others have pointed out what the Tarot deck also shows: the presence of the divine lurks in the figure of the trickster.[9] What Ginés and Rinconete do simply to show off is demonstrated on a more serious level by Cervantes' most successful heroes. Although minor figures who attain their goals appear as early as *La Galatea*, it is not until the *Persiles* that the hero himself struggles through isolation and confusion to union and victory. In earlier examples of successful quests, the hero found himself in the hands of the enemy whom he had, by deceit rather than force, to overcome. Silerio escapes the Turks and wins his lady in *La Galatea*; Ricardo deceives and destroys Turks in *El amante liberal*; the Captain deceives his Moslem captors in Algiers. But in *Don Quixote* Part II and the *Persiles*, the guile necessary for success is practiced on compatriots. Basilio fools all those at the wedding including Quiteria herself, with his false suicide, and Persiles lies to his brother and to his friend and equal, Prince Arnaldo. In the later versions of the successful hero, it seems, Cervantes no longer needs to justify deceit by having his characters practice it on unworthy opponents. Deceit becomes part of a larger view of one's place in the universe and becomes an aspect of Truth.

Combined with the emphasis on role-playing and self-knowledge in *Don Quixote* Part II is a tendency to replace violence with drama. The student fencers consider their sword battle a demonstration rather than an expression of anger. The jousts at Zaragoza toward which Don Quixote was heading until Chapter 59 also contain the battle between knights within the arena, where it becomes a show, a demonstration of skill. Everywhere Don Quixote goes he finds actors or puppeteers, or people staging situations for their entertainment, and always the emphasis is on the skill of the perpetrators in creating the illusion of reality.

What happens in the *Persiles* is that the hero begins his journey where Don Quixote, or Alonso Quijano, ended his. For Persiles the whole world is truly a stage in which he is an actor. He and Sigismunda start out in chaos, confusion and separation, and have shed every trace of their backgrounds, relinquishing even their sexual identity at the time the story begins.[10] They assume new names— Periandro and Auristela; pretend a new relationship—brother and sister; and replace their regal finery with the clothing of pilgrims. What distinguishes them from Don Quixote is that they do all of this with a grand design fully in mind, and with the consciousness of their origins fully intact. They do not identify their whole selves with the images they project. The origin and destiny that Don Quixote tried to reject by creating a new self become for Periandro and Auristela the truth which sustains them through their trials. The trials themselves, though keenly felt and suffered through, take on a symbolic quality and lose the finality that such trials without a sense of destiny have.

If Persiles and Sigismunda represent the inner selves who guide Periandro and Auristela, we see that the whole of material reality is for them in fact an illusion. But the playing out of the illusion is what serves in its turn to release Persiles and Sigismunda from the political/familial impasse that holds them apart. Illusion and truth are thus mutually sustaining elements in man's spiritual/material journey. In another article I have shown how Cervantes makes it clear through a series of secondary stories in the *Persiles* that to abandon either the spiritual or the material side of his nature is to plunge the character into failure and despair.[11] One falls into the traps of illusion only when one confuses truth with that portion of it that one considers his own. Faithful always to their origins as Persiles and Sigismunda, Periandro and Auristela use their assumed identities as a means to thread their way through the seeming obstacles that block their union. They never use force though they frequently misrepresent themselves and their intentions to potential enemies. The constancy of their affirmation of their goal stands like a beacon guiding their journey.

If not the most entertaining, by far the most complex of Cervantes' works is the *Persiles*, which succeeds not only in bringing origin and destiny into harmony with experience in time, but in showing structurally the interpenetration of matter and spirit. The solid ground from which fiction and illusion spring is found at the spiritual center where origin and destiny are one.

Don Quixote shows us that fiction and illusion are products of our material experience in time and space, and that they die when life on this planet comes to an end. What *Persiles and Sigismunda* show us, however, is that fiction and illusion need not wrest the traveler from his/her consciousness of origin and destiny. Their marriage, along with the structure of the romance in which they figure as principal characters, reveals that their physical manifestation as opposites is capable of being transcended.

In the *Persiles* Cervantes by and large abandons the techniques that characterize his age and his two *Don Quixotes*. Gone are the fictional narrators, the levels of fiction and the ironic distance. In their place is a celebration of the sense—most highly developed in *Persiles and Sigismunda*—that one is not chained to a particular viewpoint in time and space but free to manipulate the material world, secure in an all-pervading consciousness of achievable harmony and perfection. The *Persiles* enacts the mystery of the resurrection.

A curious duplication of some of the things I have been talking about here occurs in a twentieth century novel explicitly structured around the theme of the redemption of fallen matter through the power of the spirit. I refer to Pérez de Ayala's *Belarmino y Apolonio* which also ends in an epiphany and unfolds during Holy Week, the crises in the lives of the main protagonists paralleling the crisis experienced in the saga of Christ's crucifixion and resurrection.

At some point in the novel the narrator/character Pedro (don Guillén) is discoursing on the mistaken growth in the church of the belief that happiness is attainable only in the afterlife, while in this one we are to resign ourselves to misery and suffering. He says:

> La Iglesia nació como un ensayo de organización para la felicidad. En las Epístolas de San Pablo vemos, sin posible interpretación en contrario, que el Apóstol. . . creía. . . que el Salvador volvería a establecer el reino de la felicidad sobre la tierra. . . Pero sucedió en Tesalónica que algunos de los convertidos se murieron. . . El Apóstol vio al cabo que él y todos los cristianos tenían que morirse; pero como no podía renunciar a la felicidad, decidió que no se moría sino el cuerpo, y que el espíritu, inmortal, iba a la Gloria.

This is the separation that I believe Cervantes overcame in his last works, transcending thereby the perspectivist, ironic, tormented expressions characteristic of his age.

To conclude, having jumped from the Renaissance into the twentieth century, let me return to a text that takes us back to our collective origins, to Genesis. Not to the story of the fall but the first story of Creation:

> So God created man in his own image, in the image of God created he him; male and female created he them. And God blessed them and God said unto them, be fruitful, and multiply and replenish the earth, and subdue it: and have dominion over the fish of the sea, and over the fowl of the air, and over every living thing that moveth over the earth.   (I, 27-28)

This is the tradition of the power over the material world that was man's original promise and continuing challenge. This is the tradition which Cervantes, in his own work, recaptured.

UNIVERSITY OF ILLINOIS, CHICAGO CIRCLE

NOTES

[1]"Linguistic Perspectivism in the *Don Quijote,*" *in Linguistics and Literary History: Essays in Stylistics* (Princeton: Princeton University Press, 1948).

[2]The most common assumption in nineteenth and twentieth century criticism has been to see in Don Quixote a major human figure: either a misunderstood hero, or a character embarked on a mission of personal development that marks him ultimately as superior to his companions. The difficulty in apprehending the

value and purpose of the hero in *Don Quixote* is neatly summed up in John J. Allen's title, *Don Quixote: Hero or Fool?* (Gainesville: University of Florida Press, 1969). For a review, useful though strongly biased against romantic and perspectivist readings of *Don Quixote*, of critical approaches to the novel, see Anthony Close's *The Romantic Approach to "Don Quixote"* (Cambridge: The Cambridge University Press, 1978).

³See *La vida de Don Quijote y Sancho*.

⁴Some recent essays which seek to reestablish the spirit of burlesque that may have motivated Cervantes are P. E. Russell's *"Don Quixote* as a Funny Book," in *MLR*, 64 (1969), 312-26; Anthony Close's "Don Quixote as a Burlesque Hero," in *Forum*, 9 (1974), 365-78; and Martín de Riquer's "Don Quijote: caballero por escarnio," *Clavileño*, 7 (1956), 47-50.

⁵*The Art of "La Celestina"* (Madison: University of Wisconsin Press, 1956); and "The Death of Lazarillo de Tormes," *PLMA*, 81 (1966), 149-66.

⁶*The Order of Things* (translated from *Les mots et les choses*) (New York: Pantheon Books, 1971.

⁷In *Love in the Western World* (translated by Montgomery Belgion) (New York: Pantheon Books, 1956).

⁸See his *Beginnings: Intention and Method* (New York: Basic Books, 1975).

⁹In Paul Radin's *The Trickster: A Study in American Indian Mythology* (New York: Schocken Books, 1972) appear two commentaries directly related to the image of the trickster, the first by Karl Kerenyi, "The Trickster in Relation to Greek Mythology," pps. 173-91; and the other by Carl Jung, "On the Psychology of the Trickster Figure," pps. 195-211). See also Kerenyi's *Hermes: Guide of Souls* (translated by Murray Stein) (Zurich: Spring Publications, 1976). For an interesting study of the Tarot, see Fred Gettings' *The Book of Tarot* (London: Triune Press, 1973).

¹⁰Persiles and Sigismunda first find each other in Book I, after two years' separation, dressed in opposite-sex clothing.

¹¹"Three Versions of the Feminine in the *Persiles*," to be published in the Proceedings of the Fordham University Twenty-Fifth Annual Lecture Series on Cervantes, and in Spanish in *Revista canadiense de estudios hispánicos*.

Double Vision: Self and Society in *El Laberinto de Amor* and *La entretenida*

EDWARD H. FRIEDMAN

N THE WORLD OF literary creation, as well as in the world of literary theory and criticism, anti-type is as certain to follow type as the night the day. The rejection of a given mode or the choice of an alternate technique presupposes a model and an operative system of rules implicit in the model. To break rules, one must be conscious of the rules; to invent an anti-type, one must acknowledge the conventions of a prototype. When an author works with both a model and its antithetical counterpart, there may emerge a dialectical relationship between the two which gives them a greater richness as a unit than individually. Cervantes' *El Laberinto de amor* may be seen as the complication of a model, and his *La entretenida* as the deflation or parody of a model. Jointly, the plays serve as a base from which to analyze the concept of role-playing as treated by Cervantes. Ultimately, the prominent feature of the two plays may be a lack of correspondence between ideological perspectives, an intentional and insoluble hermeneutic tension, a self-defining Baroque texture. The dual context relegates

absolute values to relative values, and converts apparent truth into falsehood or enigma. In the plays, irony, ambiguity, and conceptual contradiction characterize both process and product.

The *comedia de capa y espada* may be classified as a series of variations on a theme of identity. Literary figures adopt and invent roles to overcome obstacles to love and their elaborate schemes provide complication of dramatic action and suspense, the substance, so to speak, between boy meeting girl and boy getting girl. Resumption of true identity, often synonymous with a regaining of honor, generally brings about the dénouement. Pairs of lovers are as important in this form of drama as rhyming couplets are in certain verse forms, and the *capa y espada* plays commonly end with multiple marriages or promises of marriage. In *El Laberinto de amor*, Cervantes works within this framework to create six characters in search of a marriage who attempt to control the dramatic events by becoming authors themselves, creators of plays designed to bring amorous rewards. Once the efforts have been resolved, with either resounding or qualified success, the conscious role-playing ends. Those who clearly triumph do so not because the gods have favored them, but because they have played their self-imposed roles with the greatest vigor and ingenuity.

In *La entretenida*, Cervantes presents an antithetical alternative to the triple marriage dénouement of *El Laberinto de amor*; frustrated plans rather than happy endings are the order of the day. The collective failure appears to concern Cervantes as much in this work as the group betrothal which marks the conventional *capa y espada* play. In accord with the evident intention of changing the *capa y espada* format, Cervantes uses parallel love intrigues with an opposite purpose: in *La entretenida*, representatives of distinct social classes share mutual defeat. The characters who resort to impersonation and role-playing are depicted not as ingenious and justified but as dishonest, and their schemes are finally thwarted. In effect, what works for the characters of *El Laberinto de amor* does not work for those of *La entretenida*, and an explanation of this difference may clarify the structure of both plays.

In *El Laberinto de amor*, the three female protagonists plot to win the men they love. Rosamira, together with Dagoberto, devises an elaborate plot to delay and finally to cancel her marriage to the man chosen by her father. To win her freedom, Rosamira risks being accused of dishonor, is imprisoned in a tower, and plans an escape. The other women, Julia and Porcia, run away from home while making it appear as if they have been kidnaped, adopt numerous disguises, and put their honor in jeopardy in a calculated effort to win the men of their dreams, or to turn dreams into reality. All three women are successful, Dagoberto's defiance of the social norm allows him to marry Rosamira, and Manfredo and Anastasio—even though both love Rosamira—willingly accept Julia and Porcia. Manfredo says to Julia, "Tu industria y el cielo han hecho/que les seamos esposos; /ellos son lances forçosos; /no hay sino hacerles buen pecho."[1] Porcia will marry her cousin Anastasio when they receive the expected papal dispensation.

El *Laberinto de amor* is, in essence, a fully sustained play-within-a-play. Until the final scene, no one is ever himself; each character plays a succession of roles, and the invented plots often intermix. Cervantes carries this device to its uppermost limit at the end of the second act, when Anastasio (as a farmer) asks Porcia (as the peasant Rutilio) to enter the prison as a farmgirl to deliver a message to Rosamira. This results in the exchange of clothes between Porcia and Rosamira; Porcia remains in the tower acting the part of Rosamira and Rosamira departs as a farmgirl. Thus, Rosamira, while collaborating in Dagoberto's scheme, pretends to be the farmgirl, who is really Porcia playing the role of Rutilio in the service of Anastasio, himself feigning the role of farmer. In this theatricalized universe, the only truthful story comes within fiction, when Julia in the role of Camilo interpolates an account of her unrequited love for Manfredo into the "false" story of Camilo.

If fictional creation transforms reality in *El Laberinto de amor*, it merely confirms reality in *La entretenida*. With the aid of the deceptive squire Muñoz, the student Cardenio plots to win Marcela Almendárez by pretending to be her cousin Don Silvestre, to whom she is engaged. When the arrival of the real Don Silvestre foils the plan, the projected union faces a more serious obstacle: the cousins are unable to obtain a papal dispensation for their marriage. Similarly, when Don Antonio's efforts to wed Marcela Osorio through proper means seem to be successful, Marcela asserts her own will in favor of Don Ambrosio and nullifies the permission which her father has granted Don Antonio. Marcela's written statement of her preference for Don Ambrosio will lead to marriage only if the pair can overcome the vindictive nature of her father. The kitchen-maid Cristina is both fickle and proud, and perfectly disposed to encourage quasi-chivalric struggles among her suitors. She degrades Ocaña's position as lackey while pursuing the page Quiñones and being pursued by the *capigorrón* Torrente. Ultimately rejected by Quiñones, she finds Ocaña's offer to marry her no longer stands, and Torrente's implication in Cardenio's masquerade removes him as a possible choice. Cervantes accentuates the almost total failure at pairing by calling for a series of exit lines which allude to these failures and lead to Ocaña's final speech—and the last words of the play—to the effect that ". . . acaba sin matrimonio / la comedia entretenida."[2]

The outcome supports beautifully the thesis of Thomas Austin O'Connor in his article, "Is the Spanish *Comedia* a Metatheater?" Arguing that Lionel Abel's concept of metatheater, with its emphasis on the "world as stage" and "life as dream" metaphors, is incongruous with a theocentric and moral worldview, O'Connor states: "For the Spanish dramatists the world is indeed a stage—but a real stage. Consider the ending of any serious *comedia* and one cannot help but realize that they are rejecting the idea of role-playing or falsity to a theological purpose inherent in everyday life. The man who 'plays' a part is unauthentic, false and inevitably doomed to deceiving himself about the nature of reality. The man who is true to his Christian faith is not an actor; he is being proved and tested by God. He is not playing a role; and thus, armed with faith, that implacable Spanish value, he has absolute certainty that his worldview is true."[3] Because their roles are not genuine, those who play roles in *La entretenida* are destined to fail, since—in O'Connor's words— "virtue is the humble acceptance and pursuit of one's God-given destiny."[4]

Because of her social position, Cristina—as the focal character of *La entretenida*—not only places herself in a world of literary illusion (a world of chivalric and courtly love), but she sees a possibility for upward mobility in society, actually an impossibility at that time. The literary illusion, then, is complemented by a social analogue. In Cristina's dramatization of her situation, she is a lady and her suitors are knights prepared to fight for her. Cristina is, in addition, the director of a "real" theatrical piece, a dance and an interlude, during which two of her suitors fight, though hardly in a knightly fashion. Cristina's final choice of Quiñones over Ocaña reflects her inability to "act well her role," to develop a sense of decorum, to recognize that her assigned part in the great theater of life is what is of value from the theological perspective. In terms of poetic justice, her final loss comes from not being true to herself. Similarly, Torrente cannot marry Cristina because of his earlier choice to accept a more signifant, though illusory, role in Muñoz' fictional plot over his true role in life. Ocaña, who is true to the role destiny has given him even though he laments his fate, finally has the opportunity to reject the woman who has previously scorned him. Ocaña is a poor actor, unwilling and perhaps unable to give an acceptable performance as a courtly suitor, and this ultimately works to his disadvantage. The page Quiñones, like Ocaña, only half-heartedly enters Cristina's illusion, and when he finally has to make a decision regarding marriage to Cristina, he rejects her, perhaps because he is faithful to the social hierarchy, or because he is punishing her for asking him to play a role, or because he is in fact not in love with her.

Cristina's social-climbing and her histrionic tendencies find their nemesis in Ocaña's pride. Cristina destroys what would be a perfectly acceptable match by ostracizing Ocaña on the basis of his social position, and by the time she is willing to face reality, Ocaña is unwilling to marry a woman scorned by another; as he has said earlier, there is little difference between a lackey and a page in social terms,[5] and in theological terms there is no difference. Ocaña's rejection of Cristina is to a large degree a rejection of her presumption, the presumption which keeps the true Cristina out of the play. Ocaña is the substance, and Cristina—as the spectator sees her, or fails to see her—is merely a false projection of the "true" person. The incompatability and the dénouement are logical and inevitable consequences of this mismatch.

According to the social hierarchy, Cardenio cannot possibly marry Marcela Almendárez. His aspirations to move upward in a rigidly static system lead him to resort to impersonation. Rather than remain an actor in life's (God's) drama, he becomes an actor in Muñoz' metaplay, contrived to bring riches to its author and a noble wife and a life of luxury to the lead actor. Cardenio's inability to play his natural role is mirrored in his lack of skill in Muñoz' plot. To a certain extent, the real Don Silvestre, in his attempt to marry his first cousin Marcela, is also challenging the natural order and the religious dogma which prohibits such matches. He is rejecting his role as cousin to become Marcela's husband. This is role-playing of a different sort, but it nonetheless involves destroying a "true" identity to create a false (anti-natural) self. Marcela may be seen as an innocent victim, but one could rationalize her bad luck as the result of her tendency to create fiction from reality. She creates an incestuous relationship between herself and her brother from his exhortations to Marcela Osorio; her mental fiction is an ironic analogue to the theologically incestuous relationship between her and Don Silvestre. Her perhaps subconscious wish to be the bride or beloved of her brother—that is, to change her role—may be understood as justification for her failure to find a suitable marriage partner. Marcela's confidante and counterpart, Dorotea, on the other hand, becomes so immersed in her role as friend that she does not play the legitimate role of unmarried woman, and so she remains without a husband. In the majority of the *comedias de capa y espada*, characters like Dorotea exist to be married off at the end of the play to characters left without brides, in order to complete the comic equilibrium. In the case of Dorotea, the effect is the opposite: one more person is left unspoken for.

The second Marcela, Marcela Osorio, rewrites the social scenario. She challenges that aspect of her role as daughter which dictates that she have no say in the choice of her future husband. This aspect of her role is primarily a social rather than theological condition. Marcela Osorio dramatizes the situation in a unique fashion: she is a writer; that is, she puts her ideas into writing. The case is left unresolved, and the spectator does not know whether Marcela will be successful in her assertion of will or whether her father Don Pedro will take seriously his vow to avenge the social crime. The spectator does know, however, that Marcela's plan is successful insofar as she will not be forced to marry Don Antonio, because his interest in his own honor (and thus, in appearance) makes him decide not to pursue Marcela any longer, now that she has put her feelings into writing. She has made herself the author of a document which expresses her need for independence, and this metadocument, if you will, assures her of at least partial success.

Don Antonio seems to be playing his role well. He goes through conventional channels to win the woman he loves. And yet he comes across as an actor of sorts, a man who recites and sighs rather than feels. He is playing the role of lover quite nicely, but the woman herself seems to be of little importance. Her absence, as a point of departure for his lyrical tirades, seems to be of greater value to him than her presence. Cervantes underlines this point by making Marcela Osorio a purely offstage character, a mental image rather than a woman of flesh and blood, a phantasm who would probably be of less interest to Don Antonio if she were to present herself. Somewhat ironically, the most effective passage of acting seems to have been done as well out of the spectator's range. Don Ambrosio, who like Don Antonio worships Marcela from afar, apparently has played the role well enough to make Marcela defy her father and her social role. Nevertheless, as a counterpart to Don Ambrosio. he has not been playing the role of suitor according to society's rules, and even though one obstacle (Don Antonio) has been removed, another more powerful obstacle (Don Pedro) remains.

In sum, the group failure in *La entretenida* results from the negation of the true self, as seen from various perspectives. The characters cannot fulfill their goals because these goals are misdirected and because the assumed roles are inauthentic. In the strict theological sense, then, each person should act in a manner appropriate to his station in life, for it is the quality of acting rather than the stature of the role which will bring eternal rewards. I cannot take credit for this argument because it is O'Connor's argument applied to *La entretenida*. And it is, I believe, an argument which is only half— exactly half—right. While it works for *La entretenida*, it does not work, for example, for *El Laberinto de amor.*

O'Connor stresses an axiom relating to man's true identity and a corollary which opposes role-playing as the creation of false identities and the denial of the real self. "Life is not a stage, and man is not an actor," he says. "Spain's dramatists were stressing man's theatrical or dramatic nature only by emphasizing his acceptance of the notion that life is a dream and the world, a stage, and of the falsity that that notion implies."[6] But can it be that Calderón is saying in *La vida es sueño* that life is not a dream, and in *El gran teatro del mundo* that the world is not a stage? The case is ambiguous because there exists another equally valid corollary: those who play their roles well are emulating the Christian who recognizes that to act well one's role is to win the eternal life; the effective actor in society is analogous to the good Christian on the road to paradise. The first corollary links heaven and earth, in the sense that the divine hierarchy is maintained on earth in social codes. The characters of *La entretenida* attempt to change the social order, which may be considered a reflection of a higher order; they look straight ahead when they should be looking upward, and they fail. But what distinguishes the role-playing—ultimately the cause of defeat—of these characters from that of the characters of *El Laberinto de amor*? In the latter case, those who invent the most complex and well-designed fictions fulfill their goals, as do a large number of characters of the *comedia* in general: *mujeres vestidas de hombre,* ingenious servants, lovers attempting to overcome obstacles to gain a promise of marriage.

Calderón's metaphors may be viewed in a positive theological sense. Life is a dream because it leads to an awakening to a higher life, a theater because is is a rehearsal for this higher life, and man wins eternity by acting well in this life. Segismundo's appearance in Basilio's court encompasses both metaphors in the dream-within-a-dream motif. The playing of a role will determine Segismundo's future: playing the role well, he will become king, and playing it poorly, he will return to the tower, a choice somewhat like going to heaven or hell. Life is illusory because it is incomplete, dependent on the more comprehensive concept of an afterlife, but life itself is a metaphor for this eternal life. Incidents in this life, as illustrated in Segismundo's story, are microcosms of events in the eternal life. Acting out one's destiny in life is playing a role, *El gran teatro del mundo* tells us, and this life is both a training ground for and a simulacrum of the eternal life, *La vida es sueño* tells us. Role-playing is clearly a part of this, but what is the dividing line between legitimate role-playing and illegitimate role-playing? When is role-playing to be condoned and when condemned?

One answer could be that those whose role-playing reflects good intentions and harms neither the true identity nor other people are justified in their undertakings, while those whose role-playing negates the self or true faith are wrong. Yet this explanation leads to contradictions. Cristina in *La entretenida* may live in a dream world, but she could serve God as well married to a page or a lackey. Dagoberto's plot to marry Rosamira in *El Laberinto de amor* actually does hurt Manfredo, a legitimate suitor truly in love with Rosamira.

In one play, cousins will probably be allowed to marry; in another, they will not, even though the second couple is less guilty of role-playing. The answer seems to lie not in poetic justice but in social justice. One's view of role-playing is greatly affected by his view of society, whether as an earthly counterpart of the divine order or as an agent inimical to the individual will and to the development of the true self.

If life on earth mirrors eternal life (that is, if life is figuratively a dream and the world is figuratively a stage), then man's actions on earth reflect the divine order. If man's ability as an actor—the role being his genuine identity—determines his future life, then every man should be concerned with defining and living within the requisites of his role. Yet there is sometimes a conflict between a yearning for self-fullfilment and social rules imposed by man himself. For the individual, the social restrictions interrupt the process toward fulfilment, toward the adequate performance of what he considers his genuine self. Metadrama provides the only means of dealing with social standards which need to be modified or reconsidered. In this case, the discrepancy involves only the social structure and not the divine plan. The women in *El Laberinto de amor*, for example, seem to feel that to successfully fulfill their roles as women and wives, it is necessary to choose a proper husband. The men they choose are of the same social class, are willing to marry them, and provide nothing which would be unacceptable to the divine scheme (except, in one case, kinship, which should be acceptable grounds for papal dispensation). The women, then, do not reject their roles, but attempt to play their roles better. In doing so, they challenge society, not God.

From the opposing stance, however, society's rules may be seen as analogues of God's rules. What is anti-social becomes anti-natural, so that defiance of society's rules implies defiance of the divine order which society mirrors. One who compromises his God-given role in life is making himself, rather than God, the metaphorical dramatist. A number of characters in *La entretenida*, for example, deny their genuine roles. Cristina is fully aware of her social role, but rejects this role in favor of another role in society (noblewoman) and a literary role as well (a lady in the chivalric tradition). Her interest in theatrical representation (the dance and interlude) underlines her failure to accept her given role in life. Cardenio and Muñoz cannot but recognize the moral error of their plot, but they continue the masquerade as a means of gaining stature and riches (earthly rewards) rather than looking toward the eternal life and its everlasting rewards. The marriage between Don Silvestre and Marcela Almendárez cannot take place because marriage would be anti-natural, because marriage would cause each to reject his role as kinsman.

Man's freedom to interpret the will of God leads to certain problems. Role-playing can be seen in a positive and in a negative light. Social rules may be seen as constructive and necessary or as repressive and arbitrary. Earthly life can be venerated as a microcosm of eternal life or condemned as illusory reality. This is certainly Baroque tension at play, and in his two *capa y espada* plays, Cervantes illustrates the tension by presenting both perspectives, by arguing both sides, by complicating his model and reversing it. Here, synthesis is a lack of synthesis, truth is relative, and resolution of the identity problem is a never-ending problem for the critic and the metacritic.

ARIZONA STATE UNIVERSITY

NOTES

[1] Miguel de Cervantes Saavedra, *Obras de Miguel Cervantes Saavedra*, II, *Obras Dramáticas*, ed. Francisco Ynduráin, Biblioteca de Autores Españoles, CLVI (Madrid: Ediciones Atlas, 1962), 358.

[2] *Ibid.*, p. 420.

[3] *HR*, 43 (1975), 279.

[4] *Ibid.*, 287.

[5] ". . . en mi conciencia, / que ay muy poca diferencia / entre vn lacayo y vn page. / La longura de vn cauallo / puede medirla a compás, / yo adelante, y él detrás" (BAE ed., p. 364).

[6] O'Connor, pp. 286-87. Bruce W. Wardropper has been an eloquent spokesman for the metatheatrical dimension of the *comedia*. For refutations of O'Connor's position, see Stephen Lipmann, " 'Metatheater' and the Criticism of the *Comedia*," *MLN*, 91 (1976), 231-46; and Susan L. Fischer, "Calderón's *Los cabellos de Absalón*: A Metatheater of Unbridled Passion," *BCom*, 28 (1976), 103-13, esp. 103-05.

Picaresque and Pastoral
in *La ilustre fregona*

ROBERT M. JOHNSTON

OR MANY READERS of Spanish Golden Age literature, pastoral and picaresque represent opposing generic types. Pastoral is idealistic, literary, artificial. Picaresque is characterized by an earthy realism and is anti-idealist to the point of cynicism. Pastoral treats delicate topics of philosophy and love among courtiers in shepherd's disguise, while picaresque treats lowly subjects. Pastoral romance expired due to the artificiality of its outworn conventions.[1] Picaresque novels can be seen in relation to the development of realism that leads to the modern novel.[2]

This contrast, however, is perhaps too simple. I wish to suggest that on at least one occasion, Cervantes combines conventions from both pastoral and picaresque to produce something entirely new. This occasion is *La ilustre fregona*. (A similar discussion might well focus on *La gitanilla*.[3]) *La ilustre fregona* is basically a comic romance, but Cervantes uses the world of the *pícaro* as a setting for the story in a way more usual to the green world of pastoral.[4]

The theoretical possibility of the combination of picaresque and pastoral can be inferred from Claudio Guillén in his *Literature as System*. He states: "A genre... confronts certain 'counter genres' (the picaresque opposing, for example, the pastoral or the Greek romance), with which it constitutes the 'ideal spaces' in which writers dwell before they set pen to paper."[5] He also suggests that: "the confrontation of genres may be due to a kind of coexistence on the level of experience or of the imagination, rather than to mere substitution or dialectical succession."[6] My point is that such genres and their "counter genres" may not always be mutually exclusive. While the notion of their coexistence within the same "ideal spaces" explains their confrontation, it also seems to suggest the possibility of their combining or sharing conventions.

Pastoral is not inflexible. William Empson has shown that the essence of pastoral is not dependent specifically on shepherds. Others have developed the idea, though generally not as far as Empson.[7] While this is a modern perspective, it is also true to a certain extent of the concept of pastoral in the Renaissance. In Spain, in the sixteenth century, poetry about shepherds was covered by the term *égloga*.[8] Cervantes himself uses this to refer to his pastoral romance *La Galatea*.[9] El Pinciano, in his *Philosophía antigua poética*, lists for the subject matter of eclogues not only *boyeros, cabreros,* and *pastores,* but also *pescadores, leñadores, aradores, hortelanos,* and *viandantes*.[10]

A final assumption is that of the constant change and mutation of generic forms. Alistair Fowler in his article "The Life and Death of Literary Forms" identifies three stages in the development of a genre. The first two deal with its inception and existence as a recognized literary form. The third deals with the point at which it begins to appear in new and radical ways such as "burlesque," "antithesis," and "hybrids from combination with other genres."[11] In this design, *Don Quixote*, for example, would represent a tertiary phase of the romances of chivalry. It supposes a knowledge of the conventions of that genre, but it uses them to create something opposite. By Cervantes' time, Spanish pastorals also begin to show signs of this tertiary stage of disintegration. They have been altered by, among other things, the intrusion of violence, incorporation of Byzantine-style romances, and *a lo divino* versions.[12]

After *La Galatea*, Cervantes' ideas about pastoral changed considerably.[13] This is seen in an episode in the *Coloquio de los perros* where

Berganza compares pastoral romances with real shepherds. Instead of singing songs about love, these real shepherds are busy mending sandals, picking off fleas and stealing their master's sheep. Cervantes' satire is leveled at literary shepherds mainly because they are not verisimilar. Whatever poetic truth pastoral romances may contain, since they have no semblance of truth on the level of human experience, reason finds them unattractive and rejects their fiction.[14] However, the aim of entertainment was given the highest priority by Cervantes.[15] He respected both romance of chivalry and pastoral romance for their power to accomplish this. This enchanting, "hypnotic" effect of the romances of chivalry is seen in their influence on Don Quixote.[16] The idyllic vision of pastoral demonstrates a similar power over Berganza. In spite of knowing that it is all dream and illusion, Berganza is so carried away in describing the delights of pastoral romances that Cipión must interrupt him to bring him back to reality. Cervantes recognized the potential of pastoral and chivalric romance but he wished to render them palatable for the discerning reader who was not willing to suspend totally his critical faculties. The way to accomplish this was through verisimilitude.[17]

In *La ilustre fregona*, Don Diego de Carriazo, a young farm boy from a noble family in Burgos slips away from home to become a *pícaro*. He eventually finds himself at the *almadrabas*, the tuna fisheries of Zahara on the southern coast of Spain, the *finibusterrae* of the picaresque world. When he returns, his friend, Don Tomás de Avendaño, decides to join him on a second foray. They leave home bound for study in Salamanca, but they soon evade their guardian, sell their valuables, and set out for the *almadrabas*. They are detoured to an inn at Toledo by reports of the exceptional beauty and virtue of Costanza, an innkeeper's kitchen maid.[18] Avendaño is stricken with love and their travels are suspended. He stays at the inn as the innkeeper's hired boy, and Carriazo becomes a water boy. Avendaño meets competition for Costanza from the Corregidor's son. Throughout the story, Costanza reamins a symbol of virtue, and she encourages neither of her suitors. The story ends with the arrival of Carriazo's and Avendaño's fathers. A rather transparent *anagnorisis* shows Costanza to be Carriazo's half-sister. This opens the way for a comic resolution in which Avendaño wins the hand of Costanza, Carriazo marries the Corregidor's daughter, and the son of the Corregidor marries Avendaño's sister.

While endings such as this may try modern notions of verisimilitude, for Cervantes and the Neo-Aristotelians, they were acceptable material. Though perhaps highly improbable, such events are still in the realm of the possible.[19] Other features of the story are more convincing. The *almadrabas* did exist and were a famous center for picaresque life. Domínguez Ortiz has edited memoirs of a priest who recorded actual cases of boys who ran away from home to go to the *almadrabas* and became so enamored of that life that they refused to go home.[20] There has been speculation as to an actual historical identity for Carriazo and Avendaño, and the same is true of the inn in Toledo.[21] While this speculation may never be conclusive, the fact of its existence attests to the credibility of at least that part of the fiction. These details, together with the water boys and other everyday types from Spanish town and countryside who fill in the background, lend the story a very considerable degree of verisimilitude. They also provide an appropriate context for picaresque adventures.

Though *La ilustre fregona* appears in discussions of the picaresque, critics in general have avoided calling it a picaresque work.[22] While there is no doubt that Avendaño and especially Carriazo are immersed in the world from which picaresque stories are drawn, Avendaño's Platonic love for Costanza, the discovery of Costanza's noble background, and the successful return of all characters to their original places in society are not picaresque conventions.

The hint of a different set of conventions comes early. After introducing Avendaño and Carriazo, Cervantes begins the story in this fashion:

> Trece años, o poco más, tendría Carriazo, cuando, llevado de una inclinación picaresca, sin forzarle a ello algún mal tratamiento que sus padres le hiciesen, solo por su gusto y antojo se desgarró, como dicen los muchachos, de casa de sus padres, y se fue por ese mundo adelante, tan contento de la vida libre, que, en la mitad de las incomodidades y miserias que trae consigo, no echaba menos la abundancia de la casa de su padre, ni el andar a pie le cansaba, ni el frío le ofendía, ni el calor le enfadaba. Para él todos los tiempos del año le eran dulce y templada primavera.[23]

Carriazo is so accomplished in the art of being a *pícaro*, he could give lessons to the famous Guzmán de Alfarache. But his experience differs from that of Guzmán, Lazarillo or Don Pablos. For him, all the hardships are pleasure, and all seasons are "dulce y templada primavera." While Cervantes is most obvious in his reference to the conventions of picaresque stories, these lines suggest another direction, one that leads to the constant springtime of the *locus amoenus* and pastoral. Suspension of the seasons and the benign quality of perpetual springtime are characteristics of the mythical Golden Age, and are a common point of reference in Renaissance pastoral.[24]

In addition, notwithstanding the picaresque setting, the general movement and form of the story are comparable to that of pastoral romance. Two youths of noble background disguise themselves as members of a less restricted society, and for a time they enjoy a state of freedom as they play at belonging to that society. The characters of Shakespeare's *As You Like It*, Silerio of *La Galatea*, and in some respects Grisóstomo and Marcela of the *Quixote* come to mind as parallel cases. Avendaño's becoming a stable boy for love of Costanza parallels the common pastoral motif of the courtier who assumes the shepherd's guise when love-struck by the beauty of a shepherdess. As often occurs in pastoral, Avendaño and Carriazo's sojourn is limited, and because they have not completely cast aside their identity, they return to their original position in society.[25]

Other references to pastoral conventions appear. Cervantes tells us that the *almadrabas* are to Carriazo "más frescas y verdes que los campos Elíseos" (p. 228). Later when it is apparent that they must stay at the inn because of Avendaño's love for Costanza, Carriazo exclaims:

> ¡Oh amor platónico! ¡Oh fregona ilustre! ¡Oh felicísimos tiempos nuestros, donde vemos que la belleza enamora sin malicia, la honestidad enciende sin que abrase, el donaire da gusto sin que incite, y la bajeza del estado humilde obliga y fuerza a que le suban sobre la rueda de la que llaman Fortuna! ¡O pobres atunes míos, que os pasáis este año sin ser visitados deste tan enamorado y aficionado vuestro! (pp. 265-66)

Avendaño realizes that Carriazo is making fun: "Ya veo, Asturiano, cuan al descubierto te burlas de mí" (p. 266), and invites him to take his leave and go to the *almadrabas* alone. However, friendship wins out, Carriazo stays, and the Platonic love he is jesting about becomes a reality. Carriazo's exclamation about his poor neglected tunas may be taken as a parody of the shepherd who neglects his sheep to pursue the callings of love. But it is also a sign that Carriazo recognizes the similarity between their disguise and the mask of the literary shepherd.[26] In this context one also recalls the piscatorial eclogues of Jacopo Sannazaro, Bernardino Rota, and others which set a precedent for referring to the *almadrabas* in terms usual to pastoral.[27]

The inn at Toledo also has similarities to a pastoral setting. It resembles the world of *La Galatea* in the way characters move freely in and out of its sphere. In addition, it is a place of poetry, music, and dance. Both Avendaño and the Corregidor's son write poetry to Costanza, and the latter serenades her. At one point the entire company of the inn gather for song and dance. Most like pastoral, however, is the fact that through Avendaño's Platonic love, inspired by the beauty of Costanza, the inn becomes a place where high ideals are treated in a lowly setting, and where literature is lived by the characters.

In picaresque as in pastoral, characters are impersonators. In pastoral, courtly types are disguised as rustics, in whose garb they carry on such activities as discussions of philosophy and sufferings for love. The *pícaro* impersonates nobility, at least at times, covering his lowly moral and social condition for the purpose of social climbing. Carriazo and Avendaño, on the other hand, are seeking a social level from which Guzmán and his peers are trying to escape. Furthermore, while the real *pícaro* moves, or tries to move, vertically through society, [28] Carriazo and Avendaño's aim is simply to maintain their picaresque disguise and enjoy the freedom that life affords. Such is the basic nature of the pastoral ideal which seeks freedom and shuns any ambition to rise higher either in social condition, wealth, or honor.[29]

Picaresque and pastoral have another common point of reference in the so-called "naturalism" of the sixteenth century. The question of nature as teacher and of experience as a way to truth was dealt with by the Italian Neo-Platonists and by Erasmus, hence its interest for Spanish writers of the sixteenth century.[30] In both picaresque and pastoral, the author places his characters in a state of freedom removed from the restrictions of society. In short, they both posit the return to a natural state to examine the premise that the value of man is within himself.[31]

The picaresque novel assumes that human nature, contaminated by original sin, is prone to evil; given over to freedom without sufficient moral training, man will continually make the wrong choice. Pastoral usually assumes some degree of civilization on the part of the literary shepherd and so generally avoids such pessimism. However, the garden was not only the site of the earthly paradise, it was also the place of the Fall. The potential for good or evil rests there.[32] In *As You Like It*, characters make of the forest of Arden what they wish or what their mood dictates. For Jaques it is melancholy, for the Duke, philosophy. There the pastoral setting works as a "mirror" that reflects the character to himself, and thus facilitates introspection and self-knowledge.[33] In *La ilustre fregona*, although the circumstances are different, the nature of the experience also depends on the characters themselves. For Avendaño, Platonic love makes it complete. His and Costanza's good fortune recalls the countless other lovers who have found themselves, love, and a conclusion to their stories in one of Arcadia's landscapes. For Carriazo the experience holds a potential danger, for events take a turn that could eventually lead to a picaresque outcome. Indeed, by the end of the story he is in trouble with the law for an altercation stemming from his activities as a water boy.

Possibilities for both good and evil are offered by the picaresque setting from the beginning. In the first part, when Carriazo is at the height of his career in the *almadrabas*, Cervantes states:

> ¡Allí, allí, que está en su centro el trabajo, junto con la poltronería! Allí está la suciedad limpia, la gordura rolliza, la hambre pronta, la hartura abundante, sin disfraz el vicio, el juego siempre, las pendencias por momentos, las muertes por puntos, las pullas a cada paso, los bailes como en bodas, las seguidillas como en estampa, los romances con estribos, la poesía sin aciones. Aquí se canta, allí se reniega, acullá se riñe, acá se juega, y por todo se hurta. Allí campea la libertad y luce el trabajo; allí van o envían muchos padres principales a buscar a sus hijos, y los hallan; y tanto sienten sacarlos de aquella vida, como si los llevaran a dar muerte.   (pp. 225-27)

The *almadrabas* is a wide open and free society, in which all sorts of crime and license may be found. On one hand there is hunger, violence, vice and toil, and on the other hand Cervantes sets these

negative features in balance with the promise of "poltronería," "hartura abundante," "bailes como en bodas," and "libertad." The entire
description is summed up in the first lines with the antitheses of
"suciedad limpia," "hambre pronta—hartura abundante." The apparent chaos of language in "romances con estribos" and "poesía sin
aciones" suits this society where restrictions of order and reason are
non-existent and instinct, whim, and appetite may have their way.[34]
Be this as it may, for all its wildness, the good or evil to be found in
the picaresque ambient depends on the characters themselves.

The setting at the inn also offers the characters both alterna-
tives. On the one hand, Avendaño encounters beauty and idealistic
love. On the other, evil is present in the form of the two women of
loose morals who solicit Avendaño's and Carriazo's attentions. This
alternative is the way to entrapment in the picaresque world, and
the boys reject it harshly. Armed with the virtues they bring with
them, Avendaño and Carriazo maintain a position above the pursuit
of instinct and sensual pleasure characterized by a completely natural state. At the same time, they are free from the restrictions of
regular society. This is the same position in relation to civilization
and wild nature as the pastoral world, which is situated on the
fringes of both but is engulfed by neither.[35]

The balance is all the more precarious with Avendaño and Carriazo, since it depends entirely on their inventive energies. This is a
necessary consequence of the pastoral setting being taken over by a
realistic place. On the one hand the reader is spared being asked to
accept the existence of a place in mythical geography. On the other,
for lack of a proper Arcadia, Avendaño and Carriazo must create
their own pastoral-like experience. The result is a sharper focus on
the psychological aspects of the characters. The true pastoral of *La
ilustre fregona* is an internal sort of pastoral. Instead of happening in a
place resembling the earthly paradise or the Golden Age, it exists
within the characters as a state of mind.[36] With the addition of
realistic detail and the internalization of the pastoral setting, this
sort of pastoral looks ahead to modern versions of pastoral where
the functions of the shepherd's domain are carried out by any setting close to nature or perhaps represented even by childhood itself.
Indeed, there is a suggestion of the so-called "pastoral of childhood."[37] Cervantes tells us that the fathers who tear their sons
away from the *almadrabas* do so with great regret. Perhaps for them

also that life of youth and freedom carries so great an appeal that they are casting a wistful backward glance at the lost freedom of adolescence.

A pastoral-like story in a picaresque setting may at first seem unlikely, but Cervantes is quick to remind us that he was not limited to simple imitation of existing generic models. In the prologue to his *Novelas ejemplares* he states:

> . . . yo soy el primero que he novelado en lengua castellana; que las muchas novelas que en ella andan impresas, todas son traducidas de lenguas extranjeras, y éstas son mías propias, no imitadas ni hurtadas: mi ingenio las engendró y las parió mi pluma, y van creciendo en brazos de la estampa.[38]

The term *ingenio* refers to the poet's powers of invention which work toward producing new and unusual creations.[39] However, invention and imitation are closely connected concepts and both refer to the process of encountering and selecting materials to utilize.[40] It seems probable that, among other things, Cervantes is referring here to a unique reworking and recombining of existing literary models.[41]

REED COLLEGE

NOTES

[1]Juan Bautista Avalle-Arce, *La novela pastoril española,* 2nd ed. (Madrid: Ediciones Istmo, 1974), p. 265 begins his last chapter with the assertion, "Ha muerto la novela pastoril, y atrás quedan las obras de verdadera creación."

[2]For example, Robert Scholes and Robert Kellogg, *The Nature of Narrative* (New York: Oxford University Press, 1966), pp. 250-51.

[3]W. P. Ker to my knowledge makes the earliest reference to *La gitanilla* as pastoral in "Cervantes, Shakespeare and the Pastoral Idea," in *A Book of Homage to Shakespeare,* ed., Israel Gollancz (Oxford: Oxford University Press, 1916), pp. 50-51. Frank Pierce makes several remarks about the similarity of the gypsy world to pastoral but doesn't develop the notion in "*La gitanilla*: A Tale of High Romance," *BHS,* 54 (1977), 283-94.

[4]Northrup Frye gives a brief and concise description of the place of the green world in comic romance in *The Anatomy of Criticism,* 3rd Princeton Paperback ed. (1957; reprint Princeton University Press, 1973), pp. 182-84. Joaquín Casalduero makes the following remark about *La ilustre fregona*: "Costanza hubiera podido ser igualmente una pastora y moverse en la libertad de los prados, pero entonces no sólo se la hubiera privado del medio urbano estríctamente necesario desde un punto de vista teórico y emocional en el Barroco, sino que el amor platónico hubiera adquirido la tónica renacentista de materia académica, la cual no excluía una fuerte corriente subterránea de sensualismo," in *Sentido y forma de las novelas ejemplares,* 2nd ed., (Madrid: Gredos, 1969), pp. 196-97.

[5]*Literature as System: Essays Toward the Theory of Literary History* (Princeton: Princeton University Press, 1971), p. 74.

[6]Guillén, p. 133.

[7]*Some Versions of Pastoral* (London, l935; reprint New York: New Directions, 1974). A good introduction to the variety of pastoral is Peter V. Marinelli, *Pastoral*, The Critical Idiom, 15 (London: Methuen & Co., 1971).

[8]Francisco López-Estrada, "Teoría literaria y libros pastoriles españoles," in *Homenaje a Elias Serra Rafols* (Madrid: Rivadeneyra, 1970), II, 349-51.

[9]*La Galatea*, ed. Juan Bautista Avalle-Arce, 2nd ed., Clásicos Castellanos (Madrid: Espasa Calpe, 1968), I, p. 5.

[10]*Philosophía antigua poética*, ed. Alfredo Carballo Picaso (Madrid: C.S.I.C., 1953), III, pp. 244-45.

[11]"The Life and Death of Literary Forms," in *New Directions in Literary History*, ed. Ralph Cohen (Baltimore: The Johns Hopkins University Press, 1974), pp. 91-92.

[12]Avalle-Arce treats the first two themes consistently throughout *La novela pastoril española*. *A lo divino* versions are dealt with in the final chapter.

[13]E. C.Riley, *Cervantes's Theory of the Novel* (Oxford: Oxford University Press, 1962), pp. 10-11, notes the overall change in Cervantes' notion about fiction after the *Galatea* and before *Don Quixote* I. Of course this corresponds with the publication of El Pinciano's *Philosophía antigua poética* in 1596.

[14]Riley, pp. 84-85.

[15]Riley, p. 84.

[16]Riley, p. 86.

[17]Riley, p. 20.

[18]Of course, later events show that Costanza does not wash dishes, she merely keeps the silver for the innkeeper and his wife.

[19]Riley, pp. 184-85.

[20]Antonio Domínguez Ortiz, *Crisis y decadencia de la España de los Austrias* (Barcelona: Ariel, 1969), p. 31.

[21]Agustín G. de Amezúa y Mayo, *Cervantes, creador de la novela corta española* (Madrid: C.S.I.C.,1958), II, pp 288-295.

[22]Alexander Parker includes *La ilustre fregona* in his *Literature and the Delinquent*, (Edinburgh: Edinburgh University Press, 1967), pp. 14-16, though he does not expressly label it picaresque. In describing *La ilustre fregona*, Angel Valbuena Prat uses the term "novelística idealizada," a trend within which he also locates *La gitanilla* and *El celoso extremeño*. *Miguel de Cervantes: Obras Completas* (Madrid: Aguilar, 1970), II, p. 1087. Guillén, in his study "Towards a Definition of the Picaresque," sets forth eight points he considers basic in defining the genre. In the case of *La ilustre fregona*, none of these criteria can be said to apply (*Literature as System, pp. 74-93*). Carlos Blanco Aguinaga argues that *La ilustre fregona* is in "no sense" a picaresque novel and goes on to claim that a comparison of the *Guzmán de Alfarache* with Cervantes's works which contain *pícaros* shows that: ". . . Cervantes no escribió jamás una novela picaresca—y que sus pícaros, por lo tanto, son muy distintos de los otros—porque su manera de ver el mundo y de novelar, es decir, su realismo es esencialmente antagónico al de los autores de las picarescas más famosas." "Cervantes y la picaresca: notas sobre dos tipos de realismo," *NRFH*, 11 (1957), 313-14.

[23]Miguel de Cervantes, *La ilustre fregona*, in *Novelas ejemplares*, ed. Rodríguez Marín, Clásicos Castellanos (1915; reprint Madrid: Espasa-Calpe, 1975), I, pp. 221-222. Hereafter cited in the text.

24Harry Levin, *The Myth of the Golden Age in the Renaissance* (Bloomington: Indiana University Press, 1969), p. 42. Also Marinelli, pp. 15-36.

25Marinelli, pp. 11-12, explains that the return to the city is always implicit in pastoral.

26Carriazo's reference to the pastoral quality of their situation may be Cervantes' way of disarming the reader's objections to an aspect of the story that lacks verisimilitude.

27William Leonard Grant, *Neo-Latin Literature and the Pastoral* (Chapel Hill: University of North Carolina Press, 1965), p. 204 ff. lists examples of piscatorial and other types of eclogues.

28Guillén, p. 84.

29Marinelli, p. 16.

30Manuel de Montolíu, *El alma de España y sus reflejos en la literatura del Siglo de Oro* (Barcelona: Editorial Cervantes, n. d.), p. 274.

31J. Frutos Gómez de las Cortinas, "El antihéroe y su actitud vital (sentido de la novela picaresca)," *Cuadernos de literatura,* 7 (1950), 142.

32Marinelli, p. 22.

33David Young, *The Heart's Forest* (New Haven: Yale University Press, 1972), pp. 50-51.

34Rodríguez Marín notes: "Sabido es que *aciones* son las correas de donde cuelgan los estribos, y aquí se dice *la poesía sin aciones,* por contraposición a lo de *los romances con estribos,* y en significado de suelta y en toda libertad, aun por lo jocoso y lo deshonesto." *La ilustre fregona,* p. 226 n.

35Leo Marx discusses the place of the pastoral world "in a middle ground somewhere 'between,' yet transcendent to the opposing forces of civilization and nature" in *The Machine in the Garden* (1964; reprint New York: Oxford University Press, 1973), pp. 22-24.

36Even Arcadia itself is a projection of an inner state, "the landscape of an idea," as Marinelli explains, p. 37.

37Cf. Marinelli, Chapter 5, "The Retreat into Childhood," pp. 75-81.

38Miguel de Cervantes, *Obras Completas,* ed. Angel Valbuena Prat, I, 920.

39Alban Forcione, *Cervantes, Aristotle and the "Persiles"* (Princeton: Princeton Univesrity Press, 1970), p. 327.

40Riley, p. 58.

41This paper represents a chapter in progress for my doctoral dissertation, *Some Guises of Pastoral in Cervantes.* I am greatly indebted to Professor Thomas R. Hart, my adviser, for comments, suggestions and long discussions about pastoral and Cervantes.

Cervantes and Education

BRUCE W. WARDROPPER

HE FIRST PUBLISHED works by Cervantes consist of a set of school exercises, the elegiac poems on the death of Philip II's third queen which he wrote at the behest of his master at the Estudio de la Villa de Madrid. His writing career began, then, when still a student.

Cervantes' last work, written a few days before his death, features a student. The prologue to *Persiles y Sigismunda* tells a story about the aged author's encounter with this young man. The student is warmhearted, friendly, and very appreciative of Cervantes' literary art. At the same time, he cuts a ridiculous figure: oddly dressed, he rides his donkey awkwardly. The encounter, Cervantes tells us, would have provided him with the material for a funny tale—if only he could have lived to write it.

Students were a part of Cervantes' life and art from his own student days until his death. They pass through his fiction in an unending parade. We remember the crafty, well-intentioned student in the little play *La cueva de Salamanca*, whose supposed magic conjures up the village sexton and barber in the form of devils.

Then there are the students in *El coloquio de los perros* whose attendance at a Jesuit school in Seville enables the dog Berganza to pick up a little learning. Interestingly, this tale is being read by a former student, the Licenciado Peralta. *Don Quixote* is full of students and former students. In Part I, the man determined to restore Don Quixote to sanity is a *licenciado*, the priest Pero Pérez; in Part II, it is the *bachiller*, Sansón Carrasco who assigns himself this mission. Pero Pérez is a graduate of the contemptible University of Sigüenza; Sansón Carrasco, like the great majority of Cervantes' students, attends the prestigious and ancient University of Salamanca.

Let us look at some other students in *Don Quixote* and observe how Cervantes treats them. In Part II, Chapter 22, the self-styled humanist who guides Don Quixote to the Cave of Montesinos is described as a "famoso estudiante." We will return to him later on. For the nonce, we may note that he is the cousin, the important Primo, of the unnamed Licenciado who (in Chapter 19) has defeated the Bachiller Corchuelo in a fencing match. These fractious students are presented to us readers in a curious way. After saying farewell to the Caballero del Verde Gabán, Don Quixote and Sancho Panza meet "dos como clérigos o como estudiantes." The narrator promptly begins referring to them as "dos estudiantes," making no further mention of their dubious status or their possible priesthood. When one student has told our knight about Camacho's imminent and opulent wedding, Don Quixote addresses him as "señor Licenciado." Thinking he knows better than his fictional creature, the narrator refers to this man as "el estudiante, bachiller, o licenciado, como le llamó Don Quixote." But the narrator really couldn't care less about the student's qualifications: henceforth he is identified by Don Quixote's term as "el Licenciado." Don Quixote's guess turns out to have been right, because the second student mocks the first for having only barely passed his *licencia* examination: "llevastes cola [en licencias]." Whereupon the almost not Licenciado firmly puts his friend in his place by calling him, apparently correctly, a "Bachiller." Much ado about nothing, perhaps; certainly a very funny satire of academics' punctiliousness about degrees. J. B. Avalle-Arce and E. C. Riley have analyzed this chapter to illustrate how perspectivism pervades Cervantes' narrative.[1] They are surely right. But I think that this quibbling about academic titles runs even deeper than narrative technique.

If we jump back from Part II, Chapter 19, to Part I, Chapter 19, we find a curious analogy. At night, Don Quixote and Sancho see a dimly lighted procession of what they take to be "encamisados," knights wearing shirts over their armor as camouflage for an attack under cover of darkness. The supposed "encamisados" are really mourners and pallbearers, escorting a dead *caballero* from Baeza to his burial place in Segovia; but Don Quixote does not know this. Bravely attacking the presumed knights, he routs them. The mule on which one of the mourners—Alonso López—is riding stumbles and falls heavily on López's leg, fracturing a bone. Savoring his victory, Don Quixote points the tip of his lance at the prostrate man's face, calling on him to surrender or die. Alonso López begs to be spared, pointing out that to kill him would be a sacrilege since he is a *licenciado* who has taken the first of Holy Orders. Thereupon the narrator calls him "el Licenciado," But López outsmarts the narrator by confessing, quite gratuitously, that he has lied: "no soy sino bachiller." Keeping pace with the evolving truth, the narrator instantly demotes him to "el Bachiller."

Is it not possible to detect in these parallel chapters of Part I and Part II some heavy sarcasm directed at the holders of university degrees? Is there also perhaps a trace of envy in the author's apparent superciliousness toward these ridiculous products of the University? Cervantes often seems to have scant regard for official academia.

In one of the *Novelas ejemplares* we find a further analogy to these scenes from *Don Quixote*. When Rinconete and Cortadillo begin their career of petty thievery in Seville, their first victim is described, oddly enough, as half a student, "un medio estudiante." Having filched from him a purse, "una bolsilla," Cortado ironically says to his friend: "Con ésta me pagó su reverencia del estudiante." The "reverend student" returns looking for the lost purse with which he has inadvertently paid for Cortado's services. Mischievously, Cortado consoles him for his loss with the thought that, for having laid hands on a man of the cloth, the thief will suffer automatic excommunication. "Y ¡cómo que ha cometido sacrilegio!," says the student, "que puesto que yo no soy sacerdote, sino sacristán de unas monjas, el dinero de la bolsa era del tercio de una capellanía,. . . y es dinero sagrado y bendito." Here, then, is yet another case of an academic looking more educated and priestly than he is. That appearances are deceptive is a lesson which Cervantes never tires of teaching about all walks of life; but these academics cause their appearances to deceive. They are not mistaken for something else. They misrepresent themselves; and they lie—either to cheat or for no good reason at all.

Academic pretense and fraud are more unambiguously condemned in an episode in *El licenciado Vidriera*. The Licentiate of Glass comes across an acquaintance dressed as a *letrado*. Someone addresses this man as "señor Licenciado." Knowing that he is not even a *bachiller*, Vidriera proffers him a particularly savage gibe; whereupon the student protests, insisting that Vidriera knows him to be a man of lofty and profound learning. Sarcastically Vidriera ripostes that he is a very Tantalus of learning: his learning is so lofty that it flies out of his grasp, and so profound that he cannot reach down to it.

We discover a contrasting representation of credentials in the episode in *Don Quixote* in which Sancho Panza is seen "vestido a lo letrado," riding on a mule to take posession of the *Ínsula* of Barataria. Although, as Juan Huarte de San Juan points out, a *letrado* or clerk is any man with a higher education, "en diciendo 'Fulano es letrado,' todos entendemos de común consentimiento que su profesión es pericia de leyes. . . "[2] As the butt of the Duke's jest, Sancho is, then, dressed as a lawyer. He has been forced unwittingly into academic imposture. But if, as Huarte maliciously suggests, lawyers are called *letrados* because they are "a letra dados" (p. 209), given to the letter (which we know "killeth"), Sancho is given to the spirit (which "giveth life"). Without a legal education, Sancho knows how to dispense the final purpose of the law, which is justice. For this end not education but good will and good sense are needed. Most cases of academic fakery in Cervantes do not convey such a clear spiritual lesson.

As often as not, the scholarly life is seen to produce consummate liars, as in the earlier cases we have examined. It also provides on occasion a pretext for nonstudents to lie about their scholarly prospects. In *La ilustre fregona*, when Carriazo and Avendaño decide to go to the tuna fisheries to enjoy the picaresque life, they finance the venture by telling their parents that they want to go to Salamanca to study. Avendaño had indeed been studying Greek and Latin there for three years before the wanderlust infected him. Carriazo, meanwhile, had been receiving his schooling—metaphorically at least—in the tuna fisheries: "Pasó por todos los grados de pícaro, hasta que se graduó de maestro en las almadrabas de Zahara. . . " With their generous parental allowance as students, the two prodigal sons set off for Cádiz, after first sending word to their fathers that they have changed their minds and are off to the wars in Flanders. As everyone knows, the beauty of Costanza, the illustrious scrubbing maid who is no such thing, detains the young men in Toledo. As befits the comedy which this tale is, a round of happy weddings ends their misadventures and misrepresentations. But the *pícaro* Carriazo is not, as a result of his marriage, blessed by some chips off the old block: of his three sons we are told that "hoy están todos estudiando en Salamanca." The graduate of the tunny fisheries ironically acquires bourgeois respectability as his offspring join the Ivy League.

Most of Cervantes' depictions of men of letters and students (whether explicit or ironic) are disparaging. Some of his characters, however, are identified as students when on the surface there seems no need for it. In this regard one thinks of Grisóstomo and Ambrosio (in the Marcela episode of *Don Quixote*), of Doña Clara's lover Don Luis (who falls in love with her while walking to his Estudio), of Don Lorenzo (whose father, the Caballero del Verde Gabán, wishes he would study something more practical than poetry), of Teodosia's brother and lover in *Las dos doncellas* (who are classmates at Salamanca). Are these apparently "neutral" students somehow guilty by reason of their association with the majority of students in Cervantes' work? I suspect that, taken in the context of the whole, they are indeed meant to be regarded as faintly ridiculous.

The women associated with these "neutral" students are not blessed—or afflicted—with learning. Marcela is, however, endowed with a "natural entendimiento" which enables her to press a healthy Aristotelian logic into the service of puncturing the delusions of Platonic love. Preciosa, the heroine of *La gitanilla*, possesses a lively "ingenio"; she is famous for her "agudeza." She has no need of booklearning. Gypsy life is itself a learning experience. The gypsies' teachers are "[e]l diablo y [e]l uso, que les enseña en una hora lo que habían de aprender en un año." As we shall see, coupled with native ability, "el uso"—practice and experience—was also Cervantes' most constant and effective teacher. These sympathetically portrayed women with their good minds are the antithesis of Cervantes' inept students.

Once in a while, Cervantes offers his reader a glimpse of a serious student. Such, for example, are the two young heroes of *La señora Cornelia*, who, after a long night in which their bachelor household has been suddenly enlivened by the adoption of a baby girl and the renowned beauty of Bologna, do not for an instant think of cutting next morning's classes. In *El licenciado Vidriera*, too, we have the case of a responsible student, whose commitment to scholarship borders on the fanatical. This tale contains a complex statement of what appear to be Cervantes' views on higher education and society.

Tomás Rodaja is a poor boy who will work his way through the University of Salamanca. He claims that his memory is so bad that he cannot remember the names of his parents or his native village. But later we are told that "tenía tan felice memoria, que era cosa de espanto." His lapse of memory has been deliberate. He will reveal his family name and that of his village only after he has brought honor to them both by his scholastic success. Even though Tomás becomes a famous scholar, there is a flaw in his success, and so the concealed names of his origin are never in fact disclosed. But it is the desire for fame that fuels his scholarly ambition. He wants to rise above the anonymity of his humble station in life. As he says, "yo he oido decir que de los hombres se hacen los obispos." Education makes possible social preferment.

Although Tomás adores the life of a student at Salamanca, he yields to the blandishments of a Captain Valdivia and, without enlisting, accompanies him and his regiment to Italy. As a tourist, Tomás has the detachment of an intellectual. All he can find to admire in Florence, for example, is its cleanliness. He puts everything he sees into the card file of his mind: "Todo lo miró, y notó, y puso en su punto." Tomás' learning has now been enriched by *discreción*, by worldliness. He has come out of the ivory tower.

Back in Salamanca, Tomás finishes his studies and graduates in law. He is, however, driven insane by inadvertently eating a doctored quince. In his mad state he delivers himself of a series of generally vindictive, witty sayings about all kinds of men and women, acquiring an immense reputation for his savage wisdom.

When Tomás is cured of his madness, he goes to the capital in the hope of practicing law. He has attained scholarly fame through his own merit. From the service of rich students he has reached the potentiality of freedom through the mediation of a higher education. The court denies him, however, both the fruit of his merit and the freedom he has worked for. He has no recourse but to return to a life of service, this time of military service in Flanders: "la vida que había comenzado a eternizar por las letras, la acabó de eternizar por las armas." He has studied everything, and seen everything; until his army duty he has experienced nothing. His life is a reverse reflection of Cervantes' own: what Cervantes had begun to eternalize by military prowess, he ended up by eternalizing by his literary success.

In many respects the ideal student, the Licenciado Vidriera illustrates that disenchantment with formal education which, in a less serious vein, Cervantes has shown us in the other students we have passed in review.

El licenciado Vidriera sharpens an issue of which we have so far seen only glimpses, the question whether *letras* are, or are not, superior to *armas*. It is a question to which Cervantes often returned, surely in his thinking life as much as in his writing. You will recall Don Quixote's discourse on the subject (Part I, Chapter 37), as well as the succeeding exemplification of it in the lives of the captive captain and his lawyer brother. But it crops up more unobtrusively elsewhere—in, for example, the diptych of *El casamiento engañoso* and *El coloquio de los perros*, where the experiences of the Alférez Campuzano and the Licentiate Peralta are ironically contrasted. This dual tale also encapsulates Cervantes' life. Like the soldier Cervantes, who became the famous author, the soldier Campuzano becomes the author of the dogs' dialogue.

The implications of the differences between these two lifestyles —soldiering and clerking—impinge on Cervantes' attitude to education. *Armas y letras* is a formula which spawns a set of antinomies: the practical versus the theoretical; the active versus the sedentary; the defender versus the defended; the upholder of truth versus the revealer of truth; the taker of risks versus the tenured; the gallant versus the stodgy. On the whole, Cervantes seems to opt for the superiority of *armas* over *letras*. But with his infinite capacity for perceiving nuances, he cannot bring himself to assert categorically that military life is better than academic life. The scholar, after all, must deliver to the soldier the truth which he will have to defend with his life. It is not so much that there is an interdependence between the two professions. It is rather that Cervantes has learned the fallacy of antinomies. For him there resides in each phenomenon some part of its opposite. This recognition is incarnated in Don Quixote and Sancho Panza, the madman and the fool in whom wisdom is to be found. It is a perception which Cervantes must have derived, directly or indirectly, from Erasmus' *Praise of Folly*.

The mutual interference is symbolized for Erasmus in the Silenus figurine which in Plato's *Symposium* Alcibiades had used to characterize Socrates. Socrates, says Alcibiades, "bears a strong resemblance to those figures of Silenus in statuaries' shops, represented holding pipes or flutes; they are hollow inside, and when they are taken apart you see that they contain little figures of gods."[3] Socrates' "talk too is extremely like the Silenus-figures which take apart. Anyone who sets out to listen to Socrates talking will probably find his conversation utterly ridiculous at first. . . But if a man penetrates within and sees the content of Socrates' talk exposed, he will find that there is nothing but sound sense inside, and that this talk is almost the talk of a god. . . " (pp. 110-11). Erasmus says—or more exactly, has Folly say—that "all human things, just like Alcibiades' Sileni, have dual faces very dissimilar to one another. Hence what at first sight is death, if you inspect the interior, is life; and conversely, what is life is death; what is beautiful is deformed; what is rich is poverty-stricken; what is infamous is glorious; what is learned is illiterate; what is strong is weak; what is noble is ignoble; what is cheerful is sad; what is favorable is unfavorable; what is friendly is hostile; what is healthy is noxious. In short, if you open up the Silenus, you will find all things with a different appearance."[4] In this insight of Erasmus, nothing is *this* or *that*; everything is both *this* and *that*.

Cervantes, whose intellectual formation began in the pre-Tridentine Renaissance, shared this Silenus vision with the humanists of an earlier generation. In contrasting the academic imposture of Vidriera's acquaintance with Sancho's involuntary one at Barataria, we shared in one particular Silenus perception of Cervantes. And the student in the prologue to the *Persiles*—ludicrous in his appearance, warm and friendly in his manner—is another aspect of the Silenus. Seeing all around him as ambivalent, Cervantes necessarily held complex views on education. Their complexity is increased by the fact of their expression in fiction. Because fiction is a treacherous vehicle for ideas, it is not possible to ascribe with certainty to Cervantes all the educational opinions which seem to emerge from his stories. Perhaps they were indeed moot for him. A case in point is the well-known passage in praise of Jesuit schools in *El coloquio de los perros*.

It is Berganza who pronounces the eulogy. The Jesuit fathers, with love and devotion moderated by strictness, keep their pupils on the road to virtue at the same time that they instruct them in the canon of good literature. By a variety of teaching methods—mild reproof and punishment, encouragement, and so on—they achieve the desirable educational goals they set themselves. Berganza's friend Cipión agrees with this assessment, and contributes his own glowing praise of the Jesuits' educational endeavor.

From this apparently enthusiastic and sincere passage many commentators have inferred that Cervantes is here writing as a loyal alumnus of the Jesuits, as he recalls with gratitude some time in his youth when he attended one of their schools. There is no evidence, however, that he did.

Let me briefly put Jesuit education at this period into historical context. Following the proscription of most of Erasmus' works in the Spanish Index of 1559, Erasmian thought and learning survived precariously in the teaching of such humanists as El Brocense, Mal Lara and (perhaps) Cervantes' own master Juan López de Hoyos. Their brand of Christian humanism was, however, now being supplanted by another humanism, which was associated primarily with the Jesuits. Marcel Bataillon has described this second kind as "a relaxed humanism, based on the study of Latin poets and orators. Its teaching tended above all to adorn the mind, to initiate it in the art of good speaking; it was no longer a matter of forming minds capable of confronting the [Christian] faith with its sources."[5] In other words, the critical spirit which marked Erasmian thought and scholarship had given way to an elegance of expression which went hand-in-hand with conformity. During the second half of the sixteenth century, this discouragement of criticism had taken firm hold on the lower branches of Spanish education.[6]

Writing in 1605, the learned Jesuit Father Juan de Mariana has some sharp words for the teaching carried on by his order. He recognizes the Jesuits' commanding position in the Spanish educational system: "Hanse encargado los nuestros de enseñar las letras de humanidad en los más principales pueblos de España."⁷ There would be nothing wrong with this takeover were it not that the Society of Jesus is producing few good teachers of Latin. The fathers "enseñan a los oyentes impropriedades y barbarismos, que nunca pueden olvidar, como lo demás que se les imprime en esta tierna edad. No hay duda sino que hoy en España se sabe menos latín que ahora cincuenta años." The trouble is, according to Mariana, that, because the Jesuits have gained a virtual monopoly over elementary education, those laymen—presumably Erasmians—who once taught the humanities so successfully have been driven out of the profession. There is a remarkable difference between Berganza's ecstatic view of these schools and the candid one which came out of the Society of Jesus itself.

Mariana's censure of Jesuit schools raises doubts about taking Berganza's words at their face value or as the expression of Cervantes's personal opinion. Dissimulation was after all inevitable in a nation guarded by what Bataillon has called "a spiritual police force."⁸ The great French printer Cristophe Plantin, residing in Spanish Antwerp, praised Jesuit education in terms not essentially different from Berganza's: "The schools have a genius of their own, one which tolerates nothing that is not learned, chaste, upright and simple."⁹ But when we remember that these words appear in the preface to his edition of Martial and that the edition had been mutilated by the Jesuits, it is tempting to see in them little more than an attempt to placate his censors, with perhaps even a barbed *double-entendre* on the subject of intolerance. If to this conjecture we ally the fact that Plantin, only overtly a Catholic, was secretly a member of a heretical sect, the *Familia Charitatis*, our suspicion becomes a certainty. I do not of course ascribe such a religious motive to Cervantes. But it is surely significant that in *El coloquio de los perros* the praise of Jesuit schools is folowed by a satirical comment on the method of language instruction used by the Jesuits.¹⁰

In her *Critical Guide* to this tale, Ruth El Saffar views the dogs' praise with considerable skepticism. Because Berganza is treated harshly by his master as a result of the Jesuits' objecting to his accompanying the boys to school, she concludes that the Fathers are in fact being criticized as "too powerful. . . They are too determined. They give no place to recreation and relaxation, spontaneity and pleasure. And they are too attentive to worldly influences."[11] Seen *sub specie Sileni*, the dogs' eulogy must be read as an attack.

In support of this reading it might be said that the two dogs etymologically are—and call themselves—cynics, denouncers of the hypocrisy they find in men with whom they are forced to associate. At the same time the dogs are trying very hard to avoid calumny in their exposing of insincerity. Denunciation without calumny is a hard tightrope for the dogs to walk. Just before he praises Jesuit education, Berganza has been reproved by Cipión for slandering those about whom he is talking. Berganza resolves to cure his bad habit, even though, as he says, "lo tengo por dificultoso." Each time he is tempted to speak evil he will bite the tip of his tongue until it hurts. It is right after he has made this painful resolution that he launches into his paean of Jesuit educators. Beyond the shadow of a doubt he has overcompensated. El Saffar detects "a deep rancor against the Jesuits lurk[ing] beneath Berganza's praise of them" (p. 48). "Cervantes did not get the education that would have given him easy access to the court. This may explain the overt concern in this section [of the *Coloquio*] lest resentment and frustration run away with the story." (p. 49). I would add that, even after receiving a fine education, the Licenciado Vidriera is equally denied access to the court and to preferment. It seems likely that more than the lack of formal education lay behind Cervantes' umbrage, if such it was.

I have dwelt on the vexed question of Berganza's praise of the Jesuits in order to illustrate the difficulty of deducing Cervantes' thoughts about education from his fiction. But with the Silenus vision—everything is both *this* and *that*—even an interviewer would have had difficulty getting clearcut answers from him. El Saffar's reference to Cervantes' own educational experience offers some hope that his life history might give us a few clues about how to read his fictions on education. It is reasonable to expect that the historical what-did-happen may have controlled the fictional what-might-have-been. The trouble with this methodology is that not much is known for certain about Cervantes' life. Much of what fills his biographies is conjecture.[12] The facts of his education are particularly hard to come by.

Cervantes accepted the apparently disparaging appellation *ingenio lego* with bonhomie. In the special sense that he held no university degree an *ingenio lego* is what he was. He was not a *bachiller*, like

Sansón Carrasco, or *licenciado*, like Tomás Rueda. Although he was a man of letters, he was not a *letrado*. Some of his characters too are *ingenios legos*, specifically the creative ones like Don Quixote and Ginés de Pasamonte. The world of fiction and fictionalizing properly belongs to those whose imagination has not been trammelled by a university curriculum.

Cervantes had some pre-university schooling, but very little. He may, it has been calculated, have had up to six years of formal education;[13] but this figure is admittedly based on remote possibilities rather than on credible probabilities. The constant moving of his family meant that as a boy he lived for very short periods in several cities. The nomadic life ensured that whatever elementary education Cervantes may have received was spotty and interrupted. Cervantes must have been taught to some extent by members of his family or perhaps by tutors. Most of all, Cervantes must have taught himself. However he gleaned his *primeras letras*, they were well learned.

The only documented education Cervantes received was in 1568 in the Estudio de la Villa de Madrid, under the tutelage of the humanist clergyman Juan López de Hoyos. There we know that he learned how to write poetry. Four compositions by him were included in an obituary volume which was complied by his teacher for the dead queen, Elizabeth of Valois. In this book, López de Hoyos twice refers to Cervantes as his much beloved disciple. Teachers tend to like outstading students; and Cervantes may have been brilliant. On the other hand, at the age of 20 or 21 he was some five years older than his compeers at the Estudio.[14] So it may have been Cervantes' maturity, as much as his brilliance, that endeared him to López de Hoyos. The fact that Cervantes was studying Latin

Teachers tend to like outstanding students; and Cervantes may have sketchy elementary education, he had set his sights on entering a university. If so, his precipitate flight to Italy scotched his ambition for a higher education. While in Italy, and thereafter, he learned from experience in the school of hard knocks, the same one attended by his Preciosa and his Carriazo.

Scholars have made much of Cervantes' supposed assimilation of Erasmian ideas while he was studying with López de Hoyos.[15] Bataillon gives us perhaps the most balanced statement of this assumption. Cervantes' work, he says "is intelligible only on condition that one sees in it a later fruition, ripened throughout a difficult life of adventure, but fertilized in the autumn of the Spanish Renaissance, when Cervantes received from Master López de Hoyos that somewhat confidential instruction in Erasmianism, condemned thenceforth to express itself in undertones."[16] It cannot be denied that Erasmianism shows in a great deal of Cervantes' writing. But it must be remembered that he spent only six or seven months in López de Hoyos' academy.[17] It is, moreover, far from certain that his teacher was as confirmed a disciple of Erasmus as some modern scholars have supposed. The evidence for López de Hoyos' Erasmianism is an apparently deliberate misquotation of Erasmus which argues a knowledge of two of his works.[18] We know so little about López de Hoyos[19] that it is rash to conclude from such sparse evidence that he was a convinced follower of Erasmus. What is certain is that López de Hoyos was a reader of Erasmus, that he had a high regard for his pupil, and that Cervantes' works show an Erasmian imprint. These three facts do not in themselves justify the belief that López de Hoyos introduced Cervantes to the works of Erasmus. On the face of it, it seems unlikely that a master in a municipal school would have taken the risk of placing in a student's hands books which had been prohibited just nine years earlier. It is permissible to doubt whether these few months of formal training were decisive in Cervantes' education. Some of Erasmus' works unquestionably survived their prohibition in Spain, and Cervantes may have had access to them through others than López de Hoyos. In Italy he would have had even less difficulty in obtaining Erasmian texts.

As I have suggested, experience was for Cervantes a better teacher even than López de Hoyos. As Preciosa told her lover, experience teaches as much in an hour as would otherwise be learned in a year. And the particular experience which educated the mature soldier for a career in writing fiction was the captivity he endured in Africa between 1575 and 1580. As Alonso Zamora Vicente has put it: "Before his captivity Cervantes is still a European soldier of the imperial period. He is the victorious combatant at Lepanto, the studious man acquainted with Erasmianism, the Spaniard touring the cities of Italy, devoting his youth to the double game of love and domination. . . After his captivity, on the other hand, Cervantes is a man who sees the collapse of the political and esthetic conceptions of his youth. Against the soaring Italianate world of Garcilaso he sees the rise of Góngora's baroque contorsions; against the evocation of the gilded cities of Italy. . ., the villages of Castile, with their morose barrenness, their desolate poverty. . .; against Erasmian Alcalá, Trent; against Lepanto, the Invincible Armada."[20] Out of this protracted *desengaño* of the Algerian years came the experience which would be converted into the truth expressed in much of Cervantes' fiction—not just the disenchanted sonnet on Philip II's catafalque, but *Don Quixote*, the *Novelas Ejemplares*, and even the explicitly religious *Persiles*.

A kind of learning went on in Cervantes' mind in Algiers which could not have been obtained from a university. A *letrado* could never have written his books. Only an autodidact, an *ingenio lego* with genius, was capable of that accomplishment. But the fees paid to the school of hard knocks were high. Success came to Cervantes the hard way, by the route of poverty and loneliness. While in time he surely came to appreciate the unique value of his self-education for his career, he must have concurrently resented the fact that he had no old-boys network to provide for him the social and economic advantages enjoyed by other writers. Without it he had trouble finding a maecenas who could bring official distinction to his publications.

The full force of Cervantes' rancor against those who have received a formal education is expressed in his treatment of Don Quixote's guide to the Cave of Montesinos. The self-described humanist's trashy treatises—a Guinness Book of Record Firsts, a *Vogue* magazine of fashionable liveries—are eagerly sought after not only by publishers but also by wealthy, powerful patrons. In contrast, as Don Quixote insinuates to the humanist, it was only after a long, arduous struggle for recognition that Cervantes' novels, tales, and romances won shelter under the prestige of the Count of Lemos. In the world around Cervantes, despicable scholarship is preferred to admirable fiction.

The Primo trivializes scholarship by slavishly imitating the classical poet Ovid and the English humanist Polydore Virgil. He further debases these imitations with his unbridled imagination. It is significant that, like Alonso Quijano, this scholar is "muy aficionado a leer libros de caballerías." In both characters this choice of reading matter betokens and produces an overfertile imagination as he scans authoritative books in search of useless information, information which he then perverts until it is as false as any fiction. Cervantes' fiction, on the other hand, is dignified by his perfectly controlled use of an imagination which is eminently suited to his kind of writing. The fictionalizing scholar abuses, while his creator uses, the imaginative faculty. The Cousin repeats, distorts, and vulgarizes the errors of the past; Cervantes refines the products of his imagination alone in order to produce original works of art.

The humanist and his like "se cansan en saber y averiguar cosas que después de sabidas y averiguadas, no importan un ardite el entendimiento ni a la memoria." What *does* matter, for Cervantes, is the understanding of man and his values, a true humanism of a kind alien to the self-styled humanist of *Don Quixote*.[21] This understanding comes, not from books, but from dealing with one's fellows and observing them. Cervantes aligns himself with those characters of his who have enhanced their innate talents by learning from experience. Marcela, with her natural understanding; Preciosa, with her native intelligence; even Sancho Panza, with his native peasant cunning, have sharpened their wits on "el uso," the way of the world. The self-education of these characters easily outdoes the booklearning of *bachilleres* and *licenciados*.

If Cervantes resented the poverty of his schooling, he must also have prized the education he gave himself over the education others had received from others. His own rough-and-ready education confirms for him the truth of the Silenus analogy first applied to Socrates: inside the bitter learning experience of defeat, captivity, antiheroism, and pennilessness dwells the divinity of true perception, true knowledge, and true understanding, the values of genuine Renaissance humanism. Without this most painful of educations Cervantes' fiction would have been different—less innovative, and hence less influential, and hence less significant.

Duke University

NOTES

[1]*Suma Cervantina*, ed. J. B. Avalle-Arce and E. C. Riley (London: Támesis, 1973), pp. 69-71.

[2]*Examen de los ingenios para las ciencias*, ed. Esteban Torre (Madrid: Editora Nacional, 1977), p. 208.

[3]Translation by W. Hamilton (Harmondsworth, Middlesex: Penguin Books, 1951), p. 100.

[4]My translation from *Moriae Enkomion/Stultitiae Laus, Des. Erasmi Rot. Declamatio*, ed. J. B. Kan (The Hague, 1898), p. 47. The passage is well discussed by Walter Kaiser in *Praisers of Folly* (Cambridge, Mass.: Harvard University Press, 1963), pp. 58-62. Under the motto *Meliora latent*, Sebastián de Covarrubias includes an interesting emblem of the Silenus in his *Emblemas morales*, ed. Carmen Bravo-Villasante (Madrid: Fundación Universitaria Española, 1978), f. 251; he cautiously suggests that the Spanish proverb "Debaxo de mala capa està buen beuedor" may convey something of the same notion.

[5]Translated from *Erasmo y España* (México: El Colegio de México, 1950), II, 394.

[6]See J. H. Elliott, *Imperial Spain 1469-1716* (London: Edward Arnold, 1963), pp. 363-64.

[7]"Discurso de las cosas de la Compañía," in *BAE*, XXXI, p. 601.

[8]Op. cit., II, 351 ("policía espiritual").

[9]Translated from Bataillon, II, 394-95.

[10]In an eccentric book *The Jesuits in the 'Quijote' and Other Essays* (Barcelona: Hispam, 1974), Ernest A. Siciliano concludes that the Jesuits, as depicted in the *Coloquio*, either were the only honest people in a rotten society or they were as rotten as everyone else.

[11]*Cervantes: 'El casamiento engañoso' and 'El coloquio de los perros'*, Critical Guides to Spanish Texts, No. 17 (London: Grant & Cutler, 1976), pp. 49-50.

[12]See Alberto Sánchez, "Estado actual de los estudios biográficos," in *Suma Cervantina*, pp. 3-24.

[13]Richard L. Predmore, *Cervantes*, (New York: Dodd, Mead & Co., 1973), p. 49.

[14] Luis Astrana Marín, *Vida ejemplar y heroica de Miguel de Cervantes Saavedra* (Madrid: Reus, 1949), II, 158.

[15]Particularly Américo Castro, in "Erasmo en tiempo de Cervantes," *RFE*, 18 (1931), 329-89 and 441. See also the abridged version in the author's *Hacia Cervantes* (Madrid: Taurus, 1957), pp. 167-204.

[16]Translated from *Erasmo y España*, II, 400.

[17]Astrana Marín, II, 172.

[18]Cf. Bataillon, II, 351. In an epistle (ca. 1569) to the Ayuntamiento de Madrid extoling the value of education for moral and cultural progress, López de Hoyos uses a few words from the prohibited *Antibarbarorum Liber Primus*; no doubt intentionally, he attributes the sentiment to another work by Erasmus which was still tolerated.

[19]Our knowledge of López de Hoyos derives from a series of documents published by Cristóbal Pérez Pastor in *Documentos cervantinos hasta ahora inéditos* (Madrid: privately published, 1902) II, 355-363 (in footnotes).

[20]"El cautiverio en la obra cervantina," in *Homenaje a Cervantes* (Valencia, 1950), II, 239.

[21]In his inaugural lecture in Leiden in 1915, entitled "Historical Ideals of Life" (in *Men and Ideas*, translated by James S. Holmes and Hans van Marle [New York: Meridian Books, 1959] pp. 90-91) , Johan Huizinga describes the degeneration of Renaissance humanism in terms applicable to Cervantes' Primo: "It was the enrichment [by classical culture] that mattered, not the imitation [of it]. Modern culture has not derived its vitality from a determined copying of antiquity, but from a life-giving permeation by the classical spirit and form. The industrious imitator of Cicero or Brutus became just as impossible a creature as the salon shepherd or the perfect knight. Though the historical content in the concept of antiquity was larger, that does not mean that there was less falsity in its practical expression in the lives of the humanists. The ostentatious and loquacious humanist, treacherous and hollow, a peacock in his pride, soon lost his place in the eyes of his contemporaries."

Los consejos de don Quijote a Sancho

Helena Percas de Ponseti

on Quijote le da a Sancho dos series de consejos (II, 42 y 43) en el momento en que su escudero está a punto de partir para la Ínsula Barataria a tomar posesión de su cargo de gobernador. Más tarde, por carta, añadirá algunos más (II, 51).[1] El propósito de este trabajo es dilucidar la naturaleza de tales consejos para poner de relieve qué opina Cervantes sobre la cordura de Don Quijote cuando más se maravillan de su buen juicio Cide Hamete, su biógrafo, y los duques, sus huéspedes. En estos consejos se encierra la clave de la ética personal de Cervantes, reafirmada gráficamente en el atuendo del Sancho gobernador y del Don Quijote consejero. Son, además, una magistral caracterización de Don Quijote en contraste con la igualmente magistral de Sancho. Constituyen una declaración tácita de Cervantes sobre su arte novelístico concebido para *deleitar* y *enseñar* a un tiempo, como tantas veces y de tantas maneras lo ha manifestado.

La gran mayoría de los lectores ha considerado los consejos edificantes (entre ellos, los anotadores Clemencín[2] y Rodríguez Marín[3]). Otros los han juzgado ejemplares (Casalduero,[4] Varo,[5] Bleznick[6]). Otros, moralizantes pero no insólitos (Castro,[7] Bataillon[8]). Y algunos críticos tenidos por «liberales» (May,[9] Efron[10]), no todos (Osterc Berlan[11]), los han considerado paródicos.

La crítica ha encontrado paralelos, coincidencias, y aun modelos para tales consejos entre los oradores, filósofos y legisladores, comenzando por Catón, con quien el mismo Don Quijote se compara (II, 42), hasta Erasmo y los moralistas erasmizantes (Castro,[12] Bataillon,[13] Riquer[14]), sin descartar la Biblia (Putnam[15]).

Ninguno de estos críticos ha hecho, que yo sepa, un estudio comparado detallado entre el texto de los consejos de Don Quijote y los supuestos modelos con los que se encuentran parecidos, salvo Efron quien ha analizado el primero de los consejos en función de los salmos y proverbios bíblicos. (Ver nota 24.) Un estudio comparado aun somero, pone de manifiesto que los parecidos entre los consejos y los textos clásicos son superficiales—tema y lenguaje—mientras que las divergencias son radicales—contenido y espíritu. Por otra parte, las divergencias con algunos textos modernos parecen más bien acentuar el contenido y espíritu de éstos en conflicto con los clásicos.

Podría trazarse un paralelo significativo entre Erasmo de Rotterdam y Cervantes. Las ideas de Cervantes por detrás de las del Don Quijote de los consejos podrían cotejarse con las de la *Educación del príncipe cristiano* de Erasmo. ¿Pudo conocer Cervantes la traducción hecha por Bernabé Busto para el príncipe don Felipe? Según Bataillon quedó inédita (pág. 628, n. 26). Pero hubo varios libros de educación de príncipes inspirados en el de Erasmo. El estilo de Cervantes, por otra parte, tiene mayor afinidad con el de *El elogio de la Locura* (*Moriae encomium*) del rotterdamiano, tan divulgado por España. Con este último se perciben coincidencias en técnica estilística, en espíritu y en algún tema, pero divergencias de tono y enfoque. Por tanto, me referiré a esta obra.

El espacio de que dispongo no me permite alargarme sobre este fascinante asunto de cómo utiliza Cervantes sus lecturas, pero lo tocaré brevemente considerando con mayor detenimiento, un texto que, según Menéndez y Pelayo, Bataillon, Osterc Berlan, y otros, tenía presente Cervantes al componer los consejos: el *Diálogo de Mer-*

curio y Carón de Alfonso de Valdés, admirador y discípulo de Erasmo por su propia admisión.[16]

Mi propósito es establecer que Cervantes y Don Quijote no son identificables durante la estancia del Caballero en el palacio ducal; que Don Quijote habla como el rey Polidoro (personaje del *Diálogo* de Valdés) o piensa como Felipe II, en un estilo cercano del de Fray Antonio de Guevara, mientras que Cervantes piensa como Erasmo y se expresa tácitamente en un estilo hermano del de la Locura, personaje alegórico del *Elogio*; que, a través del desorden de ideas de Don Quijote surge la unidad de pensamiento de Cervantes, y que Cervantes es barroco y renacentista a la vez, lo cual es una paradoja pero no una contradicción.

Por otra parte, la postura ética de Cervantes es perfectamente deductible del texto y contexto de los consejos sin necesidad de recurrir a ningún estudio comparativo. Basta no dejarse deslumbrar por la elegancia del estilo, el equilibrio de las contraposiciones, la armonía de los sonidos ni el resplandor de los aforismos. Cervantes mismo nos lo sugiere indirectamente a través de los juicios de Cide Hamete y de los duques. Tampoco éstos son identificables con Cervantes.[17] Todo lo cual está corroborado gráficamente, como veremos más adelante.

Los primeros consejos son «documentos»[18]—dice Don Quijote— que han de «adornar el alma» de Sancho. Los segundos «han de servir para adorno del cuerpo». En los consejos de la carta recurren las palabras *adorno, adornarse*. En efecto, ésta es su sustancia. La ironía de Cervantes es hermana de la de Erasmo quien, con menos circunspección, se refiere a la poca sustancia de «that great host of men which burden—I beg your pardon, I mean adorns—the Roman See».[19]

Cide Hamete no capta, como tampoco muchos lectores, la ironía de Cervantes tras esos adornos de que habla Don Quijote, y pregunta retóricamente, después de transcribir los primeros consejos: «¿Quién oyera el pasado razonamiento de Don Quijote, que no le tuviera por persona muy cuerda y mejor intencionada?» Sólo que, como escribe al correr de la pluma, olvida de poner los signos de interrogación. Los suplen todos los anotadores y editores del *Quijote*, tomándolos por un descuido de Cervantes. Si no se enmienda el texto original oímos la propia voz del autor «Quien oyera el pasado razonamiento de Don Quijote, que no le tuviera por persona muy cuerda y mejor intencionada».[20]

En cuanto a los segundos documentos, Cide Hamete los considera de «gran donaire». Ya, en sí, es algo insólito que algunos documentos sean graciosos. Pero también el humanista Alfonso de Valdés hablaba de las «muchas cosas graciosas y de buena doctrina» (subtítulo de su *Diálogo de Mercurio y Carón*) y del rey Polidoro. Al reemplazar *graciosos* por *gran donaire*, Cervantes dice que tienen el *don* natural del *aire*, que están llenos de aire. El chiste es al estilo conceptista popular al que también recurriría Quevedo. Don Aire, como Don Quijote. Sentido que se corrobora al terminar su frase Cide Hamete. Dice que el caballero «puso su discreción y su locura en un levantado punto.». Esto mismo podría decirse del rey Polidoro.

También los duques se maravillan de la «locura» e «ingenio» de Don Quijote cuando, por casualidad, encuentran los documentos escritos en un papel caído al suelo al pasar de manos del caballero a las del escudero.

Por el contexto se nos sugiere que las palabras encomiásticas de Cide Hamete (*discreción*) y de los duques (*ingenio*) se refieren a los consejos mientras que la despectiva de *locura* se refiere a las caballerías. Sin embargo, tanto Cide Hamete como los duques hacen sus respectivos comentarios a raíz de los consejos. Y, así, nos indica Cervantes, por segunda vez, a través de biógrafo y huéspedes que, a pesar del contexto, son los consejos mismos de Don Quijote los que contienen atributos tanto de locura como de cordura. La inversión en el orden de sus respectivos juicios (*discreción-locura*, dice Cide Hamete; *locura-ingenio*, dicen los duques) tiene la virtud de hacer de dos voces antinómicas, *discreción* e *ingenio*, dos términos casi sinónimos que se aplican por igual al mismo objeto, los consejos, ya que ambos se nos dan como antítesis de *locura*. (Ver, también, final nota 20.)

Difícilmente puede un mismo personaje, Don Quijote, ser a un tiempo *discreto*, es decir, juicioso y prudente, pero también *ingenioso*, es decir discurridor e inventivo al recordar reglas morales de doctrinales. Pero Cervantes, como autor, sí puede ser *ingenioso* al hacer *discreto* a Don Quijote para enjuiciar a través de los consejos de su personaje la ideología dentro de la cual están razonados.

También es Cervantes quien nos indica el método a seguir para discernir lo que es discreción y lo que es locura. Esta vez lo hace a través de un vocablo mal aplicado del inculto Sancho, y a través de un consejo mundano de Don Quijote a su escudero. Como Sancho no sabe leer ni escribir piensa llevarle a su confesor los documentos escritos para que se los «encaje» y «recapacite». *Encajar* significa indoctrinar, hacer recordar sin pensar. Mientras que *recapacitar* (verbo intransitivo que Sancho convierte en transitivo y en sinónimo de encajar) tiene, por contrario, el significado de repensar con sentido crítico. En cuanto al consejo de Don Quijote a Sancho, le advierte a su escudero que se fije en la *sustancia* de lo que pide una mujer hermosa y *no* en su *belleza*. Si recapacitemos, pues, sobre la *sustancia* de los consejos *con sentido crítico* sin dejarnos seducir por la *belleza* de su estilo, entramos de pleno en las sutilezas cervantinas que metamorfosean una forma barroca, equilibrada, sugerente de un contenido conservador y tradicional, en una forma renacentista, elástica, cuyo contenido responde a un pensamiento independiente del consenso, el de Cervantes.

Es preciso analizar en orden todos los consejos para darse cuenta de sus dos estructuras superpuestas. Una, circular, externa, barroca. Empezamos con Dios y acabamos con Dios. Regreso al punto de partida. Otra, espiral, interna, renacentista. El temor de Dios del principio se transforma, por inferencia, en el soborno de Dios al final. Lo cual constituye un enjuiciamiento cervantino del modo de razonar de Don Quijote. Cada consejo consiste de una primera parte positiva y una segunda parte negativa o ambivalente. O bien, un consejo pone ambivalencia en otro, o aclara una ambigüedad anterior en sentido inesperado. Esta misma técnica la he observado y descrito por extenso en los episodios que trato en *Cervantes y su concepto de arte.*

El primer consejo de la serie, «para adorno del alma», comienza con un sofisma: «Primeramente, ¡o hijo! has de temer a Dios; porque en el temerle está la sabiduría, y siendo sabio no podrás errar en nada.» Muchos consejos comenzaban con el *temor de Dios*, desde los salmos y proverbios bíblicos (*Initium sapientiae timor Domini* [salmo CX], *Timor domini principium sapientiae* [Proverbios: I, 7]) el «Teme a Dios» de Isócrates,[21] y, pasando por el «conocer, amar e temer a Dios» del Rey Sabio,[22] por el consejo del rey Polidoro a su hijo, «Ama y teme a Dios, y él te bezará todo lo demás y te guiará en todo lo que devieres hazer (»*Diálogo de Mercurio y Carón* de Alfonso de Valdés),[23] hasta el consejo de Felipe II a su hermano Don Juan de Austria (1568) de ser «muy devoto y temeroso de Dios» (*RM*, 229, n. 10). Pero concluir, como hace Don Quijote, que el temor de Dios lleva infaliblemente a la sabiduría, en vez de pensar, como en una ocasión anterior, que es «principio» de ella (II, 20) es un disparate.[24] Don Quijote razona sin discernimiento mientras está en casa de los duques, y acaba confundiendo las cosas. Poco antes pensaba que Sancho no estaba preparado para el gobierno por faltarle «merecimiento». Y que había alcanzado lo que otros no alcanzan sin mucho esfuerzo. Equívocamente, sin embargo, el *merecimiento* y el *esfuerzo* consisten en cohechar, importunar, solicitar, madrugar, rogar, porfiar, dando a entender Cervantes, a través de la momentánea confusión de ideas de Don Quijote, que más poder tiene quien manipula que quien estudia.

Cervantes saca toda la cuestión del contexto teórico, abstracto, de la filosofía (barroco) y lo trae al contexto concreto, real, de la vida (renacimiento) al hacer que Don Quijote, quien ha ensayado vivir de acuerdo con el pensamiento filosófico, regrese hacia lo teórico a través del pensamiento social. Lo cual equivale a una teoría desvirtuada por la realidad. Las cosas no son como deben ser, como eran antes. Dulcinea, la «luz», ha sido encantada. Don Quijote ha quedado en la oscuridad. Ha perdido la intuición de la verdad. Se lo dice a la duquesa. El encantamiento de Dulcinea «me la ha borrado de la idea» (II, 32).

«Lo segundo—continúa aconsejando Don Quijote—es poner los ojos en quien eres, procurando conocerte a ti mismo, que es el más difícil conocimiento que pueda imaginarse». En efecto, todas las filosofías antiguas y modernas, desde la socrática (*Nosce te ipsum*)[25] hasta la budista de la actualidad,[26] preconizan el conocimiento propio como esencial para llegar a discernir la verdad por entre las apariencias. Pero Don Quijote pretende explicar este difícil concepto filosófico simplificándolo mediante la analogía con una fábula moral y la alusión a un refrán popular, para que Sancho le entienda. Dice: «Del conocerte saldrá el no hincharte como la rana que quiso igualarse con el buey [literalmente, en tamaño; figurativamente, en categoría]; que si esto haces, vendrá a ser feos pies de la rueda de tu locura la consideración de haber guardado puercos en tu tierra». Sin la información de los anotadores difícil es aclarar el sentido. La «rueda de la locura» es alusión culta al refrán sobre el pavo real que abrió su hermosa rueda y la volvió a cerrar por vergüenza cuando miró sus feos pies.[27] Lo cual significaba que si Sancho se envanece y ambiciona subir de categoría social se avergonzará de su origen humilde. Hemos perdido de vista el autoconocimiento con el que comenzó hablando Don Quijote. Sancho pone de relieve la falta de consecuencia de Don Quijote al corregir que, de mayor, no fueron puercos sino gansos los que guardó. Posiblemente, recuerda Don Quijote el consejo del rey Polidoro a su hijo: «muestra desplazerte la ambición; si esta pudieres tener fuera de tu casa y de tu reino, entonces te puedes llamar bienaventurado» (pág. 200). El término *ambición* puede sustuirse por el de *codicia* o *pecado* o cualquier otra particularidad, y concluir con la misma bienaventuranza, una totalidad. Equivale a derivar el todo de la parte en un *non sequitur* carente de toda lógica. Con mayor lógica, en su totalmente absurdo *non sequitur* deriva Don Quijote de la totalidad, el autoconocimiento, la particularidad, la ambición de la rana y la vanidad del pavo real. Es, precisamente, la bienaventuranza, el *non sequitur* del rey Polidoro, que ha sustituido Don Quijote por el suyo al recurrir a la fábula y al refrán, si lógicamente, no consecuentemente invertidos: el envanecimiento del pavo real lleva a la ambición de la rana que se hincha hasta reventar, por lo que ya no tiene lugar el autoconocimiento del que deriva toda la analogía. De ahí, que sólo nos quedan los feos pies del pavo real: la humildad de Sancho. Si Don Quijote es falaz en su *non sequitur*, Cervantes es consecuente en su lógica paródica que niega el valor, la eficacia y la verdad a la literatura humanista pseudoculta. Mejor afirmar al estilo barroco que explicar simplificando como hace el letrado popularizador del Renacimiento. Valdés pretendía, en efecto, escribir en un «estilo que de todo género de hombres fuese con sabor leído» (Proemio al lector, pág. 3). Tambien Cervantes, pero lo hace de otro modo, afirmando lo fácil, la conducta, para que se entienda, y dejando lo difícil, la explicación, envuelta en ambigüedad, precisamente para que no se entienda y no desoriente al lector ingenuo o precipitado. El pensamiento no se transmite. Se revela.

Siguiendo su idea, Don Quijote le explica a Sancho que «los no de principios nobles deben acompañar la gravedad del cargo que ejercitan con una blanda suavidad que, guiada por la prudencia los libre de la murmuración maliciosa de quien no hay estado [—se contradice—] que se escape». ¿Es el objeto de la suavidad y de la prudencia el librarse de la murmuración maliciosa? ¿Es que los de principios nobles, quienes tampoco escapan a la murmuración, necesitan menos precauciones? ¿Recuerda Don Quijote el consejo de Isócrates: «Todo género de murmuración contra ti debes evitar»?[28] Más bien, parece recordar la advertencia de Polidoro de tener «cuidado» de comportarse con "la gravedad que conviene al príncipe» (pág. 201). Al equilibrar rítmicamente sus frases, Don Quijote convierte la *gravedad* (porte, presencia), en la *gravedad del cargo* (situación); y el *príncipe* (noble rango) en lo opuesto, *los no de principios nobles*, en los humildes con lo cual crea ambigüedades. La *gravedad del cargo* puede referirse a la situación personal del gobernante, o bien, a su responsabilidad. *Los no de principios nobles*, al origen o bien a las normas. La *suavidad* y la *prudencia*, a la táctica, o bien, a la conducta. Don Quijote y Cervantes dicen cosas distintas con las mismas palabras. Don Quijote habla de lo conveniente para un gobernador de origen humilde. Habla de tácticas. Cervantes, en cambio, habla de la falta de responsabilidad y de normas en la conducta cínica de quienes gobiernan por artimañas. Habla de principios. Don Quijote se contradice. Cervantes, no.

En el siguiente consejo le dice Don Quijote a Sancho de hacer «gala. . . de la humildad de [su] linaje». ¿No es hacer gala hacer ostentación, lo cual es equivalente a tener orgullo de su origen humilde, que acaba de ser comparado con los feos pies del pavo real? Pero es sobre todo el motivo de este consejo lo que llama la atención, pues se trata de no correrse para que otros no le corran, y no porque la dignidad y la nobleza de alma con cualidades inalienables que debe poseer un gobernador indistintamente de su origen. «Préciate más— sigue Don Quijote—de ser humilde virtuouso que pecador soberbio.» He aquí una contraposición asombrosa ya que le propone de escoger entre dos alternativas, no ya de valor desigual sino opuesto: una buena y otra mala. Para colmo, el corolario es que así se sube más alto.[29] Lo que, seguramente, quiere decir Don Quijote es que para tener éxito hay que ser virtuoso y no soberbio. El equilibrio barroco de su estilo es puramente fonético, como el de Fray Antonion de Guevara (véase nota 81 y texto correspondiente). Lleva, además, a la dudosa conclusión que el humilde virtuoso puede alcanzar por sus cualidades lo que el soberbio pecador alcanza por sus mañas. La experiencia no lo respalda.

En otro caso entramos de lleno en el tema hasta aquí medio circunvenido, el de la virtud: «Mira, Sancho. si tomas por medio a la virtud [por medio=¿sin titubear, o bien como medio para alcanzar?], y te precias de hacer hechos virtuosos, no hay para qué tener envidia a los que los tienen príncipes y señores». De nuevo una ambigüedad

imposible de resolver con sentido único, como atestiguan los vanos
esfuerzos de los anotadores.[30] Don Quijote dice que si se tiene virtud no hay para qué tener envidia a quienes tienen medios económicos por ser príncipes y señores, es decir, por venir de sangre real o
noble. Cervantes dice mucho más. Dice que los hechos virtuosos
que pasan por virtud pero no lo son, son el medio de alcanzar lo
deseado de quienes no tienen medios económicos por no venir de
sangre real o noble, la cual es el medio de quienes carecen de virtud,
de nobleza interior, aunque pasan por príncipes y señores. El elegante galimatías del breve consejo de Don Quijote resume lo que el
rey Polidoro esparce por varios. Dice Polidoro. «Si tú pusieres por
premio de tus trabajos *la virtud*. . . » (pág. 202). «Mira, Sancho—dice
Don Quijote—si tomas por medio a *la virtud*...». Polidoro, en otro
consejo: y procuras «parecer christiano [no dice *ser* sino *parecer*] no
solamente con las cerimonias exteriores, mas con obras christianas. . .»
(pág. 202). Nótese que les da todavía mayor valor a las ceremonias
que a las obras, y confunde la obra cristiana con el sentir cristiano.
Lo cual abrevia Don Quijote en: «y te *precias* de hacer *hechos virtuosos*»
(no dice: *ser virtuoso*). Polidoro, en el primer consejo : «nunca vivirás
descontento. . . y podrás dormir seguro»,[31] falacia de índole egocén-
trica que Don Quijote sustituye por otra de la misma índole, casi
imperceptible por el alambicado lenguaje: «no hay para que tener
envidia a los que los tienen príncipes y señores», final correspondiente al de un tercer consejo de Polidoro: «que no es verdadero rey
ni príncipe aquel a quien viene de linaje, mas aquel que con obras
procura de serlo» (pág. 203).

El pensamiento de Don Quijote es el de Polidoro pero se oculta
tras la ambigüedad que, por una parte, mantiene fuera del alcance
del lector desprevenido lo que en Polidoro es reducción moral u
obvia falacia (si eres virtuoso dormirás tranquilo). Por otra parte, le
permite a Cervantes de juzgar negativamente la obra de Valdés.

Don Quijote elabora su idea: «porque la sangre se hereda y la
virtud se aquista y la virtud vale por sí sola lo que la sangre no vale.».
Don Quijote utiliza el verbo *valer* en su sentido etimológico de *merecer
aprecio*; el verbo *aquistar* como cultismo por *conquistar*. Lo que él dice es
que la virtud conquistada tiene mayor valor que la sangre heredada.
Cervantes utiliza el verbo *valer* en el sentido figurado de *tener valor
adquisitivo, ser canjeable*; y *aquistar* como cultismo por *adquirir*. Lo que
Cervantes dice con sentido paródico es que el hecho virtuoso, la

virtud fabricada (no la innata) tiene todavía mayor valor canjeable en la sociedad contemporánea que la sangre adquirida (nobleza heredada y no innata). Para invocar los dos sentidos, el de Don Quijote y el propio, del aforismo «la sangre se hereda y la virtud de aquista», modifica Cervantes el refrán: «la sangre se hereda, y el vicio se pega». Sustituye con equilibrio barroco, en la segunda parte del refrán, el *vicio* por la *virtud*, y el verbo corriente *pegar* por el culto *aquistar*, de sentidos contrarios. El ritmo del refrán conocido, cuya primera parte ha quedado intacta, evoca el sentido de Don Quijote. El contenido culto y paródico de la segunda parte del aforismo revela el sentido ético de Cervantes al enjuiciar el pensamiento pseudo-erasmista de Valdés que remeda Don Quijote. Tras las pedantes cultismos de Don Quijote se encuentran los eruditos cultismos de Cervantes.

«Siendo esto así, como lo es» [que «la sangre se hereda y la virtud se aquista»], sigue aconsejando Don Quijote «que[32] si acaso viniere a verte cuando estés en tu ínsula alguno de tus parientes, no le deseches ni le afrentes [por ser de sangre humilde y presentarse sin invitación, se entiende]; antes le has de acoger, agasajar y regalar; que con esto satisfarás al cielo, que gusta que nadie se desprecie de lo que él hizo, y corresponderás a lo que debes a la naturaleza bien concertada». Es decir, no desprecies en público lo que tal vez desprecias en privado. Un lector ortodoxo puede no desconcertarse de que se ejerza la caridad por deber antes que por instinto natural. La Inquisición no se desconcertaría ya que hizo tachar la frase: «las obras de caridad que se hacen tibia y flojamente no tienen mérito ni valen nada». II, 36)[33] Pero podrá desconcertarse si considera que Dios comparte con la naturaleza la virtud teologal de la caridad que a Dios sólo se le debe. En cuanto al lector no ortodoxo podrá preguntarse si Cervantes deja infiltrar pensamientos panteístas en su filosofía cristiana, o, más acertadamente, opino yo, si está haciendo una distinción esencial entre ser virtuoso por deber (para hacer méritos) y serlo por principio (sin pensar en la recompensa: «No me mueve, mi Dios, para quererte / el cielo que me tienes prometido» dice el poeta místico). Esto último es lo cristiano. No es cristiano ni ético, aunque puede ser útil, el tomar la virtud como medio y no como fin.

Otro consejo. «Si trujeres a tu mujer contigo (porque no es bien que los que asisten a gobiernos de mucho tiempo estén sin las propias), enséñala, doctrínala y desbástala de su natural rudeza; porque todo lo que suele adquirir un gobernador discreto suele perder y derramar una mujer rústica y tonta». ¿Es que es aceptable para los no gobernantes de estar con mujeres no propias sino ajenas, como puede dar a entender el lenguaje? ¿Dos categorías de ciudadanos? ¿O es sólo una cuestión temporal?: los gobernantes, no por mucho tiempo. ¿Dos categorías de moralidad? Y, ¿cómo es que ahora se trata de enseñar, doctrinar y desbastar de su natural rudeza a la mujer, en suma, de cambiarla de naturaleza cuando hace un momento se trataba de no desechar, ni afrentar, sino de acoger, agasajar y regalar a los parientes que vienen a visitar al gobernador para corresponder así a lo que se debe a la naturaleza bien concertada? ¿Dos categorías de parientes, los lejanos y los inmediatos? O bien, ¿dos categorías de naturaleza, la de los nobles y la de los humildes, atribuyendo ahora a los nobles las buenas cualidades naturales antes atribuidas a los humildes (naturaleza bien concertada)? Pero, además, en este consejo se nos da a sobreentender que un gobernador discreto (léase, *astuto*) se hace con una fortuna que puede echar a perder una mujer rústica y tonta (léase, *sin artimañas*). La literatura moralista está llena de consejos al gobernante y al juez de no llevar a la mujer consigo debido a que la naturaleza femenina turba la paz con sus excesos, disoluciones, y temor, como también pensaban los antiguos.[34] En un estilo fonético-rítmico a lo Guevara (ver nota 81), Don Quijote coincide con ellos. Cervantes, no: dirige el dardo al gobernador *discreto* y no a la mujer *rústica* y *tonta*. De nuevo dos sentidos, uno directo y otro implícito; el moral-social de Don Quijote y el ético-crítico de Cervantes.

Lo que sigue recoge el sentido paródico que le da Erasmo a la declaración de su Locura sobre las ventajas que posee el marido de una mujer *experta*, por no decir *prostituta* (pág. 28). Sólo que Cervantes denuncia con mayor vehemencia la prostitución ideológica que la física. Ahora veremos en qué terminos.

Don Quijote no considera la rusticidad de Teresa propia para la mujer de un Sancho gobernador. Se trasluce al comienzo del siguiente consejo: «Si acaso enviudares, cosa que puede suceder, y con el cargo mejorares de consorte [pudiendo ahora escoger entre la nobleza, se entiende]. . . no la tomes tal que te sirva de anzuelo y de caña de pescar. . . y del no quiero de tu capilla [parte de un refrán que significa no lo quiero pero dámelo]; porque en verdad te digo que de todo aquello que la mujer del juez [*juez* se llama pronto al gobernador] recibiere ha de dar cuenta el marido en la residencia universal [el Juicio final], donde pagará con el cuatro tanto en la muerte las partidas de que no se hubiere hecho cargo en la vida». Es decir, no escojas a la mujer por motivos materialistas sino para asegurar la salvación del alma, porque el juez supremo las cobra cuatro veces más caras en el cielo que en la tierra. Lo que Cervantes sugiere en éste como en el anterior consejo es que hay complicidad entre el gobernador *astuto* y la mujer *maquinadora*. Su ironía y parodia va dirigida contra el utilitario consejo de Don Quijote. Pero más todavía contra quienes atemorizan y amenazan blandiendo la idea del Dios-Juez. Por encima de la moral colectiva está la ética individual.

El octavo consejo, «Nunca te guíes por la ley del encaje», es decir, por criterio propio, coincide son la opinion del satírico poeta latino, Juvenal («*Hoc volo, sic jubeo, sit pro ratione voluntas*») y de escritores del Siglo de Oro, como Mateo Alemán («Líbrete Dios de juez con *leyes de encaje* y escribano enemigo, y de cualquier cohechado»),[35] o como Pedro Espinosa («Habrá jueces lagartos, con *leyes* y dientes *de encaje* que no abrirán la boca sino con pan caliente»).[36] En lo que todos estos escritores piensan es en el abuso del juez y no, como Don Quijote, en que Sancho debe guiarse por el criterio de la ley escrita. Para Cervantes no se trata de tomar partido en el debate entre letrados y legos. Piensa, como sus contemporáneos, que hay muchos cínicos con autoridad, y no, como Don Quijote, que los letrados son infalibles. Es por la ley del encaje que gobernará Sancho y lo hará bien.[37] No sólo por carecer de memoria para recordar documentos, la letra escrita, sino por recordar refranes, la letra oral, compendio de la sabiduría popular. Como dice él mismo, sabe más refranes «que un libro» y le vienen «todos juntos a la boca. . . que riñen por salir». Pero sobre todo gobernará bien, por tener buen natural como intuye Don Quijote después del último consejo.

Los ocho consejos que siguen son, en realidad, uno sólo, y si, separadamente, parecen ostentar cualidades ejemplares, juntos revelan fondos negativos. «Hallen en ti más compasión las lágrimas del pobre, pero no más justicia, que las informaciones del rico.». Don Quijote quiere decir, como dice Alonso de Villadiego,[38] que debe tratarse con igual justicia al pobre como al rico, y con mayor compasión al pobre. Pero llevado de su predilección por el equilibrio barroco dice casi lo contrario: que se tenga más compasión por el pobre pero menos justicia que con el rico. Si queda alguna duda sobre lo que ocultan las lágrimas del pobre y las informaciones del rico se aclara con el siguiente consejo: «Procura descubrir la verdad por entre las promesas y dádivas del rico como por entre los sollozos e importunidades del pobre». Rico y pobre mienten por igual.

Dice el undécimo consejo: «Cuando pudiere y debiere tener lugar la equidad [¿es que no siempre debe tener lugar?, ¿no es ésta la esencia de la justicia?] no cargues todo el rigor de la ley al delincuente.» Impecable sentimiento cristiano que coincide con el de los consejos de Bartolomé de Góngora,[39] los del Rey Sabio,[40] o los de Zeballos.[41] Pero sigue diciendo Don Quijote: «que no es mejor la fama del juez riguroso que la del compasivo». Objetivo principal: la fama del juez; y no, como concluía Bartolomé de Góngora porque «es culpa castigar toda la culpa»: conciencia del juez. La crítica de Cervantes va, no contra el consejo, sino contra el motivo del consejo de Don Quijote.

El duodécimo consejo. «Si acaso doblares la vara de la justicia [lo que figurativamente significa cometer una injusticia, corromper un principio—la vara del juez debe ser recta—] no sea con el peso de la dádiva, sino con el de la misericordia». Cáceres, Castillo de Bobadilla, Séneca, Fray Luis de Jesús Maria, se lamentan de la perversión de la justicia a consecuencia del soborno de los jueces, que les induce a *doblar la vara de la justicia.*[42] Don Quijote quiere decir, sin duda, lo mismo, que no se deje Sancho sobornar y que sea piadoso con los indefensos, como también pedía Villadiego (ver nota 38). Pero su lenguaje retórico-legalista dice de aceptar la dádiva y pretender que el perdón es por misericordia. Lo que equivale a que el rico queda perdonado y el pobre va a galeras, como claramente se vio en el episodio de los galeotes (I, 22).[43] La alusión de Cervantes va dirigida, por tanto, contra el cuerpo judicial y, tal vez, también, contra Felipe II, si es que tuvo noticia Cervantes—difícil parece—de las instrucciones del Rey a Don Juan de Austria, aconsejándole de tomar en cuenta *la calidad* de las personas al hacer justicia. Dice Felipe II:

> De la justicia usareis con igualdad y rectitud, y *quando será necesario, con el rigor y ejemplo que el caso requiere. . .;* y juntamente, *cuando la calidad* de las *cosas* y *personas* lo sufriere sereis *piadoso y benigno,* que son *virtudes* muy *propias* de personas *de vuestra calidad.*[44]

Subrayo para mejor poner en relieve el doble criterio de la advertencia. La cual indica de hacer lo mismo que, sin darse cuenta, prescribe Don Quijote.

Otro consejo. «Cuando te sucediere juzgar algún pleito de algún tu enemigo, aparta las mientes de tu injuria y ponlas en la verdad del caso». También Villadiego habla de no ser vengativo. Y el Venerable Beda, historiador inglés, de no favorecer al amigo en causas legales.[45] De las palabras de Don Quijote (*tu injuria*) se trasluce que una de las dos partes es el mismo juez. Se trasluce también, del equilibrio barroco de lo que sigue: «No te ciegue la *pasión propia* en la *causa ajena*». (El énfasis es mío.) La razón está de parte del procesado y no del juez. La conclusión lo corrobora: «que los yerros que en ella [la causa ajena] hicieres las más veces serán sin remedio; y si le tuvieren, será a costa de tu crédito y aun de tu hacienda». Los yerros de juicio (Don Quijote) pero también equivocaciones morales cometidas sin error de juicio (Cervantes). De nuevo dos sentidos. Y en uno u otro caso puede costar caro, y, así, debe evitarse.

«Si alguna mujer hermosa viniere a pedirte justicia quita los ojos de sus lágrimas y tus oídos de sus gemidos y considera de espacio la sustancia de lo que pide, si no quieres que se anegue tu razón en su llanto y tu bondad en sus suspiros». ¿No merece la fea igual atención para considerar la sustancia de lo que pide? Claro que Don Quijote no quiere decir eso. Como no quiere decir que el hombre se olvida del deber frente a la mujer hermosa, ni que ésta esgrime contra él su hermosura, arma que no posee la fea, ni tampoco quiere decir que la única manera de conseguir justicia es comprándola, o bien ocultando le verdad, como implícitamente dice Cervantes en todo lo omitido del consejo de Don Quijote. Este estilo cervantino de hablar por inferencia sobre el poder de la belleza femenina recuerda el del discurso de la Locura sobre los poderes de la mujer. Sólo que Erasmo los presenta festivamente, como una virtud.[46] Cervantes, como artimaña del demonio.[47] Si Don Quijote habla con ingenuidad de la mujer hermosa que pide Justicia y del juez que le escucha, Cervantes habla con malicia.

«Al que has de castigar con obras, no trates mal con palabras, pues le basta al desdichado la pena del suplicio, sin la añadidura de las malas razones». ¿Puede tratarse mal con palabras al que no se castiga con obras? Don Quijote no quiere decir tal cosa sino, como Castillo de Bobadilla o como Felipe II,[48] que es indigno castigar verbalmente a nadie. Pero su debilidad por la oratoria y el ritmo de la frase le inducen a balancear las voces antitéticas, *obras* y *palabras*, sobre el pivote del verbo *castigar*. Con lo cual tergiversa el sentido y le permite a Cervantes de denunciar la actitud del cuerpo judicial.

El siguiente consejo de Don Quijote nos recuerda tanto el doble criterio judicial de Felipe II como su exhortación a mostrarse benévolo con la «lengua», «haciendo *a todos* justicia y razón» (ver nota 48), lo cual, bien pensado, es una imposibilidad técnica. Dice Don Quijote: «Al culpado que cayere debajo de tu jurisdicción considérale hombre miserable, sujeto a las condiciones de la depravada naturaleza nuestra, y en *todo cuanto fuere de tu parte, sin hacer agravio a la contraria* (el énfasis es mío) muéstratele piadoso y clemente. . . » El sentido implícito de lo que Don Quijote dice a pesar de su buena intención es: considera al culpado, culpable, y al miserable, perverso, puesto que la naturaleza humana es depravada—antes hablaba de la naturaleza bien concertada—y siempre que te sea posible [Cervantes termina la idea: hazte pasar por piadoso y clemente, aunque no lo seas]. El diccionario de la Academia da, en efecto, *culpado* como sinónimo de *culpable*; y *miserable* como sinónimo de *perverso* pero también de *infeliz*, cuyos dos sentidos son opuestos. Los sentidos negativos se derivan del concepto del pecado original de Adán y Eva por razón del cual el hombre nace con pecado aun sin culpa. En su lenguaje Don Quijote confunde el pecado original con el delito individual, y lo que es más grave, tanto el juez como el delincuente quedan exentos de responsabilidad, el primero por sus decisiones y el segundo por sus actos. Cervantes subraya y delata la irreductibilidad del espíritu de la ley divina, origen de la humana, a la práctica de la ley, no debido a la depravada naturaleza nuestra sino a nuestra incompetencia racional y mezquindad ideológica. Como el culpado siempre es el pobre por falta de dinero e influencia, por inferencia resulta que, en la práctica, el pecado original afecta sólo al pobre y no al rico.

Concluye Don Quijote la serie de los primeros consejos explicando, una vez más, por qué debe ser un juez piadoso y clemente. Pero ahora lo hace desde una premisa inesperada: «aunque los atributos de Dios todos son iguales, más resplandece y campea a nuestro ver el de la misericordia que el de la justicia». ¿Qué tienen que ver los atributos de Dios con la decisión de un juez si ya no es que el juez obra como si fuera Dios y considera que cuanto hace está bien hecho? Misericordia o justicia, lo mismo da. Por tanto, hágase lo que sea mejor para el juez: ganarse fama de misericordioso (inferencia de Cervantes). «El buen príncipe es imagen de Dios» le hace decir

Alfonso de Valdés a Polidoro recordando a Plutarco, «y el malo figura y ministro del diablo. Si quieres ser tenido por buen príncipe, procura de ser muy semejante a Dios, no haciendo cosa que él no haría» (pág. 202). Como dice Bataillon, «no es poco exigir» (pág. 402). ¿No se origina en esta identificación del monarca con Dios, la confusión de Don Quijote, tras la cual alude Cervantes a la realeza—tal vez a Felipe II—pero, sobre todo, al erasmista Valdés? El humor paródico de Cervantes es, sin embargo, hermano del de Erasmo. Hablando de los eruditos pedantes afirma Erasmo, por boca de la Locura, que tratan asuntos relativos a lo divino como si algo tuvieran que ver con lo humano (pág. 91). Y lo hacen en nombre del arte de la retórica oratoria (pág. 89). No, Don Quijote el humanista, no quiso o no debió decir cuanto ha dicho. Quiso o debió decir que el hombre, creado a imagen de Dios, debe imitar la vida de Cristo, su hijo. No su vida externa—pobreza, trabajos, enseñanzas, crucifixión —como interpreta la casquivana Locura de Erasmo (pág. 98)—¿cabe mayor orgullo?—sino su vida interior de nobleza y meditación. De nuevo coinciden Cervantes y Erasmo.

No cabe duda que Don Quijote aconseja cómo debe conducirse un gobernador para tener éxito mientras Cervantes infiere cómo no debe conducirse para gobernar bien. Lo corroboran las últimas palabras de Don Quijote a Sancho en las que fluye la tácita ironía de Cervantes: «Si estos preceptos y estas reglas sigues, Sancho, serán luengos tus días, tu fama será eterna, tus premios colmados, tu felicidad indecible, casarás tus hijos como quisieres, títulos tendrán ellos y tus nietos, vivirás en paz y beneplácito de las gentes, y en los últimos pasos de la vida te alcanzará el de la muerte, en vejez suave y madura y cerrarán tus ojos las tiernas y delicadas manos de tus terceros netezuelos». El plantel del discurso de la Locura.

Los consejos segundos «para adorno del cuerpo» son de la misma índole que los primeros. Segundan lo ya dicho, si leemos en el vocablo *segundos* un gerundio a la latina del verbo castellano segundar.[49] Don Quijote está cambiando de tema,[50] pero Cervantes, no.

Aconseja Don Quijote ser limpio y cortarse las uñas; no andar como los ignorantes que creen «que las uñas largas les hermosean las manos. . . siendo antes garras de cernícalo lagartijero: puerco y extraordinario abuso». Don Quijote habla de limpieza física, de lo externo. Cervantes habla de limpieza moral, de integridad. Pinta al que carece de ella con gráfico expresionismo: un manto rojizo (el del color del cernícalo) cuyo tinte le viene, metafóricamente, de la sangre de las inocentes víctimas que tiene al alcance de sus inescrupulosas garras negras dispuestas al juego sucio. *Puerco*, sinónimo de *sucio*, adquiere sentido figurado de obrar *sin escrúpulos*, recalcado por el vocablo *abuso*, cultismo pedantemente utilizado por Don Quijote para indicar *exceso*, pero pensado por Cervantes como latinismo, *ab uso*, compuesto análogamente a *ab initio, ab aeterno* (desde el comienzo, desde siempre). Así se refiere a la inveterada costumbre de abusar del pueblo. ¡Amarga consideración! Esto es pintar la «intención». La inconsecuencia de cortarse o no las uñas para gobernar bien la pone de realce Sancho cuando le escribe a Don Quijote que no tuvo tiempo de cortárselas por estar muy ocupado en el desempeño de sus funciones gubernatorias.

«No andes desceñido y flojo; que el vestido descompuesto da indicios de ánimo desmazalado si ya la descompostura y flojedad no cae debajo de socarronería, como se juzgó en la de Julio César.» Lo que no se dice aquí es si Julio César fue un legislador bueno o malo. La omisión de Don Quijote es el tácito comentario de Cervantes. Éste infiere que el vestir es secundario al pensar y al obrar, como claramente lo dice en *Los baños de Argel.* (Ver nota 61.) Muy consciente de su técnica elíptica pide poco después, por boca de Cide Hamete, «alabanzas, no por lo que escribe, sino por lo que ha dejado de escri-

«Toma con discreción el pulso a lo que pudiera valer tu oficio [de nuevo el verbo materialista *valer*], y si sufriere que des librea a tus criados, dásela honesta y provechosa más que vistosa y bizarra». Difícil entender qué es una librea *honesta* y *provechosa*. Aunque contrapuestos estos vocablos a *bizarra* y *vistosa* pudieran significar *modesta* y *útil*. Don Quijote se referiría a cumplir con el expediente sin hacer alardes. En la España de Felipe II se hacía ostentación entre la nobleza y en la Corte mediante la librea (Ver Percas, pág. 554). El Primo había escrito un libro «de gran provecho» titulado *«el de las libreas,* con sus colores, motes y cifras de donde podían sacar y tomar las que quisiesen en tiempo de fiestas y regocijos los caballeros cortesanos. . . » (II, 22). Era corriente, también, recoger la librea una vez terminado el servicio. El provecho, por tanto, sería para el cortesano y no para el paje. Con las palabras de Don Quijote Cervantes aludiría a quienes ostentaban una riqueza que no poseían de lo cual sacarían no poco provecho. Pero lo que sigue es lo asombroso. «si has de vestir seis pajes, viste tres y otros tres pobres, y así tendrás pajes para el cielo y para el suelo; y este nuevo modo de dar librea [léase, *de sacar provecho*] no le alcanzan [léase, *entienden,* su sinónomo] los vanagloriosos». Cervantes sugiere con sutil ironía que Don Quijote aconseja sacrificar un tanto la gratificadora vanagloria mediata en favor del agradecimiento eterno del pobre, con la consecuente compra de la voluntad divina.

Sancho no debe comer ajos ni cebollas, no por no ofender con el olor sino porque los demás no descubran su villanería (ver final de la nota 49), es decir, su origen humilde del que antes se ha dicho debe enorgullecerse.

Debe Sancho andar despacio, hablar con reposo, pero no de manera que parezca escucharse; «que toda ostentación es mala». Don Quijote infiere, inadvertidamente, que se debe ser discreto en la forma de ostentar; en vez de pensar, como Cervantes, que no se debe ostentar.

«Come poco y cena más poco; que la salud de todo el cuerpo se fragua en la oficina del estómago.» Esta moderación en el comer, como también en el beber, del consejo que le sigue, la recomiendan numerosos refranes, y algunos consejos médicos siguiendo los de Galeno. Sancho no lo necesita. Come cuando encuentra el qué. Puede decir como Quevedo: «Mi pobreza me sirve de Galeno. . . no ceno».[51] El consejo es para ricos y no para pobres que no tienen qué comer—comentario tácito de Cervantes.

«Sé templado en el beber, considerando que el vino demasiado ni guarda secreto ni cumple palabra». Cervantes: ¿Qué secreto debe guardar un gobernador, ni qué palabra cumplir mientras bebe?

«Ten cuenta de no mascar a dos carrillos ni erutar delante de nadie». El cultismo *erutar,* en vez de la voz popular *regoldar* a que tiene que recurrir el caballero porque Sancho no le entiende, le sirve a Cervantes para hacerle decir a Don Quijote que deben utilizarse los cultismos en vez de las voces populares con objeto de enriquecer la lengua.[52] Cervantes demostrará en el curso de la conversación entre Don Quijote y Sancho que ello no es cierto, que la forma no altera la sustancia, como no altera el modo de montar a caballo la naturaleza del jinete haciendo de los unos «caballeros» y de los otros «caballerizos» según afirma Don Quijote poco después. El interludio lingüístico que comento a continuación tiene por objeto llamar la atención del lector sobre la afectación de Don Quijote al hablar a lo letrado, como ha estado haciendo desde el comienzo de sus consejos, en contraste con el ingenio elíptico de Sancho al pensar al estilo conceptista popular.

Le dice Don Quijote a Sancho de no mezclar refranes con sus pláticas cuando no vienen al caso «que más parecen disparates que sentencias». Creyendo seguir el consejo de su señor dice Sancho: «Yo tendré cuenta de aquí adelante de decir los [refranes] que convengan a la gravedad de mi cargo, que en casa llena, presto se guisa la cena; y quien destaja no baraja; y a buen salvo está el que repica; y el dar y el tener seso ha menester». Esta retahila de refranes, al parecer, a despropósito, no lo son. Lo que dice Sancho es que como sabe tantos refranes (tiene la *casa*—la cabeza—llena), eligirá sin dificultad alguna («presto se guisa la cena») y con tiento («quien destaja no baraja») aquellos refranes que convengan a la gravedad del cargo (grave situación de un gobernador de origen humilde como él—sentido que también le dio antes Cervantes). Se adelantará a cualquier objeción («a buen salvo está el que repica») que pueda ponerle cualquier clase de reprobador («el dar y el tener seso ha menester»). Este último refrán es una ingeniosa sustitución del sentido de *hacienda material*, el *dar* y el *tener*, por *hacienda intelectual*,[52] *seso*, sinónimo de *inteligencia* y, figurativamente, de *prudencia*. Con lo cual está diciendo Sancho que tiene el recurso de su ingenio, *sus refranes, su hacienda,* para hablar con prudencia siempre que sea preciso. Don Quijote no le comprende. En su exasperación, no se le ocurre al caballero otra cosa que reprender a su escudero con un refrán: «Castígame mi madre, y yo trómpogelas», que si no se entiende por su sentido intrínseco (al revés de lo que sucede con los refranes de Sancho) se entiende perfectamente por el contexto: Sancho no hace el menor caso de la advertencia de su consejero. El lector se sonreirá con sola la ironía de que Don Quijote repruebe los refranes de Sancho con un refrán.[54] Pero más aún si considera que el caballero hace la concesión inconcebible de preferir la voz más idiomática y antigua de *trómpogelas* a la más sintáctica de *trómposelas*. Este vocablo de origen incierto[55] parece haberle intrigado y traído el refrán a la memoria. Él cree que viene del francés *tromper*, burlarse, engañar, como nos da a entender Cervantes haciéndoselo usar más tarde en forma «inadmisible» según Foulché-Delbosc, más cercana del francés trómpegelas (II, 67).[56] Si el refrán está bien aplicado por Don Quijote a lo que van tratando a pesar del galicismo etimológico que contiene es porque el pueblo ha torcido su sentido original al apropiárselo y hacerlo significar *porfiar*, como requiere el temperamento español, y no *engañar*, como quiere su etimología. De modo que es el uso idiomático popular que enriquece le lengua y no la voz culta. Elaborada sutileza cervantina en que, de nuevo, el barroco se metamorfosea en renacimiento si penetramos en la trastienda del pensamiento del autor. El humanismo de Cervantes no es una doctrina. Es una filosofía.

Con delicado humorismo pone Cervantes en boca de su caballero otra expresión popular igualmente bien aplicada al caso pero sin gracia en el nivel directo de lectura. Igual que la anterior carece de representación mediata para el lector. Le dice Don Quijote a Sancho que así cuadran sus refranes con lo que va tratando «como por los cerros de Úbeda.» En Úbeda no hay cerros. Don Quijote lo sabe. Y esta expresión a que se acoge después de mucho sudar para aplicarla bien, como él mismo admite,[57] contiene una alusión culta, a lo Góngora, que sólo un lector conocedor de la geografía de Úbeda puede captar en toda la extensión de su propiedad: los refranes de Sancho están tan fuera de lugar como lo están los cerros en la expresión «por los cerros de Úbeda» puesto que en Úbeda no hay cerros. El lector entiende el sentido por el contexto y por lo idiomático (como en el caso del refrán «castígame mi madre, y yo trómpogelas»). Si ha entendido, además, la propiedad de la expresión al caso concreto se percata también del acierto del «ingenioso» Cervantes al hacer que el «discreto» Don Quijote se contradiga y desmienta su teoría de que el elemento culto enriquece la lengua.

En contraste con los refranes de escudero y caballero baraja Don Quijote, a lo Antonio de Guevara[58] las siguientes sentencias morales sin relieve: «Sea moderado tu sueño: que el que no madruga con el sol, no goza del día; y advierte, ¡oh, Sancho! que la diligencia es madre de la buena ventura; y la pereza, su contraria, jamás llegó al término que pide un buen deseo». Todo retórica.[59] Como dice Sancho poco después, «las necedades del rico por sentencias pasan por el mundo».

La única vez que Don Quijote piensa estar cambiando de tema («Este último consejo que ahora quiero darte puesto que no sirve para adorno del cuerpo. . . »), Cervantes nos hace patente que el cambio es sólo superficial, que está hablando de lo mismo que antes, de lo expeditivo antes que de lo deseable en un gobernador, como el no disputar sobre linajes para no incurrir en el aborrecimiento del abatido sin recoger el agradecimiento del favorecido. En una ocasión anterior no sentía ni pensaba así. Le había reprochado a Montesinos la comparación entre Dulcinea y Belerma porque «toda comparación es odiosa» (II, 23). Entonces era cuestión de sensibilidad, de tacto, no de conveniencia. Ahora todo es cuestión de conveniencia y de apariencia: «Tu vestido será calza entera, ropilla larga, herreruelo un poco más largo; gregüescos, ni por pienso (locución familiar); que no les están bien ni a los caballeros ni a los gobernadores». Sin embargo, Don Quijote lleva gregüescos, según se infiere al mencionar las dos docenas de puntos que se le soltaron en una media (II, 44), prenda que acompañaba al gregüesco.[60] Se ve que, como consejero, piensa en términos del protocolo al uso en el vestir del dignatario, mientras Cervantes sugiere que el espíritu del caballero ha bajado de nivel. El vestido apropiado para un gobernador es la intención.[61]

Sancho ha captado muy bien el sentido utilitario de los consejos. Gobernará con mano fuerte como entiende que le aconseja su amo. Siendo él gobernador «y juntamente liberal, como lo pienso ser [—dice—], no habrá falta que se me parezca», cuyos tres sentidos, a través de su error sintáctico, son: «no habrá falta que se descubra en mí»; «no habrá falta que parezca ser mía», y, «no habrá falta que yo reconozca como tal». ¿Ha pensado todo eso Sancho o lo ha dicho sin darse cuenta entre la docena de refranes que acaba de soltar? Júzguese por lo que sigue diciendo: «No, sino haceos miel, y paparos han moscas; tanto vales cuanto tienes, decía una mi agüela; y del hombre arraigado no te verás vengado». Lo ha pensado.

Reprobado de nuevo por Don Quijote por hablar en refranes, Sancho sigue tentándole con otros cuatro que vienen «pintiparados, o como peras en tabaque». No los dirá, sin embargo, porque «al buen callar llaman Sancho». Este refrán que el escudero se apropia, si literalmente resulta mal aplicado ya que Sancho es hablador empedernido, es figurativamente exacto con respecto a su naturaleza astuta, pues calla los cuatro refranes para despertar la curiosidad de Don Quijote. En efecto, éste quiere oírlos pese a que acaba de exhortarle a no decir ya más.

Los cuatro refranes en cuestión, que empiezan siendo tres y acaban siendo seis, puesto que Sancho es incapaz de expresarse fuera de ellos—son su estilo—tienen las cualidades elípticas de la poesía y el sello del conceptismo. Refuerzan el sentido de los refranes que acaba de proferir. Se contraponen al culteranismo de los refranes de Don Quijote. Son los siguientes:

«entre dos muelas cordales nunca pongas tus pulgares», y «a idos de mi casa y ¿qué queréis con mi mujer?, no hay responder», y «si da el cántaro en la piedra, o la piedra en el cántaro, mal para el cántaro», todos los cuales vienen a pelo. Que nadie se tome con su Gobernador, ni con el que le manda, porque saldrá lastimado, como el que pone el dedo entre dos muelas cordales; y aunque no sean cordales, como sean muelas, no importa; y a lo que dijere el Gobernador, no hay que replicar, como al «salíos de mi casa y ¿qué queréis con mi mujer?» Pues lo de la piedra en el cántaro un ciego lo verá. Así, que es menester que el que vee la mota en el ojo ajeno, vea la viga en el suyo [alusión a Don Quijote], porque no se diga por él: «espantóse la muerta de la degollada», [de nuevo alusión a Don Quijote quien hace precisamente lo que le dice a Sancho de no hacer, usar refranes]; y vuestra merced sabe bien que más sabe el necio en su casa que el cuerdo en la ajena.» (II, 43)

Estas últimas palabras de Sancho son una recreación maliciosa del refrán: «más sabe el loco en su casa que el cuerdo en la ajena». No se trata de un lapso de memoria en que intercambia *loco* por *necio*. Sabe muy bien lo que dice. Con el *necio* alude a sí mismo, y con el *cuerdo* alude a Don Quijote para decirle, veladamente, que de refranes —su casa—sabe él más que su amo. El caballero no capta inmediatamente la alusión: «Eso no, Sancho. . . ; que el necio en su casa ni en la ajena sabe nada, a causa que sobre el cimiento de la necedad no asienta ningún discreto edificio.» Hermosa retórica poco después de la cual se da cuenta de la alusión y reacciona airadamente: «toda esa gordura y esa personilla que tienes no es otra cosa que un costal lleno de refranes y de malicias».

Sancho ha ganado la partida. ¿Pone Cervantes el ingenio popular por encima del culto? En un nivel más directo, sí; en otro más abstracto, no. Los refranes de Sancho y su elíptica astucia hacen el deleite del lector agudo. Los refranes de Don Quijote y su elíptica propiedad hacen el deleite del lector culto. Al nivel lingüístico el lector pondrá su juicio valorativo a favor del uno o del otro según cuál ingenio perciba. Si percibe ambos, se admirará del ingenio de Cervantes para contraponer dos clases de naturaleza humana «bien concertada», en efecto. Lo que está juzgando Cervantes no es el intelecto de Don Quijote sino su dogmatismo y su retoricismo.

En este contexto, la superioridad del Sancho refranero sobre el Don Quijote dogmático y retórico queda establecida. Pero también—

y esto es significativo—la superioridad del Don Quijote dialéctico capaz de encontrar refranes acertados cuando le hacen falta, sobre el Don Quijote aforístico, acumulador de sentencias vacuas y banales.

Don Quijote termina la segunda serie de consejos diciendo que si Sancho gobierna mal será su culpa (por necio, se entiende); y la vergüenza será para Don Quijote (por consejero, se entiende). Cervantes, en cambio, piensa que aconsejar al necio es inútil. Lo dice a través del mismo Don Quijote después de un hermoso proverbio inventado por Sancho: «más me quiero ir Sancho al cielo que gobernador al infierno». Oyendo lo cual exclama Don Quijote: «buen natural tienes, sin el cual no hay ciencia que valga». La naturaleza del hombre vale más que todos los conocimientos del mundo.

Los terceros consejos se dan por carta después del episodio amoroso-buriesco entre Don Quijote y Altisidora, el espanto cencerril y gatuno, y la velada con la dueña Rodríguez. El sentido ético de Don Quijote ha bajado todavía más de nivel. Estos consejos resumen y refuerzan el espíritu de los consejos primeros y segundos. Aconseja Don Quijote a Sancho de no ser demasiado humilde porque conviene mantener la autoridad, la cual se sustenta adornándose con el «hábito» que el oficio de gobernador «requiere» y no vistiendo como «soldado» siendo «juez». *Soldado, juez,* los dos sinónimos implícitos de *gobernador.* Además, las letras quedan limitadas a las del letrado y las armas quedan descartadas. Sigue Don Quijote diciendo que «un palo compuesto no parece palo»—desliz freudiano en que Sancho se compara a un palo y se le exhorta a componerse para no parecerlo—; que debe «ser bien criado con todos»; «procurar la abundancia de los mantenimientos» para tener a la gente contenta; hacer «pocas pragmáticas» más fáciles de guardar que cuando se atemoriza en vano; visitar (entiéndase *vigilar*) cárceles, carnicerías y plazas; no mostrarse «codicioso, mujeriego ni glotón», aunque se lo sea, como se da a entender por el verbo *mostrarse;* ser «padre de las virtudes y padrastro»[2] de los vicios». Don Quijote quiere decir *perseguirlos*, pero Cervantes piensa *encubrirlos*, como ya ha dicho aprovechando del error sintáctico de Sancho al prometer: «No habrá falta que se *me* parezca».

Todos estos «consejos» y «documentos» no hablan de justicia sino de orden público y de gastos judiciales, «ayuda de costa». Pero Sancho lo hará mejor. No decretará leyes—no sabe escribir—pero sí establecerá ordenanzas tan buenas, se nos informa, «que hasta hoy se guardan en aquel lugar, y se nombran "Las constituciones del gran gobernador Sancho Panza "». La palabra oral. La ley viva. Ley del encaje, en efecto, pero del hombre bueno y noble.

En el último de los consejos de su carta exhorta Don Quijote a Sancho a mostrarse agradecido a los duques que le han hecho la merced de nombrarle gobernador «que la ingratitud es hija de la soberbia y uno de los mayores pecados que se sabe.». Cierto. Pero el final de la sentencia reza: «y la persona que es agradecida a los que bien le han hecho, da indicios que también lo será a Dios, que tantos bienes le hizo y de contino le hace». La sugerencia de impresionar a la Autoridad Suprema recuerda el soborno de Dios que pretendía el Torquemada galdosiano. Con este último consejo se puntualiza lo que significa ese *temer a Dios* del primer consejo de la serie: el mayor atributo de Dios es castigar. Cervantes: sólo los malos temen a Dios.

El círculo aparentemente barroco se ha abierto en espiral rena-centista. El hombre sin merecimiento es eligido gobernador. Obra como juez. Y se imagina ser Dios.; Dios es reducido a juez riguroso. Se le dice que se ve con mejores ojos su atributo de misericordia que su atributo de justicia. Se le advierte que por la misericordia alcan-zará mejor fama. Y, por último, se le quiere sobornar. Esta farsa implícita sugiere a qué extremo puede conducir la falsificación de la verdad al estilo de un pseudo-letrado como Alfonso de Valdés, o de un pseudo-moralista como Fray Antonio de Guevara.

Desde el comienzo hasta el fin avanzamos por terrenos morales movedizos. Cierto que se ha hablado de justicia, de misericordia, de prudencia, de suavidad, de bondad, de clemencia ¿quién no invoca estas virtudes? pero no es dentro del contexto de lo cristiano, sino de lo social-político.

Este que ahora aconseja a Sancho no es el Don Quijote que conocíamos antes. Aquel que dijo tras soltar a los galeotes: «He hecho lo que mi religión me pide» (II, 30).[63]

Del pensamiento clásico tradicional no ha quedado nada. Con las palabras de su personaje parodia Cervantes implacablemente la moral aceptada de la sociedad contemporánea. Y, el blanco del ata-que es la clase privilegiada, la que ejerce el poder, representada por la nobleza. Por si queda alguna duda sobre ello, documenta gráfica-mente cuanto ha dicho, en los atavíos del Sancho gobernador y del Don Quijote consejero, huéspedes de los duques. También pintando habla Cervantes en distintos niveles, cada uno de los cuales elabora y matiza los demás.

Sancho va a la Insula que ha de gobernar «vestido a lo letrado» por el duque. Las armas han quedado descartadas. Por encima lleva «un gabán muy ancho de chamelote de aguas leonado» y «una montera de lo mesmo». Va montado en «un macho a la jineta» y detrás de él viene su asno «con jaeces y ornamentos jumentiles, de seda y flamantes» (II, 44).

A primera vista, la pintura de la escena es impresionista. El colorido de los atuendos, uniformemente leonado uno, flamante el otro; las desproporciones de sus formas, mayor del lado de lo apagado que de lo vivo; la textura de los paños, de prensada y lustrosa dureza le del paño de chamelote tejido de pelo de camello, o de cabra, de resplandeciente suavidad la de seda roja («flamante»), proyectan la escena sensualmente. Sancho y su asno están irreconocibles. El lector contempla con distanciamiento el grupo más grande y uniforme; con cierta seducción el grupo más pequeño y llamativo. Su simpatía está más del lado del asno que del lado del gobernador. Para el lector que se coloca en este nivel, la escena es decorativa.

Si el lector la contempla un rato percibe su sentido expresionista: el impermeable gabán de chamelote leonado, de pelo de camello o de cabra, sofoca al letrado que cabalga sobre el macho. En el simbolismo animalario jergal los camellos son hambrientos de lo que les ha sido vedado. Y, así, «se arrojan a los estudios sagrados sin preparación filosófica, por lo que confunden todo» (Covarrubias, bajo *camello*). Sancho hace ese papel y hasta intenta presentar credenciales. Inventa que fue «prioste» (mayordomo de cofradía) en su pueblo; que aprendió a hacer «unas letras como de marca de fardo que decían que decía [su] nombre». Sancho confunde voluntariamente y a sabiendas— dialéctica del pueblo—las letras divinas con haber andado por la Iglesia, y las letras humanas con haber dibujado sus signos sin saber lo que dicen. Por la picardía del escudero habla paródicamente Cervantes. Su ironía va dirigida contra los famélicos del mando bajo el reinado de Felipe II o Felipe III quienes soñaban con un cargo oficial en España y aun más en América: la Insula Barataria[64] de Sancho, así calificada a pesar de estar rodeada de tierra. Muchos no llevaban otra cosa en la cabeza (la montera leonada[65]), emblema del poder, que mandar y ser obedecidos. «Dulcísima cosa es mandar y ser obedecido» le ha dicho el duque a Sancho. Y Sancho tiene ganas «de probar a qué sabe el ser gobernador».

La cabra es símbolo de lascivia en el lenguaje jergal. El macho, cruce de caballo y burra, evoca significados jergales. El caballo, del latín vulgar *caballus* es «caballo castrado», «de trabajo» (Corominas). La burra es, figurativamente, la mujer ignorante, reacia a la instrucción, laboriosa, abnegada y de mucho aguante (Academia). El macho, cruce de ambos, es el hombre sumiso reducido al estado animal.

Pintar un ancho gabán de pelo de camello, o de cabra, leonado—color despintado del simbólico león de Castilla y de los grandes que la servían[66]—sobre un macho a la jineta—encogidos los pies en estribos cortos[67]—, es pintar un bruto, o cabrón, el gobernador, sobre un necio ignorante, el pueblo, en términos sexuales equivalentes a un verbo que no puede decirse y menos escribirse.[68]

Sancho, el pueblo, se ha pasado al gobierno. Ha sucumbido a la tentación. Pero no pierde de vista su origen. De tanto en tanto vuelve los ojos hacia su asno con cuya compañía va «muy contento». En el caso de Sancho se aplica el refrán: «El hábito no hace al monje». Poco antes ha dicho Sancho: «Vístanme como quisieren; que de cualquier manera que vaya vestido seré Sancho Panza». Cuando, más tarde, deja Sancho el gobierno, el «beso de paz» que la dará «en la frente» a su asno lo confirma. También lo confirma la pintura que nos ha hecho Cervantes del asno. Está concebida como refrán, y pensada en términos visuales al estilo conceptista del escudero: «Aunque el asno de Sancho se vista de seda, Sancho se queda». El refrán popular sobre el que está basadso reza: «Aunque la mona se viste de seda, mona se queda». «An ape is always an ape, though dressed in scarlet», dice la Locura de Erasmo invocando el proverbio griego (pág. 24). Pero Cervantes no enuncia. Pinta su pensamiento. Todo ha sido dicho gráficamente, mediante alusiones, símbolos, alegorías, y elípticos juegos de palabras en términos pictóricos.

La amarga parodia gráfica del atuendo del gobernante corrobora la parodia implícita en los sentidos de los razonamientos de los consejos de Don Quijote. La corrobora, igualmente, el atavío de Don Quijote en casa de los duques después de haber dado oralmente los consejos y antes de seguir dándolos por carta. Recuérdese su insistencia en el vestir que debe ser adecuado a las circunstancias. Y, he aquí, que, en la sociedad de su habitación, Don Quijote escoge—y ésta es la diferencia esencial entre él y Sancho—las piezas de vestir que más adecuadas le parecen para presentarse ante los duques. En su caso, por tanto, «el hábito hace al monje».[69]

Con el atuendo predominantemente escarlata de Don Quijote,

rectifica Cervantes, de nuevo gráficamente, el sentido que pretende darle la Locura al refrán: «An ape is always an ape, though dressed in scarlet». Acaba de afirmar la Locura que es error ir en contra de la naturaleza propia y asumir el color de la virtud torciendo el carácter. Lo cual es un contrasentido. La virtud es fortaleza de carácter (*virtud* viene de *virtus* = fortaleza de carácter). La Locura debió decir *vicio*, defecto adquirido por costumbre (*vicio* viene de *avezar*; deriva de *bezo* = costumbre). Con su típica sofistería confunde carácter con costumbre, bajo la capciosa pluma de Erasmo. Siguiendo el pensamiento de Erasmo, Cervantes denuncia la falacia de la Locura al pintar, no la virtud, sino el vicio en el atavío de Don Quijote.

En efecto, Don Quijote lleva «un mantón escarlata» por encima de su «acamuzado vestido», «una montera de terciopelo verde, guarnecida de pasamanos de plata», «botas de camino [de montar]» por encubrir «los puntos sueltos de sus medias verdes», su «buena y tajadora espada» en un tahelí que cuelga de sus hombros» y «un gran rosario» en las manos. Todo está fuera de lugar y nada armoniza. Es una fiesta de formas, texturas y colores. El caballero andante está irreconocible, disfrazado de Carnaval, o de Epicuro. El disfraz es emblema de libertad y desorden.[70] El desorden del atavío de Don Quijote acusa el desorden y libertad en sus ideas, así como la crisis de identidad por la que está pasando el caballero. Al aceptar la hospitalidad de los duques, Don Quijote acepta la malsana atmósfera del palacio ducal. Ya piensa, sin darse cuenta, como quienes le rodean. Se ha acomodado a sus costumbres por la ley de la convivencia, «the rule of conviviality» de que habla la Locura, y pretende, como aconseja ésta, «not to notice anything, or affably and compassionately be deceived» (pág. 38).

El retrato de Don Quijote es simbólico en varios niveles. El psicológico es el más asequible. Si mal no recuerdo Karl Ludwig Selig explicó el simbolismo psicológico de la vestimenta del caballero en una reciente sesión de la *Modern Language Association*. Si algún parecido tiene con mi lectura suya sea la palma. La montera verde a la cabeza dentro del palacio nos revela la psicología del cazador cortesano. Los «pasamanos de plata» el objeto da la casa, Altisidora, la doncella de la duquesa, quien le ha estado acechando amorosamente por los corredores del palacio. «Casa de placer» se lo llama también. El terciopelo de la montera, el refinamiento de sus táctitas: compondrá versos y cantará romances para corresponder a la doncella. Las botas de montar, sus impulsos sexuales. Las dos docenas de puntos sueltos de sus medias verdes, la debilidad de sus energías. El vistoso mantón escarlata, obsequio de los duques, su gran deseo de impresionar, reforzado por la espada que, como adorno, pende del tahelí. El rosario en las manos, su gran temor al pecado.

La actuación de Don Quijote en el palacio ducal es incompatible con su culto de Dulcinea. No la traicionará de hecho, pero sí, y esto es más grave, en espíritu. Pagará su locura en carne propia: un gato agresivo, un «demonio», un «hechicero», un «encantador», le arañará el rostro y le postrará en cama. Es representación simbólica de Altisidora, así como, también, abreviatura gráfica del león, símbolo medieval del Diablo. Diablo y Locura son sinónimos.[71] Del Don Quijote vencedor de leones (Caballero de los Leones) sólo nos queda un vago recuerdo en el «acamuzado vestido» que se vislumbra por debajo del ostentoso mantón escarlata. Su locura es compendio de los valores negativos exaltados por la Locura erasmiana: vivir bien y gozar de la vida persiguiendo el placer. La representación emblemática es la «montera verde» que le recubre la cabeza, el pensamiento.[72]

Hay un nivel metafórico-simbólico de la pintura de la indumentaria de Don Quijote que le caracteriza en el terreno de las ideas por extensión del sentido literario y popular de los colores, técnica cervantina que ya he observado en otras partes.[73] El verde, asociado en la vida y en la literatura con el placer, la concupiscencia y el sensualismo significa, por extensión típicamente cervantina, corrupción ideológica. Medias verdes bajo las botas de montar, y montera verde a la cabeza son símbolos de acciones e ideas viciadas al perseguir lo placentero antes que lo deseable. El pálido marrón del acamuzado vestido, indicativo del pudor que le causa al caballero su comportamiento habla, por extensión, de remordimiento de conciencia. La plata de los pasamanos sugerente de insensibilidad, por extensión sugiere rachas de frialdad e indiferencia. El escarlata del mantón, acusador de alegría y libertinaje, delata, por extensión, libertinaje más que libertad en las ideas. Éste es el retrato moral de Don Quijote en la casa ducal. Se ha vestido el espíritu de la sociedad dirigente. Se percatará de ello más tarde. Le escribirá a Sancho: «yo pienso dejar presto esta vida ociosa en que estoy, pues no nací para ella. . . tengo que cumplir con mi profesión. . .» (II, 51)

Hay todavía otro nivel simbólico-alegórico de la indumentaria del caballero en que Cervantes es explícito sobre el Don Quijote consejero huésped de los duques. Ha adoptado, sin percatarse de ello, las técnicas del Diablo cazador cuando se viste de verde para confundirse con la naturaleza.[74] Al ponerse medias verdes y montera verde, Don Quijote pretende confundirse con el ambiente que le rodea. En cuanto a la prenda sobresaliente de su atavío, el mantón escarlata, trae asociaciones con la religión pagana y sus dioses, por lo que Tertuliano lo llamó «pompa del diablo». También se lo llamó «púrpura real», por ser símbolo de jerarquía. Y, más tarde, «púrpura de cardenal», por reservarse para el cuerpo sacerdotal de la Iglesia.[75] Dentro del Don Quijote idealista hay un materialista; dentro del filósofo, un sofista; dentro del cristiano, un pagano. El escarlata es la información pictórica de su reducción moral. Y así corre su pensamiento. Ha aconsejado como piensa el duque cuando le dice a Sancho que para gobernar «tanto son menester las armas como las letras; y las letras como las armas». Si el sentido directo dice que tan menester son unas como otras, el sentido idiomático dice que tan menester es esgrimir las armas *como si*[77] fueran letras, como esgrimir las letras *como si* fueran armas, no las letras divinas sino las del letrado que mezcla «lo humano con lo divino» (Prólogo I). Lo vemos pintado: lleva Don Quijote la espada al cuello y el rosario en las manos. Ha tomado las apariencias por verdades. Ha confundido la letra de la ley con el espíritu de la ley, y las letras humanas con las divinas. Como Sancho, poco antes, cuando habla de haber sido «prioste» y aprendido a hacer «letras como de fardo». Sólo que la confusión de Sancho es consciente y maliciosa. La de Don Quijote es sólo a medias consciente. Éste es el sentido de su libertinaje ideológico.

Los tres niveles de pintura, el novelístico-impresionista, el simbólico-metafórico, y el simbólico-alegórico, corresponden a los tres niveles superpuestos en los consejos a Sancho: el directo novelístico, en que los consejos de Don Quijote son buenos por ser útiles y prácticos; el alusivo de los razonamientos, en que Cervantes analiza la literatura doctrinal y juzga con discernimiento y sentido crítico el pensamiento y la vida públicos, y el filosófico en que enuncia el conflicto entre la moral social y la ética cristiana. Imposible percibir la dialéctica que sustenta los consejos de Don Quijote si no le deslindamos de su creador, Cervantes.[78] Si los deslindamos no hay contradicción entre los tres niveles de lectura sino tres perspectivas nacidas de la unidad y consecuencia del pensamiento de Cervantes.

Catón, se llama a sí mismo Don Quijote. Pero ¿cuál Catón?[79] ¿Dionisio (s. IV,A.C.), el de los apotegmas morales (*Disticha de moribus ad filium*) de carácter monoteísta pero no particularmente cristianos? ¿Marco Porcio (s. I, A.C.), el filósofo suicida, de limitado sentido del deber, despreocupado del futuro, doctrinario típico, inconsciente de que su ideal es un anacronismo, y enemigo mortal del moderno legislador Julio César, de cuyo vestir descompuesto y flojo, se acuerda Don Quijote? ¿El otro Marco Porcio (s. III-II, A.C.), el estadista romano, llamado El Censor por su severidad rayana en crueldad y por su estricta justicia, perseguidor acérrimo de la corrupción, y opositor de las ideas nuevas que consideraba peligrosas? También escribió máximas (*Praecepta ad filium*) y reglas de conducta para la vida diaria (*Carmen de moribus*), en verso para más fácil retención. ¿O, aún, Publio Valerio (s. I, A.C.), el lingüista y poeta excelso, merecedor del nombre de «Catón el gramático, Latina Sirena/crítico único y creador de poetas» (*Cato grammaticus, Latina Sirena/Qui solus legit ac facit poetas*), aquel que fue el maestro de la nueva escuela lírica (*poeta novi*, como los llamó Cicerón), el que rechazó la épica nacional y el teatro en favor de las breves épicas mitológicas (*epyllia*)? La épica «también puede escribirse en prosa como en verso» había dicho Cervantes a través del Canónigo de Toledo (I, 47). El Don Quijote consejero comparte atributos con el segundo y el tercero de los Catones. El Cervantes creador comparte atributos con el primero y el cuarto de los Catones. Desde la altura de Publio Valerio Catón contempla con burlona sonrisa al presuntuoso consejero Don Quijote quién, más ostensiblemente que el petulante Fray Antonio de Guevara, se compara—creo yo—con Catón, el Censor. Fray Antonio le atribuye al censor la siguiente sentencia: «no se pierden las repúblicas por mengua de capitanes sino por falta de consejos».[80] Siguiendo la indicación del Censor, Guevara, arrogantemente humilde, le ofrece al «Serenísimo Rey de Portugal» su libro *Menosprecio de corte y alabanza de aldea* repleto de «muchas buenas doctrinas» (pág. 29). Le advierte, además, que si quiere «parescer y ser príncipe cristiano» que acepte el «consejo» y admita «el aviso»: «porque el consejo le aprovechará para lo que ha de hazer, y el aviso, para lo que se ha de guardar» (pág. 50). Bien. Como Don Quijote a Sancho: «está ¡oh hijo!, atento a este tu Catón, que quiere aconsejarte y ser norte y guía que te encamine y saque a seguro puerto de este mar proceloso [lenguaje místico que nos evoca a Fray Antonio] donde vas a engolfarte; que los oficios y grandes cargos no son otra cosa sino un golfo profundo de confusiones». No es Cervantes quien imita a Fray Antonio de Guevara en su estilo, como cree el prologuista de *Menosprecio*. . . Matías Martínez Burgos (pág. 24). Sino que Cervantes hace que Don Quijote le imite, particularmente cuando equilibra con elegancia y gravedad frases vanas y perogrulladas.[81] Le supera, sin embargo, en disimularlas debido a la sutileza conceptista con la que matiza Cervantes los cultismos de Don Quijote.

Cervantes, en cambio, parece estar de acuerdo con Erasmo. Los letrados que se meten a filósofos no hacen buenos consejeros. La Locura de Erasmo saca a relucir el famoso dicho de Platón: «Happy is the state where philosophers are made kings, or whose kings become philosophers», para negarlo recordando a los Catones:

> No, if you consult the historians you will find, as plain as day, that nowhere have princes been so baneful to commonwealths as where the rule has devolved upon some philosophaster or bookish fellow. The Catos, I suggest, give support enough to this point: one of them was always vexing the tranquility of the republic by hare-brained accusations [¿Marco Porcio, el filósofo?] while the other totally destroyed the liberty of the Roman people, defending it, all the while, as wisely as you please [¿Marco Porcio, el Censor?] (pág. 32)

Si la locura es semifalaz al relacionar estos dos Catones con el dicho de Platón, Erasmo no deja por ello de expresar por las palabras de su personaje lo que realmente piensa de ellos.

El valor de los consejos de Don Quijote a Sancho reside, pues, por inferencia, en la caracterización del caballero como intelectual desorientado, y de Cervantes como crítico magistral.

Al abandonar el palacio de los duques, reaparecerá Don Quijote armado de pies a cabeza (II, 57). Cervantes volverá a identificarse con su criatura, si no por las acciones, por el noble sentir. (Véase nota 17).

CONCLUSION

Para *deleitar* y *enseñar* a un tiempo, Cervantes pone ante los ojos el ejemplo de la realidad y ante el entendimiento la pintura de la verdad. Como la realidad tiene muchos rostros y la verdad muchos grados y categorías, según los percibe cada lector, Cervantes escribe en varios niveles. En las palabras del Canónigo de Toledo (I, 47), hay que «casar las fábulas mentirosas con el entendimiento de los que las leyeren».

No hay un solo significado que desentrañar en la ficción cervantina. Hay varios. No se contradicen. Se complementan. No hay un solo contexto. Hay varios.; No se desdicen. Se suman. No hay ejemplaridad en un solo sentido. Hay jerarquías de ejemplaridad: no todos los lectores están igualmente dotados para entender. Y, un mismo lector puede ser el niño que manosea el *Quijote*, el joven que lo *lee*, el hombre que lo *entiende*, y el viejo que lo *celebra* (II, 3).

Por tanto, no deben *intrincarse* ni *oscurecerse* los conceptos (Prólogo I). Todo lo complejo y difícil debe tratarse silenciosamente. Los consejos aforísticos de Don Quijote son fáciles de entender. Contienen cosas «buenas, santas y provechosas» como dice Sancho, y como han visto Clemencín, Rodríguez Marín, Casalduero, Varo, Bleznick. Mientras que los razonamientos que los acompañan van envueltos en un lenguaje enrevesado. Sancho los califica de «badulaques, enredos y revoltillos». Don Quijote mezcla conceptos, fábulas y refranes en sus explicaciones. Convierte ideales inválidos en otros válidos, da a escoger entre los falsos como si fueran verdaderos, cambia de tema en mitad de las frases, o distribuye el mismo tema entre varios consejos, contradiciéndose hasta el punto de concluir lo contrario de su primera afirmación. Sobre todo, tergiversa los conceptos clásicos al imitar a los letrados moralistas, en particular al erasmista Alfonso de Valdés. Y hasta piensa contradictoriamente como Felipe II. ¿Coincidencia?

Analógicamente, la Locura tergiversa, desvirtúa y confunde los textos clásicos, fuente de sus conocimientos. Da falsas interpretaciones de su sentido. Vierte verdades en sus mentiras, y al hacer crítica seria con su parodia culta afirma actitudes que son perversión del espíritu clásico. Es un personaje insensato, capcioso, cuya ironía, agudeza y bromear erudito le dan a falaz razonar apariencia de verdad siendo mentira. Ella misma se proclama sofista (pág. 8). Y admite sentir admiración por el cerdo de Epicuro que se precia de mezclar un tanto de locura con nuestros consejos («a little folly» mixed «with our counsels», pág. 105).

Don Quijote en cambio, es serio y no engaña voluntariamente. Pero con su elegancia de expresión les da a sus consejos apariencia de sabiduría siendo sólo buenos o útiles. Si el lector se acerca con sentido crítico—como hacen May y Efron—a los «badulaques, enredos y revoltillos» de las explicaciones que da Don Quijote, llega al nivel en que Cervantes hace distinciones morales y éticas dentro de la «buena conducta» invistiendo las palabras del caballero de sentidos propios. Lo bueno y lo malo que se dan juntos en la *Moria* de Erasmo al pasar sin transición de lo serio a la broma, en la obra de Cervantes se dan por separado mediante la dislocación, lingüísticamente demarcada, de Don Quijote y de su Creador. Donde Erasmo anuda, Cervantes desliga. No hay que confundir al lector.

Contrariamente a Don Quijote cuyas ambivalencias pasan desapercibidas para el lector que no se detiene a buscarlas, las de la Locura inducen a tomar gato por liebre. El caballero del Verde Gabán, cuya filiación erasmista ha probado muy convincentemente Francisco Márquez Villanueva,[82] es una de las víctimas. Porque el del Verde Gabán pertenece al vulgo mayoritario como «todo aquel que no sabe, aunque sea señor y principe», en las palabras de Don Quijote (II, 16).[83] Es a él, precisamente, a quien se lo dice. Mayor peligro, por tanto, lo constituyen quienes han modelado su espíritu, los letrados erasmistas. Al querer adaptar las ideas de Erasmo, sin captar a fondo su pensamiento, a la moral católica de la España de los Felipes reducen las ambivalencias que encuentran en la obra erasmiana, tan leída en la España de Carlos V, a una sola dimensión que pasa por la «verdad». *Le style c'est l'homme.* Y, en Alfonso de Valdés, prototipo de erasmistas, se cifran las características negativas de los imitadores del gran rotterdamiano.

Cervantes coincide con los moralistas de su época, con Villadiego, Castillo de Bobadilla, Castilla y Aguayo, Juan de Jesús María, Zeballos, Bartolomé de Góngora, como se ha visto, y con otros más, como puede observarse en las numerosas acotaciones de Rodríguez Marín. Pero no coincide con los divulgadores letrados, erasmistas o no. Igual desprecio que por el erasmista Alfonso de Valdés siente por el anti-erasmista Fray Antonio de Guevara. En las obras de ambos abundan falacias, falsedades y trivialidades. No es cuestión de tomar partido. Es cuestión de no dejar deslizar en la ficción «una palabra deshonesta ni un pensamiento menos que católico» (II, 3). Y no tenemos este *católico* sólo en su sentido literal, después de cuanto hemos dicho sobre la elasticidad de significado que sabe darle Cervantes a la lengua. *Católico* también significa *sano* (sentido figurado), *verdadero* (sentido filosófico) y *universal* (sentido etimológico). Pues no aspira a menos Cervantes. Sobre todo, no debe desvirtuarse la realidad en ningún nivel para no correr el riesgo que corrió Erasmo con el *Elogio de la Locura*, de no ser entendido del «simple» por merecer la admiración del «discreto». Cervantes no escribe para una minoría culta, como Erasmo, escribe para cada individuo lector.[84]

Su enfoque emparenta con el de los antiguos.[85] Éstos escribían en varios niveles. Ocultaban los secretos intelectuales bajo envoltura de fábulas e historias, preferentemente en verso, menos vulnerable a la desvirtuación que la prosa, para ponerlos fuera del alcance del vulgo y preservar así para la posteridad la sabiduría que encierran.

Cervantes inventa la fábula poética con el mismo objeto. Comunica su pensamiento por medio de la elipsis, de lo que no dice, de la inferencia a través de la afectación retórica de Don Quijote, a través del analfabetismo de Sancho, de las limitaciones intelectuales de Cide Hamete, y de los pensamientos perversos, cínicos o sacrílegos del Duque, fabricador de la farsa de la Insula, y escarnio de los ideales caballerescos. Cervantes pinta «la intención» (como le aconseja el amigo en el Prólogo I) por detrás de lo que dicen sus personajes, o al describir su modo de vestir. En la medida en que cada lector se detiene a pensar y debatir el sentido de las palabras con el «libre albedrío» que le otorga Cervantes (de nuevo en el Prólogo I) se acerca al pensamiento del autor.

Cervantes está más allá del debate ideológico de su época: humanismo barroco vs. humanismo renacentista. Su espíritu crítico independiente pretende rescatar en la ficción los valores universales perdidos entre la confusión moral e ideológica de la sociedad dirigente en la España de los Felipes.

GRINNELL COLLEGE

NOTAS

[1]Todas las citas sin referencia corresponden a los tres capítulos en que se encuentran los consejos, según se indica en el texto.

[2]Impresionado por la interrogación exclamativa (la pongo entera más adelante en el texto, y nota 20) del pseudo-autor Cide Hamete después de escribir los primeros consejos Diego Clemencín exclama admirado: «¡Y qué bellos documentos! ¡Qué máximas tan nobles, tan generosas, tan indulgentes, tan discretas! *El ingenioso*

hidalgo Don Quijote de la Mancha, Ed. IV Centenario con 356 grabados de G. Doré; comentarios de Diego Clemencín; estudio crítico de Luis Astrana Marín; índice-resumen de los ilustradores y comentadores del Quijote por Justo García Morales (Madrid: Ediciones Castilla, 1966), t. IV, pág. 1762, n. 36.

[3]Francisco Rodríguez Marín se siente inspirado—nos dice—para escribir un folleto que titulará: «Espejo de gobernadores/y atalaya de gobernados./Opúsculo utilísimo para los unos y los otros,/cimentado en los sanos consejos/que dió Don Quijote a Sancho Panza/cuando fué a gobernar su ínsula». *El ingenioso hidalgo Don Quijote de la Mancha*, Nueva edición crítica (Madrid: Ediciones ATLAS, 1947-49), t. VI, pág.229 n.*5. En adelante, me referiré al tomo VI por la abreviación *RM* seguida del número de la página y de la nota.

[4]Joaquín Casalduero ve en los consejos un «Doctrinal de privados» y los considera llenos de «sabiduría». Véase *Sentido y forma del 'Quijote' (1605-1615)*, (Madrid: Insula, 1966), pág. 319.

[5]Carlos Varo llama al Don Quijote de los consejos un «intelectual y teórico», y un «sabio natural» como contraposición al «hombre ridículo» en «esa doble personalidad de Don Quijote». *Génesis y evolución del 'Quijote'* (Madrid: Ediciones Alcalá, 1968), págs. 466 y 471. Northrup Frye coincide con Varo. Encuentra los consejos «surprisingly sensible». *The Secular Scripture: A Study of the Structure of Romance* (Cambridge: Harvard University Press, 1976), pág. 179.

[6]Donald W. Bleznick escribe: «Cervantes' intimate acquaintance with the *doctrinales de príncipes* that flourished during the Spanish Golden Age is revealed in the sage advice he gives Sancho. . . » *Hispania*, 40 (1957), 62.

[7]Américo Castro nada ve de «insólito» en los consejos «en cuanto a las ideas». *El pensamiento de Cervantes*, Nueva Edición ampliada y con notas del autor y de Julio Rodríguez-Puértolas (Barcelona-Madrid: Editorial Noguer, 1973; primera impresión, 1972), pág. 354.

[8]Marcel Bataillon considera los documentos de Don Quijote como «manual de sabiduría práctica» que no «traspasan los límites del vulgar recto juicio». *Erasmo y España: Estudios sobre la historia espiritual del siglo XVI* (México-Buenos Aires: Fondo de Cultura Económica, 1950), págs. 784-85 y 400, respectivamente.

[9]Para Louis Philippe May, Don Quijote es, a través de toda la novela, el expositor retórico de una verdad que no tiene aplicación en la realidad, en contraposición al Sancho Panza racional, cuyo valor se declara en el gobierno de la ínsula. *Un Fondateur de la libre pensée: Cervantès. Essai de déchiffrement de "Don Quichotte"* (Paris, 1947), págs. 44-48.

[10]Arthur Efron considera los consejos como series de yuxtaposiciones cómicas. Se extraña que hayan sido tomados en serio cuando su objeto es indicarle a Sancho cómo debe obrar para parecer virtuoso y tener éxito. En breves sustanciosas páginas capta Efron con acierto la actitud crítica de Cervantes hacia Don Quijote y la sociedad ducal (*Don Quixote and the Dulcineated World* [Austin-London: University of Texas Press, 1971], págs. 15-16 y 87-90.) Mi análisis de los consejos respalda sus observaciones. Para Efron Don Quijote es símbolo de la sociedad decadente. Para mí lo es del idealista cuyas aspiraciones no tienen aplicación posible con los métodos de una sociedad decadente.

[11]Ludovik Osterc [Berlan] considera «sabios» los consejos de Don Quijote razonados desde el consenso social a pesar de que ve todo el *Quijote* como crítica social. *El pensamiento social y político del "Quijote"* (México, 1963), pág. 262.

[12]Castro, págs. 272-74.

[13]Bataillon, págs. 784-85.

[14]Martín de Riquer, *Don Quijote de la Mancha*, 6ª ed. anotada (Barcelona: Juventud,

1969), vol. II, pág. 840, n. 4.

[15]Samuel Putnam, *The Ingenious Gentleman Don Quixote de la Mancha* (New York: Viking Press, 1949), pág. 1013, n. 6.

[16]Véase su «Proemio al lector» (Madrid: Ediciones «La Lectura», 1929), pág. 5.

[17]Si Cervantes habla a veces por boca de todos sus personajes, no puede decirse de ninguno de ellos que sea portavoz del autor. John J. Allen nos ha demostrado que el pseudo-autor Cide Hamete Benengeli y Cervantes son separables en *Modern Language Notes*, 91 (1976), 201-212. Alban K. Forcione deslinda convincentemente al Canónigo de Toledo de su autor («The Dialogue between the Canon and Don Quixote», en *Cervantes, Aristotle and the "Persiles"* [Princeton:Princeton University Press, 1970], págs 91-130.) También yo he deslindado a Cervantes de ambos personajes («El verdadero autor», «Apéndice: Cide Hamete Benengeli», y «Cervantes crítico», en *Cervantes y su concepto del arte* [Madrid: Gredos, 1975], págs. 87-104 y 139-156, respectivamente.) Por lo que a Don Quijote se refiere, percibo identificación entre Cervantes y su personaje, no sin cierta romántica auto-ironía, cuando éste se aleja de las situaciones sociales. Cuando, por el contrario, Don Quijote se reintegra a la sociedad a raíz de su vencimiento por el Caballero de la Blanca Luna, sufre una progresiva reducción espiritual, salvo en algunos momentos de lúcida rebelión. Esta reducción espiritual proviene del olvido progresivo de conocimientos que le lleva a caer en la pedantería, el error (véase nota 56), el infantilismo y la depresión antes de morir. El trabajo de Howard Mancing, «Alonso Quijano y sus amigos» (leído en el Primer Congreso Internacional sobre Cervantes, Madrid, julio de 1978), y el de Albert A. Sicroff, «La segunda muerte de Don Quijote como respuesta a Avellaneda» (*Nueva Revista de Filología Hispánica*, 24 [1975], 267-91, recogen el doble sentido barroco y renacentista a un tiempo de la muerte del caballero manchego, e indican el camino hacia una visión más coherente del sentido cervantino de la vida de Don Quijote.

[18]El llamar *documentos* a los consejos es en sí, claro indicio de alusión a los doctrinales para gobernantes. El interesado encontrará notable lista de doctrinales para príncipes y gobernantes en las noticias de Clemencín y Rodríguez Marín a los capítulos que comentamos, y en el antes citado artículo de Bleznick.

[19]*The Praise of Folly*. Trans. from the Latin with an Essay and Commentary by Hoyt Hopwell Hudson (Princeton : Princeton University Press, 1941), pág. 99. En otra parte recurre al mismo capcioso subterfugio de cometer un *lapsus linguae* significativo: «I have heard of a certain notable fool—there I go again! I meant to say scholar—» (pág. 89).

[20]Sigo con la paráfrasis explicativa: «solamente se disparaba [descabellaba (Cide Hamete); se separaba del consenso (Cervantes)] en tocándole en la caballería [ideas caballerescas (Cide Hamete). idealismo de caballero (Cervantes], y en los demás discursos [comentarios (Cide Hamete); digresiones (Cervantes)] mostraba tener claro y desenfadado entendimiento [sin complejidad y sin causar enfado (en sentido encomiástico, Cide Hamete; en sentido peyorativo, Cervantes)] de modo que, a cada paso, desacreditaban sus obras su juicio, y su juicio sus obras». Cide Hamete y Cervantes están en desacuerdo sobre el origen del descrédito, pero de acuerdo en que las obras y juicio se desacreditan mutuamente. No se trata ya del cuerdo-loco como en casa de Don Diego de Miranda, sino de Locura total.

[21]Lo recuerda Castro, pág. 354.

[22]Rodríguez Marín recuerda más de un lugar en la Partida II del Rey Sabio (ley IX, tít. vii [pág. 229, n. 10]) que ofrece puntos de contacto con los consejos de Don Quijote.

[23]Pág. 209. Osterc Berlan también lo recuerda (*loc. cit.*).

[24]Lo advierte Arthur Efron y muestra cómo tuerce Cervantes el sentido de las tres

referencias bíblicas (Salmos 111:10, Proverbios 1:7 y 9:10) indicadas por Putnam como fuentes de este consejo (*loc. cit.*).

25Rodríguez Marín lo recuerda (pág. 230, n. 3).

26Desde el siglo VI A.C. hasta la actualidad los sacerdotes budistas ponen el autoconocimiento como primer paso hacia el Nirvana, anonadamiento en la esencia divina.

27Dice el refrán: «Mírate a los pies, y desharás la rueda» (*RM*, p. 230,. n. 5).

28Castro cree que hay «análogo espíritu» y «estrecha semejanza» entre ambos escritores. Tal vez sí. Yo me inclino a creer que hay una reflexión entre festiva y amarga sobre la inutilidad del esfuerzo por evitar la murmuración.

29Lo dice un refrán: «De pobres pañales, obispos y cardenales» (*RM*, pág. 232, n.*3). Clemencín ha encontrado tres ejemplos de personajes que, en su juventud, guardaron, precisamente, puercos (pág. 1761, n. 22): un agorero, un emperador y un papa. Falta saber si tan lejos llegaron por sus virtudes, defectos o habilidades. Pero lo cierto es que no son «innumerables» los que «de baja estirpe nacidos han subido a la suma dignidad pontífica e imperatoria»,. como afirma Don Quijote.

30A Rodríguez Marín le parecen «clarísimas» las palabras del texto, y se extraña que tantos anotadores no las hayan entendido (pág. 232, n. 5). Con todo, explica la ambigüedad de manera incomprensible: «no hay que tener envidia a los [sujetos] que los tienen [los hechos] principescos y señoriles». No creo que su explicación se entienda mejor que las de Pellicer, Hartzenbusch, Benjumea, Juan Calderón, cuyas versiones ofrece. Clemencín es quien a mi parecer, más cerca llega a ver los dos sentidos que ofrece la ambigüedad: «Es probable que Cervantes empezó a poner en su manuscrito otra cosa de la que hay, y luego se le olvidó borrar lo supérfluo». Pero como Clemencín no distingue dos voces, la de Don Quijote y la de Cervantes, concluye que es un error lingüístico en vez de caracterización indirecta de Don Quijote, y acaba corrigiendo el texto (pág. 1761, n. 25).

31También Osterc Berlan piensa en este consejo (*loc. cit.*). Encuentra espíritu análogo en lo que Polidoro y Don Quijote dicen. Sí, pero quiero puntualizar que no lo hay entre Polidoro y Cervantes quien, al falsear en las palabras de Don Quijote el pensamiento de Valdés, pone de manifiesto la falta de vuelo de este letrado.

32Ese *que* es estilo legal (como el *ítem*) que se infiltra en el estilo quijotesco ambivalentemente calificado por sus autores «de gran donaire».

33*Indice expurgatorio del cardenal Zapata en Sevilla*, 1632 (*RM*,pág. 132, n. 2).

34Véanse las citas en *RM*, pág. 234, n. 17.

35En *Guzmán de Alfarache*, parte I, libro I, cap. 1 (*RM*, pág. 235, n. 12).

36Única manera de hacerle soltar el bocado, como explica Rodríguez Marín (*loc. cit*).

37La prueba la aporta el mismo escudero: «yo entré desnudo en el gobierno y salgo desnudo dél.» (II, 57).

38«No se mueva por ruegos ni por lágrimas; mas en caso igual y dudoso se debe inclinar a favorecer al huérfano, y al pobre, y a la viuda, y al peregrino, y a las personas semejantes. . . » (*Instrucción política y práctica judicial* [Madrid: Luis Sánchez, 1612], fol. iii vuelto, según *RM*, pág. 235, n. 2).

39«Y en la sentencia penal ha de aver moderación de clemencia, y es culpa castigar toda la culpa», dice en *El corregidor sagaz* (fol. 31, vuelto, según *RM*, pág. 235, n. 2).

40«. . . ca como quier que la justicia es muy buena cosa en sí, e de que deve el Rey siempre vsar, con todo esso fazese muy cruel quando a las vegadas non es templada con misericordia» (ley II, tít. x, Partida II). En otra parte añade: «porque los juezes deuen ser siempre piadosos e mesurados; e más les deue plazer de quitar o aliuiar el demando que condenarlo o agrauiarlo» (ley XVII, tít. xxii, partida III, informa *RM*, pág 237, n. 7).

[41]En su *Arte real para el buen gobierno de los Reyes y Príncipes* (fol. 159, vuelto, citado por *RM*, pág. 237, n. 7) Zeballos se expresa con poética lucidez: «La justicia tiene los ojos inclinados al rigor de la ley; en ella mira y en ella se entretiene; dura cosa es, pero assi lo halla escrito; pero la clemencia sabe muchas reglas de philosophia, haciendo argumentos y silogismos que corrijan su rigor». Creo que este modo de concebir y sentir la justicia equivale a guiarse por la ley del encaje de un juez humano.

[42]*RM*, págs. 236-37, n. 6.

[43]Del episodio se los galeotes se deduce que más criminal es el juez que se deja sobornar que el galeote que ha enviado a galeras.

[44]Palabras citadas por Rodríguez Marín de las «Instrucciones dadas en Aranjuez, 23 de mayo de 1568» (pág. 229, n. 10 y pág. 235, n. 2). Juan de Castilla y Aguayo concibe la justicia a la inversa: «quanto más calidad ilustre tienen los cavalleros y gente principal en puestos de autoridad tanto 'más afables' deben ser 'con la gente ordinaria que con ellos tractare.' Como por el contrario lo suelen hazer los que en esto de la cavallería no tienen su negocio el más bien entablado del mundo, porque ponen su autoridad en la mala criança . . . » (*RM*, pág. 231, n. 5). Coincide con Castillo de Bobadilla y con las palabras—¿y la intención?—de Felipe II. (Ver nota 48.)

[45]Dice Villadiego: «al Corregidor no se le dió el cargo para vengar sus injurias» (folio 122 vuelto); Bartolomé de Góngora en *El corregidor sagaz* (folio 6) recuerda las palabras de Beda de su libro *El Reyno de Dios*: «El que sentencia el negocio de su amigo de otra manera que el de su enemigo, balança engañosa tiene, contra la Lei; sean las balanças yguales» (Leído en *RM*, pág. 237, n. 3).

[46]Women «have the gift of beauty, which with good reason they prefer above all things else. Assisted by it, they wield a tyranny over tyrants themselves. . . And by what other sponsor are they better recommended to men than by folly? What is there that men will not permit to women? But for what consideration, except pleasure? And women please by no other thing than their folly. The truth of this no one will deny who has considered what nonsense a man talks with a woman. . . » (pág. 24).

[47]A la hermosa Camila de la novela de *El curioso impertinente*, calificándola de «el enemigo», le atribuye el narrador, en términos militares, el poder de «vencer con sola su hermosura a un escuadrón de caballeros armados» (I, 33-35). No es la primera vez que un personaje femenino, indistintamente de su caracterización, está pensado en los mismos términos. Por ejemplo, la admirable Catalina en *La gran sultana* (Véase Percas, pág. 302).

[48]Castillo de Bobadilla advierte que «aunque se muestre el juez terrible, sea aborreciendo el delito, pero no injuriando al delincuente. . . » pues no «es incompatible tratar con decencia al que ha de ser castigado con aspereza». Felipe II advierte a Don Juan de Austria «no decir *a ningún hombre* palabra que sea de injuria ni ofensa suya, y que vuestra lengua sea para honrar u hacer favor, y no para deshonrar a nadie. Y los que erraren y ecedieren, hacerlos heis castigar, haciendo a todos justicia y razón; y este castigo no ha de ser por vuestra boca, ni por las palabras injuriosas, ni por vuestras manos» (citado por *RM*, pág. 239, n. 3). Nótese que el lenguaje de Felipe II delata una contradicción básica si también deben considerarse la *calidad* de las *cosas* y *personas* para ser *piadoso* y *benigno*, como dijo antes. Análoga contradicción refleja el lenguaje de Don Quijote.

[49]En otra parte, «The Painter and the Writer are One and the Same», conferencia leída en *Cervantes Lecture Series* de Fordham (5-8 dic., 1977) en cuya Memoria se publicará, he hablado de la originalidad cervantina en el uso neológico de dos latinismos *Giranda* y *Miranda*, referentes, en el nivel directo, a una veleta y a un apellido, y en el

nivel alusivo a una mala y a una buena aplicación del latín, la primera, por parte de Sansón Carrasco, el bachiller que no hace más que *bachillear*, como él mismo dice; la segunda, por parte de Cervantes, el gran lingüista que sabe decir varias cosas a la vez, una para cada nivel de ficción en que escribe. Clemencín comenta que Cervantes utiliza *segundar* por *repetir*, y en el *Persiles* por *seguir*, acepciones poco frecuentes. En cuanto al vocablo *segundos*, para Clemencín se trata de una imprecisión cervantina (III, pág. 1089, n. 14). No percibe la analogía etimológica con el latín. En otra parte incluye *segundar* en una lista de palabras inventadas, o introducidas y acreditadas por Cervantes (IV, pág. 1763, n. 8), entre ellas, *villanería*, referente a *extracción, linaje, alcurnia* (IV, pág. 1762, n. 6). Con este sentido la utiliza Don Quijote en uno de los consejos. La palabra corriente *villanía* se refiere a la moral. Sospecho que es voluntaria por parte del autor la doble connotación que sugiere *villanería: villanía*, y lo relativo a la *villa*.

⁵⁰La justificación del cambio de tema se encuentra en la interdependencia de cuerpo y espíritu tan frecuentemente asociados en los escritos del Siglo de Oro español. Sobre esta interdependencia habla Bleznick en el artículo antes citado (véase pág. 64 y n. 4).

⁵¹Leído en *RM*, pág. 248, n. *2. Sobre la moderación en el comer y beber véase *Refranero español*, colección de ocho mil refranes populares, ordenados, concordados y explicados, precedida del *Libro de los proverbios morales* de Alonso de Barros, Ed. y recop. de José Bergua, 6a. ed. (Madrid: Ediciones Ibéricas, 1961), págs. 136-138; Clemencín (pág. 1763, n. 7); Rodríguez Marín (págs. 248-49, notas 2, 3 y 1); Castro cita a Isócrates (pág. 354); Bleznick comenta estos preceptos en función de la tradición aristotélico-galénica (pág. 63).

⁵²Opinión debatible a juzgar por los comentarios de lingüistas y anotadores del *Quijote*.

⁵³Explícitamente lo dice poco más adelante en la conversación: «¿A qué diablos se pudre de que yo me sirva de *mi hacienda*, que ninguna otra tengo ni otro caudal alguno, sino refranes y más refranes» (II, 43).

⁵⁴No será la primera vez que lo hace. Ni tampoco la última. Sancho lo observa más tarde: «Estáme reprehendiendo que no diga yo refranes, y ensártalos vuesa merced de dos en dos» (II, 67).

⁵⁵Véase el diccionario etimológico de Corominas bajo *trompa*.

⁵⁶R. Foulché-Delbosc considera este *trómpogelas* como error de imprenta («Trómpogelas», *Revue Hispanique*, 6 [1899], 143). Pero yo creo que no es error de imprenta sino de Don Quijote. En el mismo episodio se equivoca sobre música, sobre etimología, y una tercera vez sobre la definición de *refrán*. La equivocación sobre música aparece poco después de una explicación de *albogues*, instrumento musical mencionado entre varios otros harmoniosos: *churumbeles, gaitas zamoranas, tamborines, sonajas, rabeles.* Cuando Don Quijote menciona *albogues* por primera vez esta pensando en más de un *albogue*, especie de flauta o dulçaina o trompeta (Covarrubias, Corominas). Pero como utiliza el plural, *albogues*, se equivoca y da la definición de otro instrumento del mismo nombre que tiene forma plural siendo singular porque está formado por dos platillos (análogamente a *tijeras* o *pantalones*). Y luego, como se ha confundido de instrumento, rectifica su primera afirmación de que es música lo que produce y ahora dice que da un «son que, si no muy agradable ni armónico, no descontenta. . . »

A raíz de *albogues*, de origen árabe, comete Don Quijote un segundo error, esta vez, etimológico. Con un «conviene a saber» de lo más académico (expresión favorita de Antonio de Guevara, págs. 88, 113, 136, 145 de su obra *Menosprecio. . .* Ver además, la nota 58) afirma que todas las palabras que empiezan por al son de origen árabe. Y suelta algunas (almohaza, almorzar, alhombra, alguacil, alhucena, almacén, alcancía). Entre ellas, *almorzar* no es de origen árabe. También afirma rotundamente que sólo tres palabras que terminan en *í* son de origen árabe: borceguí, zaquizaní y maravedí. *Borceguí* es, sin embargo, de origen dudoso. Y, sin transición, añade otras dos (alhelí y alfaquí), que clasifica como árabes tanto por el *al* primero como por el *í* en que acaban, reafirmando su primer error (*al*) y contradiciendo su propia teoría (*í*). Véase sobre este asunto Joan E. Ciruti, «Cervantes and the Words he says are Arabic» (*Hispania*, 40 [1957], 70-72).

Por último, en la misma conversación con Sancho da una definición falsa de los refranes atribuyendo la sabiduría que encierran a «la experiencia y *especulación* de nuestros antiguos *sabios*» (subrayo para mayor claridad), cuando tiempo atrás sabía que los refranes «son sentencias sacadas de la mesma experiencia» (I, 21), como también lo sabía el Cautivo: «sentencias breves sacadas de la luenga y discreta experiencia» (I, 39). No de la *especulación* de ningún sabio. Al día siguiente de la atribución de los refranes a la experiencia y especulación de los antiguos sabios, reconoce Don Quijote que es el pueblo quien los ha creado: repite un refrán que le ha oído decir a Sancho.

De nuevo, hay que distinguir entre lo que *sabe* Cervantes y lo que *no sabe* Don Quijote. La caracterización que hace Cervantes de Don Quijote es la de un noble idealista, algo pedante, dogmático como siempre, que envejece a rápidos pasos y se equivoca cada vez con mayor frecuencia sobre los hechos y, más profundamente todavía, sobre las doctrinas.

[57]«. . . para decir yo uno [refrán] y aplicarle bien, sudo y trabajo como si cavase» (II, 43).

[58]Júzguese por el estilo de las siguientes frases sacadas al azar de *Menosprecio de la corte y alabanza de aldea* (Edición y notas de M. Martínez de Burgos [Madrid: Espasa-Calpe, 1931], reproducción facsimil de la edición «La Lectura» de Clásicos Castellanos, 1928): «Es privilegio de aldea que allí sean los hombres más virtuosos y menos viciosos. . . » (págs. 134-35); «. . . los que allí moraren, puedan de su hazienda guardar más y gastar menos, del qual previlegio no gozan los cortesanos. . . » (pág. 136); «. . . en tener sanctos propósitos ningún sancto me sobrepujó, y en ser pecador ningún pecador me igualó» (pág. 243). Véanse también notas 59 y 81.

[59]Desde que está en casa de los duques la retórica ha venido a formar parte de la manera de pensar de Don Quijote. Por ejemplo, cuando se entera de que Sancho ha sido nombrado gobernador comenta: «. . . y aquí entra y encaja bien el decir que hay buena y mala fortuna en las pretensiones» (II, 42). Don Quijote puede ser sentenciador tanto como pensador original.

[60]Nos lo recuerda Clemencín (IV, pág. 43, n. 20).

[61]Explícitamente lo dice en *Los baños de Argel* por boca de Juanico: «porque si nuestra intención / está con firme afición / puesta en Dios, caso es sabido / que no deshace el vestido / lo que hace el corazón». (*Obras de Cervantes*, BAE, tomo 156 [Madrid, 1962], pág. 147).

[62]*Padrastro* se llama a sí mismo Cervantes (Prólogo I). Un sentido de este vocablo es el *denunciador* o *censor*. (Para más datos véase Percas, pág. 46). No es sin inmensa ternura que maltrata Cervantes, el padrastro, el Censor, tan despiadamente a su personaje haciéndole ridículo y patético para decir que los fines deben ser los medios y los medios los fines.

[63]Claro que hay un equívoco en esto de «mi religión». Don Quijote confunde los atributos de la caballería con los de la religión cristiana: «a los caballeros andantes no les toca ni atañe averiguar si los afligidos, encadenados y opresos. . . van de aquella manera, o están en aquella angustia por sus culpas, o por sus gracias; sólo les toca ayudarles como a menesterosos, poniendo los ojos en sus penas, y no en sus bellaquerías» (I, 30). El blanco de Cervantes es el interlocutor de Don Quijote, el Cura.

[64]Las connotaciones de *Barataria*, vocablo derivado del verbo *baratar*, común a todos

los romances hispánicos, son en el Siglo de Oro español, *permutar, trocar,* (Corominas). Barataria es nombre antonomástico. Pudiera aludir, como pensó Fermín Caballero en *Pericia geográfica de Miguel de Cervantes*. . . (Madrid, 1840, pág. 36) a algún lugar de
España, tal vez Alcalá de Ebro «que si no es isla, está casi circulada de aquel gran río»
donde los duques de Villahermosa tenían un castillo-palacio y jardines, denominados
de Buenavía, junto a su cercana villa de Pedrola (*RM*, VII, pág. 9, n. *8). Y, por
extensión alegórica, a toda España y a toda América. Si seguimos con la alegoría y con
las connotaciones más obvias de Barataria, ser barata o entregada por nada, y más
lejanas, como la de *baratarios*, o cristianos a quienes se permitía ejercer el comercio en
ciudades musulmanas del norte de África (*RM, loc. cit.*), los duques, dueños de Barataria, vendrían a ser apóstatas, si no de hecho, de espíritu. Lo cual cuadra con el
comercio que ejercen, el de entretenerse jugando con las almas de dos ingenuos, el
simple de Sancho y el idealista de Don Quijote.

⁶⁵El representar lo que hay en la cabeza por lo que recubre, técnica pictórica
expresionista, es elemento recurrente en el estilo cervantino. El caballero de los Espejos, armado de pies hasta casi la cabeza, lleva primero un sombrero de plumas de
«diversas colores»—diversas ideas—que más tarde se reducen a tres que flotan sobre
su yelmo cuando se confronta con Don Quijote. Éste, vencido por el caballero de la
Blanca Luna, prefiere dejarse matar a renunciar a su idealismo: no se quita el yelmo ni
se alza la visera. En casa de los duques, en cambio, Don Quijote se pone una montera
de terciopelo verde guarnecida con pasamanos de plata, cuando se prepara para ace-
char a su acechadora Altisidora. A esto me referiré en el texto. Ver, también, en
Percas, la montera de terciopelo leonado de Don Diego de Miranda (págs. 335-38), el
turbante al modo turquesco de Belerma (pág. 472), y el capuz de bayeta morado de
Montesinos (págs. 554-57).

⁶⁶Véase «Gestación del símbolo del león» en Percas, págs. 325 y nota 11; 328-38.

⁶⁷Sobre el origen y connotaciones simbólicas de *montar a la jineta* he tratado en mi
libro, pág . 362.

⁶⁸Invoco aquí las palabras de Manuel Durán sobre las suciedades estéticas y la
degradación paródica de la cultura renacentista, que con mayor tacto que en Rabelais
encontramos en Cervantes (véase «El *Quijote* a través del prisma de Mikhail Bakhtine:
carnaval, disfraces, escatología y locura», pág 84).   Agrego que el mayor tacto de
Cervantes se debe a que sus alusiones son elípticas.

⁶⁹He tratado de los gráficos juegos de ideas sobre el refrán: «El hábito no hace al
monje», y su reverso, «El hábito hace al monje» (que no es refrán), al hablar de la
historia del Cautivo y Zoraida (Percas, págs. 251-53), del morisco Ricote (págs. 265,
267), de su hija Ana Félix (págs. 259-60), y de la gran sultana, Catalina (págs. 300-
302); en otro contexto, al comparar las armaduras del Caballero de los Espejos, luego
de la Blanca Luna con la armadura de Don Quijote (págs. 308-15), y los atavíos del
Caballero del Verde Gabán con los de Don Quijote (págs. 336-39). Con mayor detalle
estudio la emblemática en estos dos últimos casos en la ponencia leída en el Congreso
de Fordham, antes mencionado.

⁷⁰De nuevo me refiero al trabajo de Manuel Durán, pág. 79.

⁷¹ Sobre la identidad entre *Diablo* y *Locura* véase «An Emblematic Interpretation of
Sansón Carrasco's Disguises» de Pierre L. Ullman, en *Estudios literarios de hispanistas
norteamericanas dedicados a Helmut Hatzfeld con motivo de su 80 aniversario.* Compilados y
editados por Josep M. Solá-Solé, Alessandro Crisafulli, Bruno Damiani (Barcelona:
Ediciones HISPAM, Colección Lacetania, 1974), págs. 224-25.

⁷²Francisco Márquez Villanueva ha documentado ampliamente el sentido emblemático del *verde* como indicación de locura (*Personajes y temas del "Quijote"* [Madrid: Taurus, 1975], págs. 219-27). Véase tembién su ponencia «La locura emblemática en la

segunda parte del *Quijote*, págs. 93-94). La emblemática didáctico-moralista fue muy difundida por la España barroca. Véanse los sustanciosos trabajos de Karl Ludwig Selig, «La teoria dell'emblema in Ispagna: i testi fondamentali» (*Convivium*, New Series, 2 [1955] anno XXIII, 409-21); y de Roy L. Tanner, «La influencia de la emblemática en 'El Cisne de Apolo'» (*Cuadernos Hispanoamericanos*, núm. 328 [Octubre, 1977], 1-24). También Cervantes recurre al emblema, pero como se ha visto lo hace coincidir con la realidad psicológica de modo tan natural que apenas si se lo percibe.

[73] Véase Percas, págs. 320 «III. El Caballero del Verde Gabán» (332-82, más específicamente 338, 361, 366, 385), y «El verde como símbolo (386-95); también, la antes mencionada ponencia «The Painter and the Writer are One and the Same» en la que se considera el simbolismo del verde en conjunción con el de otros colores, y con el de las formas y texturas de la indumentaria de varios personajes.

[74] El diablo cazador vestido de verde se encuentra en buena parte de la literatura medieval. Sin ir más lejos, en las *Canterbury Tales* de Chaucer: Prólogo a la historia de Reeves: «For in oure wyl ther stiketh evere a nayl,/To have an hoor heed and a grene tayl,/As hath a leek; for thogh oure myght be goon,/Oure wyl desireth folie evere in oon» (Versos 3877-80); y en la historia del Mercader: «Though I be a hoor, I fare as dooth a tree/That blosmeth er that fruyt ywoxen bee,/And blosmy tree nys neither drye ne deed./I feele me nowhere hoor but on myn heed;/Myn herte and alle my lymes been as grene/As laurer thurgh the yeer is for to sene» (Versos 1461-66). Véase, también, el significativo artículo: «Why the Devil Wears Green» de D. W. Robertson, Jr. (*Modern Language Notes*, 69 [1954], 470-72).

[75] Véase Meyer Reinhold, *History of Purple as a Status Symbol in Antiquity* (Bruxelles: *Latomus*, Revue d'Études Latines, Vol. 116), págs. 63, 70 y 56 respectivamente.

[76] No es la primera vez que Cervantes interviene cruelmente en la vida de Don Quijote. Bajo la figura de Merlín, quien sabía «un punto más que el diablo» encantó a Dulcinea en la cueva de Montesinos y le puso a Don Quijote ante los ojos, descarnada y desnuda, la visión de la realidad (Percas, «Fuentes de la cueva de Montesinos», en particular, págs. 497, 549, 552).

[77] El uso del adverbio *como* con dos sentidos opuestos ya lo he observado por lo menos en otro lugar del *Quijote*, cuando dice Cide Hamete Benengeli, hablando de las novelas del curioso impertinente y del Capitán cautivo, que están «como separadas de la historia» de Don Quijote. Este *como*, equivalente a un *como si*, puede ser tanto afirmativo como negativo (Percas, págs. 165-66).

[78] Es preciso disociar a Don Quijote de Cervantes. No como lo hacía Unamuno por creer a Cervantes «ingenio lego», inconsciente de la grandeza de su creación. Cuando se puso Cervantes ese nombre antonomásico de «ingenio lego» (*Viaje del Parnaso*, VI, terceto 58, verso 3) quiso decir que su ingenio era profano y no letrado, que venía de naturaleza y no de indoctrinación. *Lego*, del latín *laicus*, que no es clérigo, y *laicus*, a su vez, del griego λαιχοσ profano, perteneciente al pueblo. No quiso decir, que fuera ignorante ni inculto, aunque sí insinuar con picardía todo lo contrario. Humanista de verdad. Bruce W. Wardropper hace esta misma observación sobre el Cervantes hombre de letras, pero no letrado («Cervantes and Education», págs. 188-89).

[79] Algunos anotadores, Pellicer, Rodríguez Marín (RM, pág. 229, n. 5), Martín de Riquer (6a. ed. Juventud [Barcelona, 1969], pág. 840), lo identifican con Dionisio Catón. Otros, John J. Allen (ed. Cátedra [Madrid, 1977], pág. 340), Luis Andrés Murillo (ed. Castalia [Madrid, 1978], pág 357), con Marco Porcio, El Censor.

[80] *Menosprecio. . .,* pág. 49. Guevara menciona a Catón por lo menos seis veces (págs; 31, 47, 49, 215, 221, 222) en tres de las cuales le atribuye dichos y hechos imposibles de documentar en las biografías e historias que hablan del estadista

romano, según M. Martínez de Burgos, su anotador (págs. 31, 215, 222). Sancho le atribuye a «Catón Zonzorino un refrán: «y el mal, para quien le fuere a buscar» (I, 20), que inventa cuando le sobrecoge el miedo en la aventura de los batanes. Cervantes parece estar pensando en Guevara.

[81]Véanse algunas de las equilibristas frases de Guevara tomadas al azar. «. . . antes favoresced al predicador que reprehende el vicio que al cavallero que es vicioso» (pág. 50). Como este consejo de Don Quijote: «Préciate más de ser humilde virtuoso que pecador soberbio». Guevara: «. . . si uno ha estado en la corte. . . llama a todos pacatos, moñacos. . . motejándolos de muy desaliñados en el vestir» (pág. 196). Ahora que está en el palacio de los duques, como si dijéramos en la Corte, por primera vez le dice Don Quijote a Sancho que le tiene por «porro» y que no debe andar «desceñido y flojo». Creo que Cervantes tiene presentes estas y otras frases de Guevara cuya obra, que tanto se leyó por la Europa del XVI, considera insustancial y, tal vez, nociva. El propósito de Guevara era entretener, no enseñar, a sus lectores, lo cual va en contra de todo lo que piensa, siente y hace Cervantes. De Guevara habla en el Prólogo al *Quijote* I con incontenido desprecio: para mostrarse un hombre «erudito», si quiere hablar de «mujeres rameras ahí está el obispo de Mondoñedo (Guevara), que os prestará a Lamia, Laida y Flora, cuya anotación os dará gran crédito». Poco crédito podía dar quien inventa citas, autores, personajes, leyes, anécdotas, épocas y lugares, como hace Guevara. Me remito al estudio de Francisco Márquez Villanueva, «Fray Antonio de Guevara o la ascética novelada» (*Espiritualidad y literatura en el siglo XVI* [Madrid-Barcelona, 1968]págs. 17-66), para respaldar mi opinión sobre el limitado valor intrínseco de la obra de este escritor que tan importante fue en su tiempo por su espíritu creador y revolucionario, así como por la frescura de su lenguaje. Un importante y documentado trabajo de reivindicación de Guevara que tendrá que tomarse en cuenta, sin embargo, es el de Augustin Redondo: «*Antonio de Guevara (1480?-1545)* et l'Espagne de son temps (Genève: Librairie Droz, 1976), 883 págs. Sospecho, sin embargo, que Cervantes no comparte la admiración del profesor Redondo por Guevara.

[82]*Personajes y temas del "Quijote"*, págs 147-227, en particular 208-227.

[83]Cito el texto entero porque se ve claramente lo que significa el «a los que los tienen príncipes y señores» del consejo antes comentado (notas 30, 31 y texto correspondiente). «Y no penséis, señor, que yo llamo aquí vulgo solamente a la gente plebeya y humilde; que todo aquel que no sabe, aunque sea señor y príncipe, puede y debe entrar en número de vulgo».

[84]De nuevo remito al trabajo de Bruce W. Wardropper (pág.190-91) en el que tan perspicazmente distingue el valor de la experiencia en el humanismo renacentista de Cervantes en contraste con el valor más teórico del humanismo renacentista de Erasmo.

[85]Me lo ha hecho observar Michael McGaha a raíz de un comentario sobre mi libro *Cervantes y su concepto del arte* en el que describo varios niveles estilísticos y temáticos superpuestos sobre las mismas palabras. Por su gentileza tengo a la vista el texto de Leone Ebreo, *Dialoghi d'Amore*, trad. por F. Friedeberg-Seeley y Jean H. Barnes (London: The Soncino Press, 1937), págs. 110-114.

NOTES ON THE CONTRIBUTORS

JOHN J. ALLEN is Professor of Spanish at the University of Florida. Born in Kansas in 1932, he studied at Duke University and Middlebury College and received the Ph.D. from the University of Wisconsin in 1960. He has taught at the University of Florida since then, except for the year 1977, when he was Visiting Professor at the Rijksuniversiteit te Utrecht. During the years 1976-78 he was a Regional Delegate to the MLA Delegate Assembly. His book *Don Quixote: Hero or Fool?* is a very influential study of Cervantes' narrative technique; it appeared in Florida in 1969 and a second part will be published in 1979. His edition of *Don Quijote* was published by Ediciones Cátedra in Madrid in 1977.

JUAN BAUTISTA AVALLE-ARCE is William Rand Kenan, Jr., Professor of Spanish at the University of North Carolina. Born in Buenos Aires in 1927, he studied at St. Andrew's School, the Colegio Nacional de Buenos Aires and the University of Buenos Aires and received the A.B., M.A., and Ph.D. from Harvard University, where he served for a time as Teaching Fellow. He has taught at The Ohio State University and Smith College and has been at the University of North Carolina since 1969. He was a founding member of the Asociación Internacional de Hispanistas and has served on the editorial board of *Renaissance Quarterly, PMLA, Romance Notes, Hispanic Review* and *Hispanófila*. His extensive publications on Cervantes include the books *Conocimiento y vida en Cervantes* (Buenos Aires, 1959), *Deslindes cervantinos* (Madrid, 1961), *Nuevos deslindes cervantinos* (Barcelona, 1975) and *Don Quijote como forma de vida* (Madrid, 1976). He has also produced editions of *La Galatea,* (Madrid, 1961; 1968), the *Persiles* (Madrid, 1969) and *Don Quijote* (Madrid, 1979). In collaboration with E. C. Riley he edited the critical anthology *Suma cervantina* in 1973.

JUAN COROMINAS is Assistant Professor of Spanish at California State University, Dominguez Hills. Born in Spain in 1924, he received

the Licentiate in Philosophy from the Pontifical University Angeli-
cum in Rome in 1962 and holds two M.A. degrees—one in philosophy and the other in Spanish—from the University of Southern
California, where he also received the Ph.D. in Spanish in 1977. He
has lectured in Spain, Mexico, Argentina, Paraguay, the Phillipine
Islands, Japan and the United States and has contributed articles to
literary and philosophical journals in Spain.

Manuel Durán is Professor of Spanish and Chairman of the
Department of Spanish and Portuguese at Yale University. Born in
Barcelona in 1925, he studied in Spain, France, Mexico and the United States, obtaining the degrees of Licenciado en Derecho and
Maestro en Letras at the Universidad Nacional Autónoma de México
and the Ph.D. in Romance Languages and Literatures at Princeton
University, where he studied with Américo Castro. His book *La
ambigüedad en el Quijote* (Xalapa, Veracruz, 1960) has been recognized
as one of the most distinguished contributions to Cervantean criticism in recent years. He is also the author of the volume on Cervantes in the Twayne World Authors Series.

Ruth El Saffar is Professor of Spanish at the University of Illinois at Chicago Circle. Born in New York in 1941, she studied at
Colorado College and received the Ph.D. from Johns Hopkins University in 1966. She has taught at Johns Hopkins, Colorado College,
the University College of Baghdad and the University of Maryland
and has been at the University of Illinois at Chicago Circle since
1968. In addition to numerous articles she has published three books
on Cervantes: *Novel to Romance: A Study of Cervantes' "Novelas Ejemplares"*
(Baltimore, 1974), *Distance and Control in "Don Quixote"* (Chapel Hill,
1975) and *Cervantes' "El casamiento engañoso y el coloquio de los perros"* (London, 1976).

Edward Friedman is Assistant Professor of Spanish at Arizona
State University. Born in 1948, he studied at the University of Virginia and received the M.A. and Ph.D. from Johns Hopkins University, where he wrote his dissertation on "The Unifying Concept: An
Approach to the Structure of Cervantes' *Comedias*" in 1974. His articles on Cervantes' theater have appeared in *Revista de Estudios Hispánicos, Neophilologus* and *Hispania*. He has also written on some of the
Novelas ejemplares and on Calderón, Ruiz de Alarcón, Lope de Vega,
Juan de Timoneda, Unamuno, Pedro Salinas and Alfonso Sastre.

Robert M. Johnston is Assistant Professor of Spanish at Reed College. He has studied at Portland State University and the University of Pavia, Italy, and is presently a doctoral candidate at the University of Oregon, where he is writing a dissertation entitled "Some Guises of Pastoral in Cervantes." He spent the year 1976-1977 as a Fulbright scholar in Barcelona.

Francisco Márquez Villanueva is Professor of Spanish at Harvard University. Born in Seville in 1931, he studied at the Università per Stranieri in Perugia and received his Ph.D. from the University of Seville in 1958. He has taught at the University of British Columbia, Rutgers, Middlebury College, Queens College of the City University of New York, the University of Pennsylvania and Princeton before accepting his present post at Harvard in 1978. Readers of this volume will be particularly interested in his books *Fuentes literarias cervantinas* (Madrid, 1973) and *Personajes y temas del Quijote* (Madrid, 1975).

Michael D. McGaha is Associate Professor and Coordinator of Spanish at Pomona College. Born in Texas in 1941, he studied at the University of Dallas and the University of Madrid and received the Ph.D. from the University of Texas at Austin in 1970. His articles on Cervantes have appeared in *Romance Notes, Anales Cervantinos, Hispano-Italic Studies, Revue de Littérature Comparée* and *Comparative Literature Studies*. He is the author of the book *The Theatre in Madrid during the Second Republic, 1931-36.* (London, 1979) and has also written extensively on the Spanish theatre of the Golden Age.

Luis Andrés Murillo is Professor of Spanish at the University of California, Berkeley. Born in Pasadena in 1922, he studied at the University of Southern California and received the Ph.D. from Harvard University in 1953. His important book *The Golden Dial: Temporal Configurations in "Don Quixote"* appeared in 1975, and his annotated edition of *Don Quijote* accompanied by an impressive bibliography was published in Madrid in 1978. Professor Murillo is the founder of the California Cervantes Society.

Helena Percas de Ponseti is Seth Richards Professor of Spanish at Grinnell College. Born in Spain, she studied in Paris and at Barnard College and received the Ph.D. from Columbia University in 1951. She has taught at Barnard College, Russell Sage College,

Columbia University and Queens College and has been at Grinnell since 1957. Her exhaustive study on the Cave of Montesinos episode in the 1615 *Don Quijote* appeared in *Revista Hispánica Moderna* in 1968 and her two-volume work *Cervantes y su concepto del arte* was published in Madrid in 1975.

ELIAS L. RIVERS is Professor of Hispanic Studies at the State University of New York, Stony Brook. Born in Charleston, South Carolina in 1924, he studied at the College of Charleston and at Georgetown University and received the Ph.D. from Yale University in 1952. He taught at Dartmouth College and at The Ohio State University and was Professor of Spanish at Johns Hopkins University for fourteen years before moving to Stony Brook in 1978. He is Secretary General of the Asociación Internacional de Hispanistas and has served as associate editor of *Modern Language Notes.* Best known for his editions and his critical studies of the works of Garcilaso de la Vega, he has also published a number of important articles on Cervantes.

Born in Spain, EDUARDO URBINA studied at California State University at Hayward and has recently received the Ph.D. from the University of California, Berkeley. While at Berkeley, he has taught as an Instructor and was awarded the Charles E. Kany Graduate Scholarship in 1978. His dissertation, written under the direction of L. A. Murillo, is on "Sancho Panza, 'escudero sin par': parodia y creación en el Don Quijote."

BRUCE W. WARDROPPER is William Hanes Wannamaker Professor of Romance Languages at Duke University. Born in Scotland in 1919, he studied at King Edward's School and at Cambridge University and received the Ph.D. from the University of Pennsylvania in 1949. He has taught at the University of Pennsylvania, Johns Hopkins University, The Ohio State University, Harvard, the University of Pittsburgh and the University of North Carolina.He served on the executive board of the Asociación Internacional de Hispanistas from 1971 to 1977 and has been a member of the editorial committees of *Modern Language Notes, PMLA,* and *Revista Hispánica Moderna.* His numerous books and articles reflect wide-ranging interests and an encyclopedic knowledge of Spanish literature of the Golden Age.

Index